# THE AMERICAN CENTURY

D0025786

# The American Century
## A History of the United States Since the 1890s, 7e

By Walter LaFeber, Richard Polenberg, and Nancy Woloch

*Also available in two separate volumes:*

## The American Century
A History of the United States from 1890 to 1941, 7e


## The American Century
A History of the United States Since 1941, 7e

# THE AMERICAN CENTURY

## Volume 1
## A History of the United States
## from 1890 to 1941

Seventh Edition

## Walter LaFeber, Richard Polenberg, and Nancy Woloch

*M.E.Sharpe*
Armonk, New York
London, England

The EuroSlavic fonts used to create this work are © 1986–2013 Payne Loving Trust.
EuroSlavic is available from Linguist's Software, Inc.,
www.linguistsoftware.com, P.O. Box 580, Edmonds, WA 98020-0580 USA
tel (425) 775-1130.


**Library of Congress Cataloging-in-Publication Data**

LaFeber, Walter.
  The American century : a history of the United States since the 1890s / by Walter LaFeber,
Richard Polenberg, and Nancy Woloch. — Seventh Edition. —
    volumes cm
  Includes bibliographical references.
  ISBN 978-0-7656-3483-2 (hardcover : alk. paper)—ISBN 978-0-7656-3484-9 (pbk. : alk. paper)
  1. United States—History—20th century.  2. United States—History—21st century.  3. United
States—Foreign relations—20th century.  4. United States—Foreign relations—21st century.
  I. Polenberg, Richard.  II. Woloch, Nancy, 1940–  III. Title.

E741.L45 2013
973.9—dc23                                                                      2013004357


Volume 1: A History of the United States from 1890 to 1941; ISBN 978-0-7656-4044-4


Printed in the United States of America

The paper used in this publication meets the minimum requirements of
American National Standard for Information Sciences
Permanence of Paper for Printed Library Materials,
ANSI Z 39.48-1984.

IBT (p)    10    9    8    7    6    5    4    3    2    1

# Contents

# List of Maps

# Preface

We are most grateful for the response to the first six editions of *The American Century*. That response has confirmed the need for a concise text that is both highly factual and, at appropriate points, interpretive. In this seventh edition, we have adopted suggestions and corrections given to us by instructors and students. We are issuing this first volume separately for the first time, in response to instructor requests.

This volume, like the second (covering 1941 to the present), stresses the importance of economic, social, and political change; but also, we devote feature sections to art, architecture, sports, and other topics. Since its inception, this book has given equal attention to U.S. foreign and domestic policies, at points noting how the two are necessarily related. To help students understand that foreign (and often domestic) policy, we include brief analyses of developments elsewhere in the world.

We are especially indebted to the staff of M.E. Sharpe, above all to Steven Drummond, Executive Editor for History, for his encouragement, friendship, unfailing good advice, and awesome patience; and Kimberly Giambattisto and Henrietta Toth for their care and professionalism in handling editorial and other issues that invariably and unexpectedly arise.

# THE
# AMERICAN
# CENTURY

# CHAPTER ONE

# 1890s

## The Beginnings of Modern America

Henry Ford in his first model car, completed in 1896. *(AP Photo/Ford Motor Company)*

Modern America emerged during a forty-year crisis that began with the Civil War (1861–1865) and ended with the war against Spain in 1898. The crisis, which recast every part of the nation's life, climaxed in the 1890s. At the Chicago Columbian Exposition of 1893, Americans celebrated their triumphs in industry and technology while, ironically, enduring the nation's worst economic depression. A young historian, Frederick Jackson Turner of the University of Wisconsin, delivered a speech at this world's fair that helped explain the irony. The vast open lands of the West, Turner asserted, had shaped American social and political institutions. According to the 1890 census, however, these lands had finally been settled. Turner concluded: "And now, four centuries from the discovery of America, at the end of a hundred years of life under the Constitution, the frontier has gone, and with its going has closed the first period of American history." Scholars later agreed that Turner overemphasized the importance of the frontier in the shaping of American character, but few, then or since, would deny that a different America was indeed born in the last years of the century. The birth pains were promising—and terrifying.

## THE SCULPTOR OF MODERN AMERICA: THE CORPORATION

Between 1860 and 1900 no birth was more notable than that of the modern industrial corporation. Barely conceived of before the Civil War, it quickly came to dominate Americans' lives by determining what they possessed and where they worked and, in general, by producing everything they needed from their baby food to their tombstones.

Before the Civil War, state and national governments had created corporations largely to operate public highways and banks. But shrewd business executives soon realized that merely by obtaining a charter of incorporation from a state government, they suddenly had the right to acquire great sums of capital through sales of stock. At the same time, the liability of each investor was limited to the amount he or she invested. It was like magic. The new creature first appeared to build railroads during the 1850s boom. It was the Civil War, however, that shaped the industrial corporation.

The mammoth armies of the North and South created an immense market that demanded rapid production of goods. Through privately owned corporations, such men as Gustavus F. Swift (meat), Gail Borden (dairy and groceries), and Andrew Carnegie (railways and later steel) got their start by supplying the sinews of war. Equally important, when Southerners deserted Washington in 1861, unopposed Northern politicians were able to whip legislation through Congress to aid their section's factories. Between 1862 and 1865 members of Congress consequently built a tariff wall insulating American producers against foreign competition, passed bank laws to standardize and liberalize the monetary system, and allowed owners to import cheap labor from Europe. Most striking, Congress simply gave away tremendous amounts of land and mineral resources to corporations that were building the transcontinental railway (completed in 1869) and other transportation systems. By the early twentieth century, the government had given private railway builders free land equivalent to the areas of Maine, New Hampshire, Vermont, Massachusetts, Rhode Island, and much of New York. Some of this acreage held rich deposits of coal, lead, and iron ores.

This was hardly "private enterprise." Corporations obtained incalculable favors from government to develop the country's wealth. An intimate, sometimes questionable, relationship developed between business and government. One member of the House of Representatives observed in 1873 that Congress had become like an "auction room where more valuable considerations were disposed of under the speaker's hammer than in any other place on earth." More cynically, one presidential candidate advised another during the 1870s that businessmen wanted "men in office who will not steal but who will not interfere with those who do." The result was historic: in 1850 the laws had shaped the corporation, but by 1900 the corporation shaped the laws.

The railroads even changed how Americans told time. Until the 1880s, the country was a chaos of time zones. Wisconsin alone had thirty-eight such zones. But cross-country travel required a better system, so in 1883 the railroads imposed four time zones on Americans— Eastern, Central, Rocky Mountain, Pacific—and in 1918 Congress finally made this system law. The isolated, rural "island communities" of the 1870s became part of an integrated and more homogeneous America. Small local firms suddenly faced competition from giant producers and either copied or merged with the giants or were wiped out by them.

Inheriting a chaotic and decentralized America, the corporation streamlined and centralized the nation's economic life. It also produced unimagined wealth that marked the beginning of an affluent America. In 1860, 31 million Americans turned out manufactures valued at $2 billion, traveled on 30,000 miles of railroads, and produced little iron or steel. Forty years later, 75 million people produced manufactures worth $11 billion, used 200,000 miles of rails, and overtook Great Britain and Germany to become the world's greatest iron and steel (and soap) producers. The corporation helped create such new cities as Chicago, Atlanta, Kansas City, Minneapolis, and Dallas.

## THE NEW TECHNOLOGY: EDISON, ENERGY—AND SECRETARIES

The new corporation was the child of the new machines. For in the late nineteenth century American technology, which had lagged behind British and French technology, suddenly developed and transformed the world with the electric light, typewriter, telephone, thermionic valve (which made possible radio and, later, transistors), automobile, and airplane. All of these discoveries and products appeared in the forty years after the Civil War.

To develop the technology Americans wanted to sell overseas and use in their own homes required two particular ingredients: scientific knowledge and money. The lonely inventor living on a shoestring, whose sudden discovery changed the world, was becoming rare. Thomas Edison's laboratory, which developed the incandescent bulb in 1879, had by 1901 turned into the General Electric Corporation's laboratory employing hundreds of skilled technicians. The garage where Henry Ford tinkered on his first horseless carriage had become a mechanized industrial complex. Only the corporation could provide the range of management skills and the amount of money needed for developing much of the new technology.

But from the start, government at both the state and the national level was also necessarily involved. The 1862 Land Grant College Act had established new universities and poured resources into other schools, which were to "teach such branches of learning as are related to agriculture and the mechanic arts." These schools began producing professional engineers who drove the United States to the forefront of world technology. An American people that too often is thought of as anti-intellectual actually built its twentieth-century civilization on scientific discoveries and technology that demanded the most rigorous intellectual training and application.

The transformation of the business office exemplified the changes. Before 1860 the office usually had a few male employees who, with their pens, handled a wide range of tasks and acted as both managers and secretaries as they tried to work their way up. Men continued to be the managers, but by 1900 the office was a large enterprise with many women who performed specific tasks (such as typing and filing) with such new machines as the typewriter, which appeared in the 1870s. Women left their homes to become wage earners. With no hope of moving up the corporate ladder, they were the new proletariats of American business. The office was becoming routinized, bureaucratized, and—most important—mechanized and corporatized. And so was much of American society.

The creators of this society naturally believed it was the best of worlds. In 1886 Andrew Carnegie looked at his vast, efficient steel empire and observed, "If asked what important law I should change, I must perforce say none: the laws are perfect."

## BOOM HIDDEN IN BUST

Not all Americans agreed with Carnegie. During the quarter-century following 1873, the country suffered from increasingly severe periods of economic depression. The 1873 panic was triggered by overexpansion and stock exchange corruption. The economic crisis worsened until labor violence erupted in 1877, 1886, 1892, and then sporadically between 1893 and 1895. Overproduction caused this twenty-five-year crisis. Industries and farms produced so much that markets were glutted, prices fell, and both farmers and laborers suffered. Pig-iron production, for example, doubled between 1873 and 1893, while its price dropped from $50 to $13 a ton. Production of cotton, traditionally the nation's leading export, increased more than 50 percent during these years; Americans eventually produced more cotton than the entire world could consume. Some corporations, like some farmers, could not stand the competition and went bankrupt.

As men such as Carnegie learned that efficiency and cost cutting were necessary for survival, they tended to drive others out of business until such vital industries as sugar refining, oil, steel, and tobacco were dominated by one or two companies. In these fields, competition increasingly disappeared. Prices were then determined not by many sellers in an open marketplace, but by a few corporations based on their own costs and whatever return they thought desirable on their investment. Companies banded together to fix prices in "pools" or formed giant combinations known as "trusts," which destroyed competition. To form a trust a number of corporations would join together, giving a group of trustees the power to set prices for all of them. Thus the corporations fixed prices and cut out competition. Their profits skyrocketed.

But at the very moment competition was vanishing and opportunity narrowing, belief in the self-made man flourished. Business tycoons helped popularize the idea that success came to those who worked hard and saved their money. The view that there was room at the top for all who were virtuous received its most popular formulation in the novels of Horatio Alger. The typical Alger hero, such as "Ragged Dick" or "Mark the Match Boy," began life as a poor orphan. But he was "manly and self-reliant" and through honesty and hard work attained a position of solid respectability with the further assurance that he would "go far." The belief that success resulted from virtue sanctified corporate practices and led Americans to praise entrepreneurial liberty ("free enterprise") as the highest social value.

When state or national legislatures tried to control corporations, the courts often stopped them. Carnegie might have believed the laws were perfect, but the Supreme Court tried to improve on perfection. It did this by radically changing the idea of "due process," a basic tenet of American law. Before the 1880s due process referred to procedure. For example, the Constitution's Fifth Amendment provides that no person can "be deprived of life, liberty, or property, without due process of law," that is, be subjected to arbitrary arrest, unlawful forfeiture of property, and the like. In 1868 the Fourteenth Amendment strengthened this guarantee by providing that no state government can take away individual rights without due process. This amendment was aimed especially at preventing Southern states from depriving black citizens of voting and other rights. The Supreme Court, however, interpreted it in quite another way.

Between 1886 and 1898 the Court ruled on whether the Minnesota and Nebraska legislatures could regulate railroads in those states. The judges held the state laws invalid, not because the legislatures had violated *procedural* due process in passing the regulations, but because in the Court's opinion the laws were unfair *in substance* to the railroads. The Court asserted the right to decide whether the railway rates were reasonable, instead of deciding, as it had in the past, whether the procedures used in passing the laws were constitutional. Judges thus declared that their own views, rather than those of elected officials, should determine the substance of these particular state laws.

This was potentially an explosive situation, for the Court had put itself above elected officials in order to protect private corporations. Justice Stephen J. Field, who served on the Supreme Court from 1863 to 1897, often shaped its view. His beliefs, in turn, had been molded by his experience as an ambitious businessman on the California frontier (where in self-defense he learned the art of shooting to kill without taking the pistol out of his pocket) and from his reading of classical economists who believed an open marketplace existed in which everyone competed equally.

In the *Wabash* case of 1886 the Court struck down an Illinois law regulating railroads that crossed state boundaries. The Court declared that since the railway was in interstate commerce, only Congress could deal with it. This decision forced Congress in 1887 to establish the Interstate Commerce Commission (ICC) to stop such unfair practices as rebates to favored customers. At first the railroads fought the ICC, but shrewd railway lawyers, such as Richard Olney of Boston, adopted different tactics. Olney argued that the ICC was inevitable because public opinion demanded it; therefore, the railroads should simply ensure that their friends controlled the agency. This was one reason why the ICC proved ineffectual; the other was a series of Supreme Court decisions that stripped the ICC of any powers to set fair rates. The same fate paralyzed the Sherman Antitrust Act, passed by Congress in 1890 to outlaw business combinations that tried to monopolize markets or engaged in "restraint of trade" in interstate commerce. The impact of the Sherman act was so pitiful that the spectacular merger and trust movement followed it between 1897 and 1902.

Americans, who have always professed reverence for both efficiency and competition, found by the 1890s that they could not always have both. With the aid of the Supreme Court they chose efficiency. Some critics might tag the corporate leaders of the cut-and-thrust post–Civil War era "Robber Barons." Most Americans, however, were willing to overlook the brutal, often illegal, practices if Rockefeller could deliver cheap, dependable oil for home lamps, or if Cornelius Vanderbilt's New York Central Railroad could reduce the price of bread by cutting transportation costs for flour from $3.45 a barrel in 1865 to only 68 cents in 1885. When writers debated whether Shakespeare or Vanderbilt had contributed more to the human race, Shakespeare inevitably lost.

The Robber Barons corrupted politics, undercut laws, and stifled competition, but many people nevertheless agreed with Carnegie's assessment. "It will be a great mistake for the community to shoot the millionaires," he said, "for they are the bees that make the most honey, and contribute most to the hive even after they have gorged themselves full." For these Americans who questioned whether they should obediently serve such queen bees as Carnegie, alternatives seemed quite limited. The crucial question became: What kind of checks could the society produce to limit the corporation's spreading power? Queen bees, after all, are quite brutal.

## THE COLLAPSE OF THE FIRST BARRIER: THE SOUTH, WHITE AND BLACK

Five forces in American society might have made the corporation more responsible: the South, labor unions, protest movements, organized religion, and the political parties. During the 1880s and 1890s each of these either finally accommodated itself to the new industrial America or else was swept aside.

Historically the South had led opposition to the corporation's dominance, for that section had fought for low tariffs, agrarian values, and easy credit. However, Southern resistance halted after the Civil War as Northern capitalists followed Union soldiers into the defeated South, making the area a virtual colony of the North. Spurred by new wealth, cheap labor, and nonexistent taxes, the South doubled the number of its industrial laborers and tripled its investment in manufacturing between 1880 and 1900. By 1900 the region contained half the nation's textile mills. In 1870 one house stood at a rail intersection in Alabama; thirty years later this site, named Birmingham, produced $12 million of manufactures annually and competed with Pittsburgh as leader in world steel production. Yet the South industrialized only as rapidly as the rest of the country. Its spectacular development simply allowed it to keep pace with the North.

Much of the new southern industry, moreover, depended on northern capital. Many southerners, knows as "redeemers," rushed to make their own fortunes by cooperating with the entrepreneurs from above the Mason-Dixon line. The redeemers sacrificed tax income, thereby sacrificing schools and community facilities, in order to induce industry to build in their towns. One redeemer believed that "it were better for the state to burn the schools" than levy heavier taxes on corporations to pay the state debt. The thirteen southern states together had less taxable property than the single state of New York and spent $3 million less each year on education than did New York. In 1890 illiteracy afflicted nearly half of all southerners and more than three-quarters of the section's African-Americans. State universities in the South were nearly bankrupt. In 1890 Harvard alone received more income than all southern colleges combined. The institutions that did thrive, such as Vanderbilt in Tennessee and Johns Hopkins in Maryland, depended on northern funds. Even in higher education, the North colonized the South.

The agrarian South did not disappear, but its character greatly changed. The average farm, approximately 350 acres before the Civil War, shrank to less than half that acreage afterward. Meanwhile the number of farms doubled to over 1 million, one-third of them operated by tenants or sharecroppers for absentee owners. This was hardly an economic base from which the South could challenge the mighty corporation.

Blacks particularly depended on tenant farming or sharecropping. White farm owners preferred former slaves to white workers, for as one owner remarked, "No other laborer [than the Negro] . . . would be as cheerful or so contented on four pounds of meat and a peck of meal a week, in a little cabin 14 by 16 feet with cracks in it large enough to afford free passage to a large sized cat." During the 1890s, however, race relations underwent a transformation. On the farms African-Americans saw that tenant farming renewed their slave ties to the land, now without even the relative security that slaves had possessed. When blacks tried to gain employment in the new factories, bloody clashes with whites resulted.

During the late 1880s radical whites attempted to weld the poor of both races into a class movement that became the Populist Party. But redeemers broke up this coalition with racist attacks that first split apart the whites and then turned them violently against blacks. Racism proved stronger than common economic interests shared by both blacks and whites. Lynchings multiplied until they averaged 188 a year during the 1890s. "The government which had made the Negro a citizen found itself unable to protect him," black antilynching crusader Ida Wells-Barnett claimed in 1895. "The white man's victory became complete by fraud, violence, intimidation, and murder." So-called Jim Crow laws were rushed through state legislatures, segregating schools and transportation into supposed "separate but equal" facilities. In 1896 the Supreme Court upheld such laws in *Plessy v. Ferguson*. The Court brusquely overrode the lone protest of Justice John Marshall Harlan, who argued, "our Constitution is colorblind." By 1900 the illiteracy of African-Americans was six times as great as that of whites.

When the United States declared war against Spain in 1898, many African-Americans insisted they be allowed to fight for the liberation of Cubans and Filipinos from Spanish control. After overcoming considerable white opposition, President William McKinley finally allowed the creation of four black regular regiments and a volunteer force that reached about 10,000 men. The regulars distinguished themselves in Cuba, but when black soldiers returned home they found conditions worse than before. The president would do nothing. The *New York World* published a cartoon showing McKinley studying a map of the Philippines. In the background a figure pulled back a curtain to reveal the murder and lynching of blacks. The caption read: "Civilization Begins at Home."

Most African-American leaders responded to this crisis by accepting the policies of Booker T. Washington, a black educator. Washington advised acceptance of segregation, stressed the need for nonviolent accommodation to white society, and urged blacks to achieve equality ultimately by means of economic gains, particularly through vocational training. "The opportunity to earn a dollar in a factory just now is worth infinitely more than the opportunity to spend a dollar in an opera house," he observed. Washington hoped that self-help measures would eventually tear down most racial barriers. "In all things purely social we can be as separate as the fingers, yet one as the hand in all things essential to mutual progress." In effect Washington promised that African-Americans would constitute a docile labor force. "The Negro is not given to strikes," he noted.

Some black elders dissented. T. Thomas Fortune, a New York editor, founded the Afro-American League in 1890. It protested strenuously against the spread of Jim Crow institutions but died out within a short time. W.E.B. DuBois, who began teaching at Atlanta University in 1897, also criticized the accommodationist doctrine. He asserted that Washington's emphasis on vocational training cheated blacks of the cultural advantages of a liberal education and deprived them of leaders. But the great majority of black clergymen, professionals, and politicians flocked to Washington's side. His popularity grew when such corporate leaders as Carnegie applauded his policies and when President Theodore Roosevelt asked him to dine at the White House—the first black ever invited as a guest to the mansion. The ensuing antiblack uproar ensured that he was also the last of his race invited to the White House by Roosevelt. By the turn of the century it was impossible for either a black movement led by Washington or a South whose industry and culture were largely dependent on northern capital to check the new corporation.

## THE COLLAPSE OF THE SECOND BARRIER:
## LABORERS AND UNIONS

Like the South, the labor movement initially fought the corporation, then accommodated to it. Between 1860 and 1900 the number of industrial workers increased from 2.7 million (or 40 percent of all workers in farms and factories) to 13 million (65 percent). Several union movements attempted to organize laborers after the Civil War but fell victim to racism, the economic depression, and internal political divisions. The continual economic crises after 1873 drove workers to the breaking point, and some organized in small local groups. Nearly 24,000 strikes occurred during the last quarter of the century. Several were especially dangerous.

The general railroad strike of 1877 nearly paralyzed the nation, frightening some Americans into urging a third presidential term for General Ulysses S. Grant because he was the best hope to head off "another French Revolution." Nine years later the Haymarket Riot began when two laborers were killed during a clash with police during a strike in Chicago. At a protest meeting the next night in Haymarket Square, a bomb was thrown. Eight policemen were killed. The bomb thrower was never caught, but amid the hysteria the anarchist movement, which preached individual freedom by abolishing all state controls, was conveniently blamed. Four anarchists were hanged; a fifth committed suicide in his prison cell. The Haymarket became a symbol to critics of the new corporate system. The riot inspired a number of works that fundamentally criticized industrialism, among them Mark Twain's *A Connecticut Yankee in King Arthur's Court* (1889). Twain ends his novel with the freewheeling Yankee entrepreneur using his industrial ingenuity to kill 25,000 people. The image of capitalism did not improve in 1892 when strikers at Carnegie's Homestead works in Pittsburgh were fired on by hired Pinkerton detectives.

The new corporate America was born amid bloodshed and violence. The terrible depression of 1893 to 1896 worsened matters, as labor uprisings threatened to paralyze many cities. The most serious was a strike against the Pullman Company in Chicago. The trouble began when management sliced wages by 25 percent and fired many workers but refused to reduce costs in the model town of Pullman, where most employees lived. The American Railway Union, led by Eugene V. Debs, refused to move Pullman coaches. The railroad owners then declared that they would not run trains without those cars and blamed the union for disrupting transportation. On the advice of Attorney General Richard Olney, President Grover Cleveland obtained an injunction against the strikers and then, over the protest of Illinois governor John P. Altgeld, sent federal troops into the city. The ostensible reason was to keep U.S. mail moving, but the effect was to break the strike for the benefit of a private corporation. In 1894 the Supreme Court upheld this use of a sweeping injunction, and Debs went to jail.

Labor's only major success occurred when Samuel Gompers organized the American Federation of Labor (AFL) in 1886. This union survived the horrors of the 1890s largely because Gompers reached an accommodation with the new corporation. One leader of an earlier, short-lived union had urged his members to become politically active in order to "strangle monopoly." But Gompers refused to identify labor's interests with those of any one political party, choosing instead to work for whichever candidates seemed most friendly at the time. Gompers, moreover, had little desire to "fight monopoly." Instead he tried to counter big corporations with big labor, using union techniques such as strikes and boycotts directly against a particular corporation in order to obtain recognition and benefits. He concentrated on organizing skilled workers along craft lines because he believed that only they could exert much leverage on employers. This policy excluded not only most men in the industrial work-force but almost all women factory workers, who tended to hold unskilled jobs. By 1900 the AFL had organized only 3 percent of the nation's nonfarm employees, but it had established the roots for its twentieth-century triumphs. Gompers survived by accepting the corporation and by accepting as well the antianarchist, antisocialist, and, to some extent, nativist fears of most Americans.

The immigration question proved especially important. Through the mid-nineteenth century the country received over 2 million newcomers each decade, but this number doubled in the 1880s and 1890s. The source of the migration changed from western Europe to eastern and southern Europe, which in turn meant accepting increased numbers of Roman Catholics and Jews. Both old-stock Protestant Americans, who considered the newcomers racially inferior, and segments of organized labor, which disliked the added competition for jobs, favored attempts to restrict immigration. The long-cherished notion that the country could transform immigrants into acceptable citizens through the so-called melting pot of schools and churches began to fade. In 1882 the first exclusion law in American history was passed; it was limited to keeping out Chinese.

## THE COLLAPSE OF THE THIRD BARRIER: PROTEST MOVEMENTS

Farmers already knew about the closed frontier. Following the 1873 depression, the great American West changed for them from a promise to a hell. During the next quarter-century, the cost of growing wheat and corn was sometimes considerably more than the price the crops brought on the market. With new machinery and vast lands, farm output soared. Farmers produced so much that they had to rely on exports to other nations to absorb surpluses. But on the world market, Americans had to compete with cheap grains from newly opened fields in Argentina and Russia. Terrible winter storms followed by intense heat and drought during the 1880s left many farmers with no crops at all. Some farmers tried to escape to the growing cities but others tried to fight. They organized such political movements as the Grange, the Greenback Party, and the Populist Party. The Populists hoped to improve the farmer's condition by gaining control of the federal government and then using it to regulate the railroads and trusts, provide more credit, impose graduated income taxes, and clean up corrupt politics. Corporate leaders attacked the Populists, and so did many urban laborers who feared that "farm power" might mean higher bread prices. The Populists' demand for government help led to their being labeled "radical" and "socialist." Such terms were beside the point,

## FRANK LLOYD WRIGHT
### ARCHITECT OF THE OLD FRONTIER
### AND THE NEW CITY

Frank Lloyd Wright and his wife, Olgivanna, reading in the living room at Taliesin, Wisconsin. *(Wisconsin Historical Society)*

"American architecture," a critic acidly observed in 1891, "was the art of covering one thing with another thing to imitate a third thing, which, if genuine, would not be desirable." Houses and office buildings were mere boxes, banks resembled Greek temples, government buildings looked like ancient Rome. There was little that could be called American architecture. Then Frank Lloyd Wright burst upon the scene.

Fallingwater, the famous split-level house designed by architect Frank Lloyd Wright and built in 1936. *(Time & Life Pictures/Getty Images)*

Wright was born in Wisconsin in 1869. His work by twentieth century's turn exemplified key American characteristics. Like the frontier thesis of Frederick Jackson Turner, Wright's genius emphasized the importance of space and the natural frontier environment in American life. "Intimacy with Nature is the great friendship," he insisted, then built structures that followed the land's contours and harmonized with the environment. His houses were not mere boxes ("more of a coffin for the human spirit than an inspiration," he sniffed), but a "prairie architecture" that would not be "on a hill," but "*of* the hill." Inside, room flowed into room, space into space, like the prairies outside, instead of being artificially separated by walls. These were the first ranch houses. In Wright's plans, they were to be wholly American and functional for Americans, much as Greek temples were useful for Greeks, but less so for American business executives.

During the 1890s many Americans became frightened that machines would soon strangle the natural environment. Wright, however, saw no conflict between machines and nature. In building his prairie architecture he was the first designer to use products of the industrial revolution that transformed the nation between 1870 and 1900. He innovated with such new building materials as steel, reinforced concrete, and, later, plastics. Like Carnegie and Rockefeller, moreover, Wright was an ambitious American entrepreneur, and he hated any governmental interference in either his art or his business. "I believe in the capitalist system," he declared. "I only wish I could see it tried some time."

Yet he was too much of an individualist and nonconformist to be accepted by his countrymen. Scandal plagued him, particularly after he left his wife and children to travel in Europe with the wife of one of his clients. For his new love, he built the ultimate prairie-style house, Taliesin, in Wisconsin. In 1914 a crazed servant killed the woman and six others, and then burned Taliesin. Wright rebuilt it, but after the scandal had difficulty obtaining work. Nearly bankrupt in 1929, he was saved by a commission to build the Johnson Wax Company's administration building in Racine, Wisconsin. He then entered his last, greatest period, creating magnificent homes, the entire campus of Florida Southern College, and a radical tubular structure for the Guggenheim Museum in New York City. He rightly considered himself the world's greatest architect, condemning cities that would not take his advice (on Dallas: "Seems to be made of rubber bath-mats"; on Pittsburgh: "Abandon it"). He died at ninety years of age, having completed 700 buildings and while working on plans for a mile-high, 528-floor skyscraper that would reach upward like the great trees of the American West. His epitaph was written by a French newspaper editor: "Nothing was ever more deliberately and more profoundly American than the personality and career of Frank Lloyd Wright."

## Web Links

**www.delmars.com/wright/index.html**
A virtual look at Wright's work with links to collections and resources.

**www.FrankLloydWright.org**
The site of the Frank Lloyd Wright Foundation, with a tour of Taliesin and lists of sites open to the public.

for corporations had been growing rich from government legislation since the Civil War. The real struggle was over who would use the government.

In 1892 the Populist presidential candidate, James B. Weaver, received more than a million popular, and twenty-two electoral, votes. The party also elected governors in Kansas, North Dakota, and Colorado. Two years later, in the congressional elections, Populist candidates received nearly 1.5 million votes. That was the peak of the party's power. The last hope for a racially tolerant party that could make important changes in industrial America disappeared when William Jennings Bryan and the Democratic Party absorbed most Populists in the 1896 presidential campaign.

Another reform movement more effectively challenged the social values of the new corporation. The women's rights organization began in 1848 at Seneca Falls, New York, when a group of feminists resolved that since "all men and women are created equal" and since men refused women the vote and thus made them "civilly dead," any law that treated women as inferior to men would have "no force or authority." In 1869 Wyoming territory gave women the vote. By the 1870s, moreover, feminist leaders attempted to build on the Seneca Falls declaration by urging massive social change that would go far beyond the vote ("that crumb," as one leader termed it): the reform of divorce laws, an end to job discrimination, legal equality (in many states married women could not testify in court against their husbands or hold title to property), and a marriage institution in which the partners would be more equal.

Every feminist reform seemed to threaten social stability. Critics frequently linked the feminists to anarchists and strikers as threats to social order. Business leaders, even as they transformed the nation, tried to retain the image of tranquil, stable society that rested on the family and on a clear division of labor within the family. The prospect of women voting brought dire predictions of role reversal, domestic disorder, and social anarchy. In an early debate over the suffrage question, one senator charged that if women were given the vote, they would turn society "into a state of war, and make every home a hell on earth."

The woman suffrage movement split into conservative and liberal factions, then reunited into an organization that, led by Susan B. Anthony and later by Carrie Chapman Catt, dropped demands for drastic reforms in order to gain the vote. To accomplish this goal, suffragists shrewdly used the arguments of their male opponents: women were concerned primarily with taking care of the family and consequently should have the vote since their concern for spiritual and traditional values, as opposed to men's money-grubbing, would raise the moral level of politics. But women were also capable of appealing to other prejudices. Suffragists in the South exploited racial fears by asserting that the enfranchisement of white women would ensure white supremacy in the voting booths. Elsewhere, native, white, Protestant women, indignant because they could not vote—whereas male immigrants ultimately could—spoke with disdain of "the ignorant vote." The drive for the franchise thus gained momentum. But in narrowing their program, feminists—like the South, the AFL, and Populists-turned-Democrats—had gone far in accommodating themselves to the America of the industrial corporation. In the end, conflicts in the post–Civil War era revolved not around the question of whether conservatives could carry out a class solution, but around the question of which class would succeed in carrying out a conservative solution.

American socialists never capitulated in quite the same fashion. Neither, however, did they gain many followers. In the United States, unlike England and Germany, no close bonds ever developed between the socialist movement and organized labor. The socialists who achieved the widest recognition sought to modify Marxist ideology by smoothing its rough edges. The Christian Socialists, for example, sharply attacked the new corporate order and the suffering it caused, but called for the creation of a cooperative society in the name of traditional Christian morality. They rejected Marx's materialism and belief in the inevitability of class struggle.

No one carried the attempt to reconcile socialism with American values further than Edward Bellamy, whose best-selling *Looking Backward* (1888) led to the creation of "Nationalist Clubs" across the country. Bellamy's novel described a society in the year 2000 that was organized according to socialist principles, one in which cooperation had replaced competition. But his utopia differed substantially from Marx's. Bellamy did not condone class conflict or assume that the working class was a repository of special virtue. He emphasized change in the United States rather than around the world; he found a place for religious worship in his new order; and he saw the new society developing in a gradual, peaceful way. One character explains: "Evolution, not revolution, orderly and progressive development, not precipitate and hazardous experiment is our true policy . . . prudence and conservatism are called for." This moderate approach helps explain why Bellamy gained such a large following.

## THE COLLAPSE OF THE FOURTH BARRIER: CHURCHES

In an earlier America the church had been an outspoken critic of men who sought profit rather than godliness. By the post–Civil War era, however, both Protestant and Roman Catholic leaders in the United States had largely lost their capacity to make fundamental economic or political analyses. "Our churches are largely for the mutual insurance of prosperous families, and not for the upbuilding of the great under-class of humanity," a leading New York City clergyman commented in 1874. Church leaders, moreover, confronted not only the complexities of the new industrialism, but an intellectual revolution that transformed every branch of knowledge.

Discovery of the quantum theory in physics demonstrated that energy is not emitted in predictable, continuous steps, but in unpredictable and interrupted stages. This discovery threatened to replace the ordered seventeenth-century world of Isaac Newton with an uncertain, rapidly changing universe that apparently had few if any absolutes. Sigmund Freud's investigations in Austria revealed new, treacherous depths in the unconscious. Such findings triggered the dilemmas that would characterize, and haunt, twentieth-century thought.

Some church leaders worked to reconcile the new science with their religious beliefs. The most popular response, however, was the new revivalism led by Dwight L. Moody, who condemned outright Charles Darwin's discoveries that species had evolved over the ages and were not created in a particular moment, as the biblical version seemed to indicate. Moody handled such problems by proclaiming that reason was less useful in religion than emotion. His message was particularly well received in college communities. John R. Mott, a Cornell University graduate, responded to the new revivalism by spearheading the spectacular growth of the Young Men's Christian Association. Some churchgoers tended to solve their intellectual confusion through sheer activity.

By 1900 the church had failed utterly to lessen the oppressiveness or the power of rampaging industrialism. Its failure was so marked that new organizations, such as the Salvation Army, had developed to aid the human casualties in the urban slums. By 1902 coal mine owner George F. Baer could oppose strikers with the remark: "The rights and interests of the laboring man will be protected and cared for—not by the labor agitators, but by the Christian men to whom God in his infinite wisdom has given the control of the property interests in this country." Few church leaders disputed Baer. The question thus became: Would these "Christian men" indeed care for—or exploit—their fellow men and women?

## THE COLLAPSE OF THE FIFTH BARRIER: THE POLITICAL PARTY SYSTEM

Some scholars believe that the last, best hope to check the corporation's rising power was the political system and particularly the choice it provided voters in the 1896 presidential election. This is doubtful. Given the experiences of the social groups discussed above, the issue had been decided before 1896. The triumph of William McKinley over William Jennings Bryan in that election did no more than confirm a prevailing trend. It also established a political pattern that would govern the United States for nearly forty years.

The roaring depression of 1893 was the destroyer. It struck while a Democratic president, Grover Cleveland, and a Democratic Congress held power. The 1894 elections consequently brought about the largest turnover of congressional strength in the nation's history. The Democrats lost 113 House seats; their Capitol Hill leadership was virtually wiped out. In New England only a lone Democratic congressman survived (John F. Kennedy's grandfather, John "Honey Fitz" Fitzgerald), and even such southern states as Texas and Virginia elected Republicans.

Until this point, voters had been able to separate Democrats from Republicans rather neatly. Democrats preached limited government and noninterference in the affairs of individuals, states, and corporations. The marketplace, not the government, was supposed to encourage or regulate the society. As one Democratic leader proclaimed, "We are never doing as well as when we are doing nothing." The Republicans, on the other hand, urged a more active government and greater centralization of power. They used government to erect protective tariffs, give land to railroads, and make the monetary system more efficient for business. Republicans, however, did not plan to use power to reform or regulate. The corporations, therefore, had nothing to fear from Democrats and much to expect from Republicans.

But after the 1894 disaster, Democrats searched desperately for new blood. They found it when Bryan, a former Nebraska congressman, electrified the party's 1896 national convention with his "Cross of Gold" speech. He urged increased coining of silver (which was cheaper than gold) to create more money and thereby enable farmers and other depression victims to pay their debts. The proposal found no support from leading businessmen. They feared that mixing silver with gold, as Bryan proposed, would so cheapen the nation's currency that the banking and credit system would sink. Nor did urban wage laborers like Bryan's plan, for it could mean they would be paid in cheaper silver dollars and have to pay higher grocery prices.

The Nebraskan also had another major problem. Since the 1840s and 1850s, American politics had been increasingly influenced by close-knit, well-organized ethnic and cultural groups (such as the Germans and Irish) that were concentrated in the cities. These ethnic groups sought to preserve such traditions as beer fests and nonreligious activities on Sunday afternoons. The Democratic Party, with its tolerant view of pluralism and ethnic traditions, offered little interference and these groups had consequently become highly important in the party organization. Bryan was a Democrat, but he represented a largely rural view and constituency, was a "dry" on the burning question of whether alcoholic beverages should be prohibited, and practiced a religious fundamentalism abhorrent to many Roman Catholics and liberal Protestants in the Democratic Party. He argued for an activist government that would move decisively in both the society and the economy.

McKinley, meanwhile, transformed the Republican Party. Republicans had long been friends of business, but since the antislavery crusade of the 1850s they had also become identified with attempts to impose their own moral and political standards on ethnic groups and newly arrived immigrants. When Republicans preached the evils of alcoholic drink and the need to reserve Sunday for nothing but quiet meditation, Irish, German, and Jewish immigrants tended to vote Democratic. As a rising star in the political jungles of Ohio, however, McKinley had learned how to moderate such zeal so that he could win votes from ethnic settlements and "wets" in Cleveland and Cincinnati, as well as from traditional Republican rural areas. During the 1896 campaign he blurred the lines between the parties by welcoming the ethnic Democrats, whom Bryan was driving out, while keeping most traditional Republicans.

The confrontation was one of the most dramatic in the country's political history. An unprecedented number of voters turned out to give McKinley a triumph. His administration raised the tariff and then, with the help of rising prices in 1897 and 1898 caused by new discoveries of gold and increased agricultural exports to Europe, the president killed any hope for modifying the currency by having Congress pass the Gold Standard Act. With these issues decided, Americans began staying away from the polls on Election Day. One-party states became fixtures. Democrats owned the South (especially when African-Americans were kept from voting after the 1890s). Republicans controlled much of the Northeast and Midwest. A new era of American politics began, characterized by a diminished concern for elections, little party competition in many states, and Republican power. The new corporate industrialism had little to fear from Washington.

## THE UNITED STATES BECOMES A GREAT WORLD POWER

Not coincidentally, the United States saw its economy mature at the same time that it became a world power. It joined England, France, Germany, and Russia in the great-power class when the Europeans were most imperialistic: between 1870 and 1900 they conquered more than 10 million square miles (one-fifth of the earth's land) and 150 million people. (Imperialism may be defined as one sovereign people subjugating and controlling an alien and formerly sovereign people.) The United States, however, did not join the rush for land. It thus differentiated its empire from that of the Europeans, who sought colonial areas—that is, territory that the Europeans could formally control and populate. After the Civil War, Americans sought empire primarily for trade, not territory, and preferred to allow native inhabitants to rule themselves under informal U.S. protection. This was the Americans' "new empire," as it was termed in the late 1890s.

The old empire, developed between the seventeenth century and the 1850s, had been based on the land conquered by Americans in their march across the continent. This old empire ended with the settlement of the Pacific coast, the close of the frontier, and the consolidation of the continent by the corporation. The last act had been a series of vicious Indian wars that climaxed a determination to drive Native Americans from lands in the Dakotas, Oklahoma, and Wyoming that had been given to them earlier in the century. These lands had been thought barren, but settlers rapidly encroached upon them after the Civil War, whereupon the federal government concocted devices to expel the American Indians. Between 1887 and 1934 they lost to whites about 86 million of their 138 million acres. One Sioux chief asked the obvious: "Why does not the Great Father put his red children on wheels, so he can move them as he will?" When some tribes refused to budge, the U.S. Army struck. "We must act with vindictive earnestness against the Sioux, even to extermination, men, women and children," General William Tecumseh Sherman proclaimed in the late 1860s. Sherman was especially ruthless. He destroyed buffalo herds, and then attacked Indian camps in midwinter so he could burn all provisions and thus cause mass starvation. The tribes were exterminated or reduced to begging. Their great chiefs—Geronimo, Big Foot, and Chief Joseph—died or fled, while Sitting Bull, the famous conqueror of Lieutenant Colonel George Custer's cavalry in 1876, ended as an exhibit in a circus.

Perhaps the ultimate horror occurred at Wounded Knee, South Dakota, in 1890. After troops disarmed cooperative Sioux, someone fired a rifle. The cavalry opened full fire, and then unloaded large cannons, which exploded nearly a shell a second in the defenseless camp. "We tried to run," one Sioux woman recalled, "but they shot us like we were buffalo." At least 150 and perhaps 250 of the original 350 men, women, and children were murdered. The American Indian campaigns sharpened the military's effectiveness. More important, they gave many Americans a rationale for warring against peoples of other colors.

Racism, however, did not trigger American imperialism in 1898. Its taproot lay in the post-1873 depressions and the need to find overseas markets for the overly productive factories and farms. That need became imperative during the strike-ridden days of the mid-1890s, when, in the words of Secretary of State Walter Quintin Gresham, "symptoms of revolution" appeared among unemployed laborers and farmers. Riots and strikes from Brooklyn to Chicago to San Francisco were capped by a march of thousands of unemployed (the so-called Coxey's Army) on Washington, DC, in 1894. The "symptoms" would disappear only with employment, and that required expanded markets. "The prosperity of our people," the secretary of the treasury announced in 1894, "depends largely upon their ability to sell their surplus products in foreign markets at remunerative prices."

The United States exported less than 10 percent of its manufactures and about 18 percent of its farm products, but these figures were misleading. Products that formed the economy's backbone heavily depended on external markets: 70 percent of the cotton crop had to be sold abroad, as did 40 percent of the wheat, 50 percent of the copper, 15 percent of the iron and steel, and even 16 percent of the agricultural equipment. These figures were impressive, but they were also inadequate, for the magnitude of exports did not prevent a quarter-century of depressions. Even greater overseas markets were required. There was, of course, an alternative. Americans could reorient their system, making more equal the distribution of wealth. Business and political leaders, who instead preferred greater production and expanded markets, never seriously considered that alternative. The needed world outlets, however, were coming under the control of the aggressive Europeans. If Americans were to find overseas buyers, they needed the aid of the State Department and perhaps the U.S. Army and Navy. As one prominent Republican observed in 1897, "Diplomacy is the management of international business."

Two business possibilities suddenly opened dramatically, one in Asia, the other in Latin America. In 1895 a surging Japan humiliated China in a brief conflict that revealed the loser to be a paper dragon. The European powers rushed to carve out areas of China exclusively for

President William McKinley, c. 1900. *(Library of Congress)*

their own trade and investment. This flew directly in the face of a half-century of an American policy known as the "open door," whose objective was to trade with a whole, sovereign China. McKinley knew that major American interests were deeply endangered, particularly after iron and textile exporters implored him to stop the European moves. The president's hands were tied, however, by another crisis ninety miles off the Florida coast.

Since 1868 Cubans had revolted against the domination, corruption, and inefficiency of their Spanish rulers. The United States had barely avoided involvement during the 1870s. The conflict simmered down during the next decade, but burst into flames once again in 1895. Under the leadership of José Martí, the Cubans announced the establishment of their own independent government. Several restraints initially kept Americans out of the struggle. For one thing, they feared that intervention might result in their having to annex Cuba, which they wished to avoid because of the racial, constitutional, and political problems that would inevitably arise. As it was, they were experiencing enough difficulty just keeping their own nation together during the 1890s. Moreover, the business community, with which McKinley was in close contact, did not at first want war. The depression at last seemed to be lifting in 1897. Finally seeing the light at the end of a gloomy economic tunnel, businessmen feared that the demands of a war economy would threaten the growing prosperity.

In early 1898, however, both restraints disappeared. The first problem evaporated when Americans began to understand that they did not have to govern a free Cuba. They needed only a veto over certain Cuban actions so that, for example, the island could not fall under British power. The inhabitants could otherwise be allowed to govern themselves. McKinley and Congress devised a classic solution in which the United States would enjoy power over, but have little daily responsibility for, the Cubans.

The second restraint disappeared in March 1898, when the business community and McKinley began to fear that a continuation of the Cuban struggle endangered $50 million worth of American investments on the island. A political threat also existed. If McKinley let Cuba fester and uncertainty continue, Bryan might oust the Republicans in 1900 with the cry of "Free Cuba and Free Silver." "Look out for Mr. Bryan," remarked McKinley's top political adviser, Mark Hanna, in February 1898. But, he was asked, would not the Democrats hesitate before offering the nomination again to Bryan? "Hesitate?" Hanna replied. "Does a dog hesitate for a marriage license?"

In late January 1898 McKinley sent the warship *Maine* to Havana to protect U.S. property. Two weeks later the warship blew up, killing more than 250 Americans. The causes have never been determined, but the nation (although not the president) quickly blamed Spain. War sentiment grew, fueled by an increasing fear that the United States would not be able to protect its growing interests in China until the Cuban problem was solved. On March 25 a close political adviser in New York City cabled McKinley: "Big corporations here now believe we will have war. Believe all would welcome it as relief to suspense." Two days later the president presented an ultimatum to Spain. The Spanish acquiesced to two of his demands by promising to stop their brutalities and to declare an armistice. But they refused McKinley's request that they promise eventual independence to Cuba and allow him to act as a mediator in the negotiations. Any Spanish government that accepted that demand would have immediately fallen from power. On April 11, McKinley asked Congress to declare war. Not for the first or last time, Americans concluded they would have to fight abroad in order to have peace and prosperity at home.

## "THAT SPLENDID LITTLE WAR"

It would be one of the weirdest and most significant of wars. The first action occurred not in Cuba, but thousands of miles away in the Spanish-controlled Philippines. Six weeks before declaring war, McKinley had ordered Admiral George Dewey, the American commander in the Pacific, to take the Philippines should war erupt. Dewey's force was not overly imposing. When it left Hong Kong to fight the Spanish fleet, British naval officials remarked that the Americans were "a fine set of fellows, but unhappily we shall never see them again." Dewey, however, easily blockaded, then in less than six hours smashed a decrepit Spanish flotilla, killing or wounding 400, while only a few Americans suffered scratches. The United States suddenly became a major military power in the Far East as the result of Dewey's victory at Manila Bay in May 1898.

The campaigns in Cuba were not as spectacular. The American army numbered only 28,000 regulars before the war, and when augmented with 200,000 volunteers it was short of modern rifles, had inadequate medical supplies, ate food that was unfit for human consumption, and wore uniforms designed for duty in Alaska. The War Department proved so ineffectual that McKinley had to fire his secretary of war amid a national scandal. Americans escaped additional humiliation only because Spain was even more inefficient and corrupt. A broken-down Spanish navy struggled across the Atlantic only to be blockaded in Santiago. American troops overcame the heat and malaria long enough to win the heights overlooking that Cuban city. Theodore Roosevelt, who had the good taste to have his uniform custom-tailored by Brooks Brothers in New York City, led one charge up the heights, thus leading the troops directly into the enemy fire. They were saved only by the inability of the Spanish garrison to hit slowly moving targets. Americans held their precarious position for two days, in part because of the heroism of African-American units. Spain's navy was thus forced out into the harbor and then destroyed easily by the American fleet. Madrid asked for peace.

A war that lasted only three months made the United States a great world power. Roosevelt groused, "there wasn't enough war to go around." Americans now held a commanding position in Asia and the dominant role in the Western Hemisphere. At home they felt only the exhilaration, for they never had to consider curtailment of their individual liberties or rationing of foodstuffs in order to fight the war. Only 500 Americans died in battle, but four times that number fell victim to diseases. It was an unreal war. One reporter noted that as an American warship shelled a Spanish fort in Cuba, the sailors "whispered and chuckled. . . . Meanwhile from below came the strains of the string band playing from the officers' mess. . . . War as it is conducted at this end of the century is civilized." The horrors of 1873 to 1897 were over, with the new corporate system preserved and dramatically expanded by what Secretary of State John Hay called "that splendid little war."

## THE PEACE: CLOSING CUBA, OPENING CHINA

McKinley had limited diplomatic objectives. He did not want to copy the Europeans by obtaining a large, expensive, unmanageable colonial empire. After obtaining Cuba, therefore, he allowed the Cubans to write their own constitution but forced them to accept the Platt Amendment passed by the U.S. Congress. This legislation gave the United States the right

Emilio Aguinaldo, commander of Filipino insurgents. *(The Granger Collection, NYC)*

to land troops in Cuba to maintain law and order, limited the amount of debt the island could accumulate, and later made Guantanamo a U.S. naval base. "There is, of course, little or no independence left Cuba under the Platt Amendment," the U.S. commander in Cuba accurately observed. Supposedly independent, the island would actually be controlled and exploited by the United States for sixty years. The president in addition took Puerto Rico from Spain and made it an unorganized territory of the United States.

He also acquired the Philippines, but the Filipinos reacted quite unexpectedly. McKinley had decided that they were unprepared for self-government and that if left to themselves they would be victimized by some European power. He did not want all of the islands, only the magnificent port of Manila, from which American merchants and warships could develop and protect interests in China. Manila, however, would be threatened if the remainder of the islands fell into European hands. McKinley therefore decided reluctantly that he had no alternative but to take all of the Philippines. As he later explained to missionaries who visited the White House, he had constantly prayed about the problem; then one night a voice told him to annex the Philippines for, among other reasons, "we could not turn them over to France or Germany—our commercial rivals in the Orient—that would be bad business and discreditable." Apparently everyone who had endured the post-1873 depressions knew the horrors of "bad business," even ghostly voices. The Filipinos, however, were not impressed. Led by Emilio Aguinaldo, they declared themselves independent and fought 120,000 American troops in a three-year struggle. Some 2,000 Americans and perhaps as many as 200,000 Filipinos died. The United States used increasingly brutal methods to end the insurrection. After some American troops were massacred, one general ordered the killing of every Filipino male over the age of ten. This order never took effect, but lesser barbarities continued until 1902, when Aguinaldo had been captured and resistance finally broken.

At home, anti-imperialist groups, led by conservative businessmen, intellectuals, and some Democrats, organized to blast McKinley's Philippine policy. "G is for guns / That McKinley has sent / To teach Filipinos / What Jesus Christ meant," went one anti-imperialist poem. But despite financing from Andrew Carnegie and literature written by such figures as Mark Twain, these groups received little support. In the election of 1900 Bryan tried briefly to gain the support of the anti-imperialists, but he decided to soft-pedal their cause in order to emphasize again the free-silver issue. Nothing could save either the anti-imperialists or Bryan. McKinley and his vice presidential running mate, Governor Theodore Roosevelt of New York, won a landslide victory larger than the Republican triumph of 1896.

Despite the Philippine bloodshed, the president had scored notable victories, including an end to the depression, solution of the Cuban problem, and establishment of the United States as a great power in Asia. The last was particularly important. Using Dewey's victory as leverage, McKinley moved to stop the carving up of China by the Europeans. Viewed another way, he sought to keep all of China open to American exporters and missionaries. In 1899 and 1900, Secretary of State John Hay issued two "open door" notes asking the other powers to promise that they would keep China open on an equal basis to all outsiders; meanwhile Chinese sovereignty would be recognized in all parts of the empire. The other powers, particularly Russia, grumbled, but Hay publicly announced that everyone had accepted the American position. This was not accurate, for the Russians, and later the Japanese, would not agree that China should become a marketplace open to all. They believed that their proximity to the China market gave them—indeed, required that they have—favored positions for their own economic and political interests. Hay and McKinley nevertheless insisted that American businessmen and missionaries enjoy an open door to compete for Chinese customers and souls on the same terms as anyone else, even Russians and Japanese. American statesmen would hold to that insistence until the 1940s.

The Civil War and the ensuing economic crisis mark the most threatening forty-year era in U.S. history. But McKinley's triumph at the end of the dark years gave Americans new optimism and reaffirmed their traditional belief that the nation had a special mission to perform in the world. The country had not simply survived the terrors of the post-1860 years. It had done great works. Americans had developed the modern corporation, an almost magical instrument for ordering and expanding wealth. With the conquest of Spain and the issuance of the open door notes, the nation stood on the world stage as one of the great global empires. Frederick Jackson Turner had been proven correct: a new period was indeed opening in American history. With the continental frontier apparently closed, Americans were seeking new frontiers.

In September 1901, McKinley explained why to the Pan-American Exposition in Buffalo, New York. The United States possessed "almost appalling" wealth, the president announced, and must therefore move into the world market to trade: "Isolation is no longer possible or desirable." The next day an anarchist shot McKinley. Theodore Roosevelt, a most outspoken expansionist and a student of Turner's theories, moved into the White House.

# CHAPTER TWO

# 1900–1917
# The Progressive Era

Suffragists on a picket line in front of the White House. One banner reads, "Mr. President How Long Must Women Wait For Liberty." *(Library of Congress)*

An interest in reform has always characterized American history. What varied over time has been the things people identified as evils, the intellectual justifications and political techniques used to eradicate those evils, the obstacles reformers encountered, and the degree of support those reforms received. Seldom has a larger proportion of the population favored social improvement than during the opening years of the twentieth century, when Americans first tried in a systematic way to control the forces of industrialization and urbanization. Because the United States was becoming a major world power, the successes and failures of the Progressive movement affected not only Americans but also people around the world.

## THE REFORM IMPULSE

Although progressivism followed on the heels of the Populist revolt and sometimes echoed certain Populist demands, the two movements differed in important respects. Populism had drawn support primarily from farmers and had always remained a sectional force; progressivism won backing from city dwellers, including the middle classes, and had as wide a following in New York and California as in Kansas and South Carolina. Populists had sought for the most part to improve conditions in the countryside; Progressives devoted considerably more attention to political and social problems in the cities. Precisely because Progressives drew on a wider constituency and were concerned with a broader range of issues, they achieved a measure of influence at the city, state, and national levels that had eluded the Populists.

Progressives did, however, pay a price for this success. So many different people wanting so many disparate things styled themselves "Progressives" that the movement often seemed to lack a clearly defined program. Progressivism attracted surprisingly diverse groups: small businessmen who favored a curb on monopolies, and big businessmen who sought to extend their economic influence and eliminate their competitors; native Americans who feared the influx of eastern European immigrants, and settlement-house workers who appreciated the newcomers' contributions to American culture; southern whites dedicated to the preservation of Jim Crow, and northern blacks just as fully committed to its eradication; social scientists who believed that planning held all the answers to human progress; and prohibitionists who imagined that closing the saloons would usher in a new world.

Yet for all its diversity, there was a distinctly Progressive approach to social problems. Progressives saw industrialization and urbanization as potentially disruptive forces. The burgeoning cities and corporations seemed to endanger social stability and to undermine older ideals of individual initiative and equal opportunity. To restore a sense of order, to impose a reasonable measure of control on the forces transforming American life, Progressives used the power of government in an unprecedented fashion. In some respects the concern with democratizing government through the direct election of senators, the initiative and referendum, and woman suffrage followed logically from this conviction that government had to play an expanded role. Progressives were optimists, activists, and rationalists. They assumed that society was malleable and devoted their energies to molding it in the proper way.

## BIG BUSINESS

One major impetus to progressivism was an awareness of the social problems resulting from explosive economic growth. Between 1880 and 1900 the United States took over world leadership in industrial output. Not only did production increase, but also it became concentrated in the hands of relatively few corporations and trusts, which often found it both possible and profitable to control market conditions. The creation of the United States Steel Corporation in 1901 symbolized the growth of industry, its consolidation, and its domination of the market. By purchasing Andrew Carnegie's steel interests, J.P. Morgan established the first billion-dollar corporation and controlled 60 percent of steel output. Yet this was only the most spectacular in a series of mergers that took place at the time. By 1904, 1 percent of American companies produced 38 percent of all manufactured goods.

Recognizing that the existence of mammoth trusts called for a measure of public control, reformers were divided over what course to pursue. Some wished to restore competition by dismantling the trusts, outlawing monopolies, and encouraging small enterprise. Others believed that big business was highly efficient. They saw nothing wrong with trusts so long as the government ensured that the benefits of efficiency were passed on to the public in the form of low prices and that profits were kept within reasonable bounds. Despite sharp differences of opinion on this matter, Progressives agreed on the desirability of bringing private economic power under a larger measure of public control. Most reformers thought that government should regulate railroad rates, lower the protective tariff, and protect consumers from impure or unsafe products. What distinguished Progressives was less their unanimity on a solution to economic problems than their agreement that unruly economic forces required some form of discipline.

Those most directly affected by the growth of industry were factory workers themselves. Efforts to improve their conditions centered on three issues: compensating workers injured on the job, regulating the hours and wages of working women, and restricting child labor. Reformers channeled most of their energies into enacting laws for these purposes at the state level. Not until relatively late in the Progressive Era did they turn to federal legislation, and then they met with only partial success. In 1908 a major obstacle to state regulation crumbled when the Supreme Court, reversing an earlier ruling, held in *Muller v. Oregon* that fixing a ten-hour day for women did not violate the Fourteenth Amendment's guarantee against deprivation of property without due process. Equally important, the Court based its decision on documentary evidence concerning the harmful social effects of long working hours, thereby accepting a key argument of reformers.

## CITIES AND SLUMS

The United States became more highly urbanized as it became more highly industrialized. Progressivism represented a response to the city as much as to the corporation. Between 1890 and 1920 the number of people living in cities increased by 300 percent, while the number of rural dwellers increased by only 30 percent. Urban population grew by 11.8 million in the decade after 1900, so that by 1910 more than 44 million Americans—45.7 percent of the total population—lived in areas defined as urban by the Census Bureau. The largest cities grew at a spectacular rate: by 1910, 1.5 million people lived in Philadelphia, 2.1 million in Chicago, and 5 million in New York. Not only did big cities grow bigger, but there were also more of them. In 1860 there were nine cities with a population over 100,000; in 1910 there were fifty. This urban expansion reflected a natural increase in population as well as the effect of both migration from rural areas and immigration from Europe.

Because cities grew so swiftly, contained such a diverse population, and furnished some people with a chance to acquire fabulous wealth, they were plagued by mismanagement. Investigations into municipal government unearthed officials who took bribes or who, for the right price, granted lucrative gas and streetcar franchises to private corporations. Where city government was not corrupt it often seemed archaic, administratively unable to cope with the needs of modern urban life. Above all, there was what Jacob Riis termed "the blight of the tenement": dimly lit, badly ventilated slums, jammed with more people than it seemed they could possibly hold. To Progressives the slum was "the great destroyer of individuality" and as such posed a threat not only to the health of its residents but also to the health of the state. "Democracy was not predicated upon a country made up of tenement dwellers," said one reformer, "nor can it so survive."

Progressive solutions for these problems were as varied as the problems themselves. Some reformers concentrated on modernizing and depoliticizing urban government. They favored extending the merit system, streamlining municipal administration, freeing cities from state control, and transferring powers traditionally exercised by mayors to impartial city managers or commissions. Other Progressives, including mayors Samuel "Golden Rule" Jones of Toledo and Tom Johnson of Cleveland, emphasized the benefits of municipal ownership of public utilities. Many reformers sought to tear down slums by enacting building codes that imposed structural and sanitary safeguards. New York City adopted such a tenement-house law in 1901, and other cities followed suit. Finally, there were those in the city planning movement who wished to create a more rational urban environment.

## MORALITY AND DEMOCRACY

Some Progressives wanted to protect Americans not only from the perils of urban and industrial life, but from their own impulses as well. Moral uplift was an important element in reform, and perhaps nothing revealed this relation more clearly than the link between progressivism and Prohibition. Not everyone who supported Prohibition was a Progressive in politics, but a large number of reformers favored a ban on alcohol and, what is more significant, justified their stance on thoroughly Progressive grounds. Starting with the premise that the saloon functioned as the home of the political boss and a breeding ground for corruption, reformers concluded that if they ended the sale of liquor they would take a long step on the road to urban reform. Moreover, many believed that liquor caused workers to squander hard-earned wages and neglect their families. A Boston social worker thought that ignoring Prohibition was like "bailing water out of a tub with the tap turned on; letting the drink custom and the liquor traffic run full blast while we limply stood around and picked up the wreckage." In this view, Prohibition seemed an indispensable weapon in the effort to stamp out poverty.

To achieve any of these goals—business regulation, urban reform, social justice, moral uplift—required, in the view of Progressives, the extension of political democracy. Reformers favored the election of senators directly by the people rather than by state legislatures, and in 1913, after several states had made this change, it was incorporated into the Seventeenth Amendment. Similarly, Progressives endorsed the preferential primary, which gave voters a larger voice in the selection of candidates; most states adopted some variant of this system. Progressives also favored the initiative and referendum. By 1915, twenty-one states had accepted such plans, under which citizens could introduce a measure into the state legislature and vote on it at a general election. Finally, reformers supported woman suffrage, in part because they expected women to vote in behalf of social reform. A litmus-paper test for progressivism might well have involved attitudes toward popular rule.

## WOMEN AND THE PROGRESSIVE IMPULSE

If Progressives counted on woman suffrage to provide votes for social reform, they had reason. Middle-class women supported the Progressive agenda. In women's clubs, temperance locals, social settlements, and other reform associations, they strove to foster urban improvement, moral uplift, and social justice. Such activism not only served Progressive ends, but also bolstered the arguments of suffragists, who based their claim to the vote on the good that women would do for society if they were enfranchised.

A great swell of female organization, well under way by the 1890s, laid the groundwork for women's involvement in Progressive reform. The first women's clubs, formed after the Civil War, had been devoted to cultural projects. In 1892, when the National Federation of Women's Clubs began, clubwomen decided to "contemplate our own social order" and steered their attention to urban improvement. Contributing to libraries, settlements, and hospitals, they advocated better city services, protection for women and children in factories, and finally, in 1914, woman suffrage. Members of the militant Women's Christian Temperance Union, meanwhile, followed leader Frances Willard's injunction to "Do everything." In addition to campaigning for Prohibition, they endorsed a gamut of causes—pacifism, labor reform, social purity, and city welfare work. Many temperance workers were also drawn into the suffrage movement.

The city provided a broad arena for women's collective efforts. As the new century began, women created new reform organizations to improve urban life and to serve as bridges between social classes. The National Congress of Mothers (1897) sponsored playgrounds and kindergartens, battled urban problems and promoted "all those characteristics which shall elevate and ennoble." The National Consumers League (1899) sought to curb hours of women wage earners in stores and factories and to ensure the safety and cleanliness of products bought by homemakers. The Women's Trade Union League (1903), whose members included women factory employees as well as their middle-class "allies," hoped to unionize women workers. With major bases in New York and Chicago, the league burst into action. In New York's shirtwaist strike of 1909–1910, when some 30,000 garment workers walked off the job, league members masterminded strike publicity and joined waistmakers on the picket line. They protested the infamous Triangle Fire of 1911, when scores of women garment workers, locked in the upper stories of a shirtwaist factory, were incinerated or leaped to their deaths. Since unionization proved difficult, the league supported the passage of protective laws to ensure women workers a minimum wage, limited working hours, and safer working conditions. Between 1908, when the Supreme Court voiced approval of such laws in *Muller v. Oregon*, and 1917, some twenty states enacted them.

The most significant achievement of Progressive women was undoubtedly the settlement house. In 1889, Jane Addams founded Hull House in Chicago and a group of women college graduates started the College Settlement in New York. By 1900, 100 settlements existed; by 1905, 200; and by 1910, 400. Located in the immigrant ghetto, the settlement house responded to neighborhood needs by providing clubs and social services. It answered what Addams

People lined up to identify the bodies of victims after a fire at the Triangle Shirtwaist Company in New York City that killed 146 workers on March 25, 1911. The disaster drew attention to inadequate fire regulations and poor working conditions in the city's sweatshops. *(Hulton Archive/Getty Images)*

called the "subjective need" of young educated women who wanted to contribute to public life. (Men worked in settlements, too, but they were in a minority.) It gratified, in one settlement worker's words, a "thirst to know how the other half lived." The settlement house also became an urban social science laboratory, investigating local conditions and transforming its findings into legislative proposals. Settlement house residents supported juvenile courts, compulsory education laws, housing laws, factory regulation, and sanitation measures. Finally, the settlement house propelled its leading residents into positions of civic responsibility. Florence Kelley of Hull House moved on to become a state factory inspector, consumer advocate, and lobbyist. Julia Lathrop, another Hull House resident, became the first head of the federal Children's Bureau, founded in 1912.

The suffrage movement capitalized on the activism of urban reformers, labor advocates, and settlement house workers. Hull House leaders such as Lathrop and Kelley spoke at suffrage conventions. Addams, too, served as an officer of the National American Woman Suffrage Association. In her articles and speeches, she argued for the vote by appealing to Progressive sensibilities. The complexity of city government, Addams claimed, demanded "the help of minds accustomed to . . . a responsibility for the cleanliness and comfort of other people." Modern urban problems could not be solved by mere business expertise, she argued, but required "the human welfare point of view." When the Progressive Party first convened in 1912, it endorsed woman suffrage and invited Jane Addams to make a major seconding speech for nominee Theodore Roosevelt. When a "great party" pledged itself to protect children, care for the aged, and promote industrial safety, Addams explained, it was "inevitable that it should appeal to women and seek to draw upon the great reservoir of moral energy so long undesired and unutilized in politics."

The energy generated by Progressive reform pervaded the women's movement and ranged across the political spectrum. In the decade before World War I, women established a peace movement. They joined the campaigns against prostitution and "white slavery." College students formed suffrage societies and social service clubs. Progressive educators sought to reform classroom teaching and to promote vocational education. Through the Young Women's Christian Association, women reformers offered residences and services to young working women. On the left, socialist women contributed to labor reform and suffrage campaigns. Elizabeth Gurley Flynn, an organizer for the Industrial Workers of the World, mobilized workers in the Lawrence, Massachusetts, and Paterson, New Jersey, textile strikes. Anarchist and free speech advocate Emma Goldman toured the nation and voiced her views in *Mother Earth* (1906–1918). Decrying the "conventional lie" of marriage and woman's role as "sex commodity," Goldman defended free love, contraception, and women's emancipation. Public health nurse Margaret Sanger, following Goldman's example, campaigned for sex education, contraception, and other radical causes. Her short-lived periodical, *The Woman Rebel* (1914), where the term "birth control" was first used, brought her a multicount federal indictment for violation of the obscenity laws. Radical efforts were not necessarily appreciated by the Progressive mainstream of the women's movement, which was devoted primarily to woman suffrage and social service, but they contributed to a rising feminist tide.

An influential feminist of the era was Charlotte Perkins Gilman, who was less interested in the vote than in women's emancipation from economic dependency. In *Women and Economics* (1899) and subsequent works, Gilman denounced the home as an archaic institution that imprisoned women, transformed them into nonproductive consumers, and clogged the wheels of progress. "Only as we think, feel, and work outside the home, do we become humanly developed, civilized, and socialized," she wrote in 1903. To foster women's economic independence and liberate women from the home, Gilman proposed large apartment units, collective housekeeping arrangements, and child care facilities. Although her ideas diverged from those of mainstream feminism, which tended to emphasize women's homemaking expertise, Gilman's views won admiration both within the women's movement and outside it. Progressive America was receptive to all facets of reform.

## SIN AND SOCIETY: THE MUCKRAKERS

That receptivity, in turn, was fostered by a group of journalists known as muckrakers who set out to document the social costs of urbanization and industrialization. The development of this literature of exposure reflected technological changes in magazine publishing. In the decade of the 1890s new developments in printing and photoengraving made the publication of inexpensive magazines feasible. As the price dropped from 25 or 35 cents to 10 cents, the magazine-reading public tripled and advertising revenue soared. Not only could writers reach a wide audience, but that audience apparently wanted to read about what was wrong with America. Articles of a muckraking nature began to appear, and in 1901 *McClure's* published "In the World of Graft," which exposed the alliance between police and criminals in various cities.

In 1902, *McClure's* circulation was boosted by the start of two major muckraking series, Lincoln Steffens's probe of corruption in municipal government, "The Shame of the Cities," and Ida Tarbell's exposé of the development of John D. Rockefeller's Standard Oil trust. From 1903 to 1912 nearly 2,000 articles in this genre appeared. Virtually no area of American life escaped the muckrakers' attention. They exposed corrupt city officials and U.S. senators who never cast a vote without consulting business interests. They zeroed in on fraudulent business deals. They described what it was like to live in a slum or work in a sweatshop. The muckrakers told of vermin scurrying around the floors of meat packing plants: "The rats were nuisances; the packers would put poisoned bread out for them; they would die, and then rats, bread and meat would go into the hoppers together." They depicted workers horribly maimed when factories failed to install safety devices. They threw a harsh light on those who made a living from gambling, liquor, or, worst of all, the white-slave trade—"the recruiting and sale of young girls of the poorer classes by procurers." The muckrakers taught consumers about food adulteration and dangerous patent medicines.

Behind these journalistic assaults rested characteristically Progressive assumptions. Muckrakers went after the inside scoop. They believed that the truth lay beneath the surface, that things were not what they seemed, that as the historian Richard Hofstadter observed, "reality was the inside story. It was rough and sordid, hidden and neglected." In trying to get to the bottom of things, journalists often sought real-life experiences. Jack London served time in a county penitentiary before he described the brutalizing effects of the prison system. Upton Sinclair worked in the Chicago stockyards before he wrote *The Jungle.* John Spargo recounted his attempt to do a child's work in a coal mine: "I tried to pick out the pieces of slate from the hurrying stream of coal, often missing them; my hands were bruised and cut in a few minutes; I was covered from head to foot with coal dust, and for many hours afterwards I was expectorating some of the small particles of anthracite I had swallowed." Muckrakers usually wrote fact, not fiction; they were concrete; they named names. They spent more time criticizing specific evils than proposing broad solutions.

## THE REFORM IDEOLOGY

The muckrakers, by calling attention to social evils, helped create a climate conducive to reform. Similarly, a group of intellectuals, by developing a new approach to economics, law, and history, lowered another barrier to change. This barrier had taken the form of an ideology that rejected state aid for the victims of industrialization and urbanization. Conservatives, following what they believed to be Charles Darwin's path, reasoned that society, like nature, evolved through a struggle that assured the survival of the fittest. In economics conservatives stressed laissez-faire; in law they worshipped precedent; in history they dwelt on the sanctions for private property written into the Constitution. In each instance society was a captive—of natural law, of precedent, of the past. William Graham Sumner, perhaps the most prominent American social Darwinist, summed up this outlook in the title of an essay: "The Absurd Attempt to Make the World Over."

Unlike Sumner, a group of reform-minded economists reasoned that the attempt to make the world over was anything but absurd. Rather, it seemed to them the height of common sense. Richard T. Ely of the University of Wisconsin denied that natural laws governed the workings of the economic system or that laissez-faire was an adequate guide to public policy.

Thorstein Veblen, in *The Theory of the Leisure Class* (1899) and other works, pointed to the inefficient and unproductive aspects of the profit system as well as to the waste involved in conspicuous consumption and conspicuous leisure.

During the Progressive Era the courts often acted as an obstacle to reform. But at the same time men like Oliver Wendell Holmes Jr., who was appointed to the Supreme Court in 1903; Louis D. Brandeis, appointed in 1916; and Roscoe Pound of Harvard Law School, began to transform the law from a bulwark of the status quo into a vehicle for change. Although they would not always be found on the same side of an issue, Holmes and Brandeis shared a similar conception of the relationship of law to society. Holmes believed, "the life of the law has not been logic: it has been experience." If the law was rooted in human history rather than in abstract principles, if people made laws to fulfill their needs, then the law must change as new needs arose. Pound, in "The Need for a Sociological Jurisprudence" (1907), held that law must conform to "the general moral sense" of the community. It could do so by placing a higher value on social justice than on individual property rights.

Once legal scholars had reached this point, it remained only for Progressives to interpret the Constitution itself as the product of particular social interests. A number of historians did so, but none captured more attention than Charles Beard did in *An Economic Interpretation of the Constitution* (1913). Beard shared the Progressive concern with unmasking the "real" forces in history. He attempted to demonstrate that the upper classes, who had not been making out well under the Articles of Confederation, had organized the movement for adoption of the Constitution; that the document lacked widespread popular support; and that "the Constitution was essentially an economic document based on the concept that the fundamental private rights of property are anterior to government and morally beyond the reach of popular majorities." Once Americans realized that the Constitution was a biased document, as one reformer believed, they would not allow it to stand in the way of necessary change.

Muckrakers and intellectuals played the complementary roles of popularizing and rationalizing reform. Both showed less interest in how society was supposed to function than in how it really did. Both sometimes regarded ideology as nothing more than a cloak for economic interest. Journalists and scholars assumed that just as a bad environment made bad citizens, so a good environment could work wonders, for "to up build human character in men you must establish for them the right social relations." While they ranged over the political spectrum—from the socialist Upton Sinclair to the rather conservative Oliver Wendell Holmes—their work resulted in a diagnosis of social problems and a theory of state action that provided the underpinning for progressivism.

## NATIVISM VERSUS THE MELTING POT

In their search for social harmony, reformers discovered no greater sources of dissonance than the twin issues of ethnicity and race. Progressivism coincided with a massive wave of immigration. In the twenty-five years before World War I, 18 million immigrants came to the United States, nearly four-fifths of them from Italy, Russia, Poland, Greece, and other countries in southern and eastern Europe. By 1917 one of every three Americans was an immigrant or the child of one. With the nation becoming more urban and industrial, these immigrants, more so than those who had arrived earlier, settled in big cities and took jobs in manufacturing. Some had left Europe to escape political or religious persecution and some

Immigrants on deck of S.S. *America*, c. 1907. *(Library of Congress)*

left to avoid military service, but most were drawn by the magnet of economic opportunity. Industrialists who needed a supply of cheap labor often encouraged migration. Immigrants themselves wrote home urging their friends to join them. One Polish immigrant reported, "Let nobody listen to anybody but only to his relatives whom he has here, in this golden America."

Many Americans, Progressives among them, believed that the new immigrants were racially inferior and therefore incapable of becoming good citizens. In 1910 this view drew support from the report of a commission headed by Senator William T. Dillingham. The commission concluded that people from southern and eastern Europe did not assimilate as well as older immigrant groups, but rather committed more crimes and had a higher incidence of alcoholism and disease. A few Progressives, such as Edward A. Ross, rested their nativism squarely on racial grounds; Ross saw new immigrants as "beaten members of beaten breeds" who "lack the ancestral foundations of American character."

Most Progressives who wished to restrict immigration, however, wanted to do so for reasons of reform rather than of race. A number of reformers believed that immigration injured American workers. Not only did the immigrants depress wages by working for next to nothing, but also they retarded the growth of trade unions. Employers understood all too well that a labor force in constant flux, composed of men and women of different nationalities speaking different languages, could not very easily be organized. Progressives often located the source of poverty in the boatloads of immigrants who, with few skills and little prospect of employment, placed an intolerable strain on existing charities and social services. Reformers also thought that immigrants provided the main prop for boss rule in the cities and believed that without such votes political machines would die a natural death.

Although most Progressives appear to have viewed immigrants as their racial inferiors or as impediments to reform, there were some who took a considerably more tolerant position. Either they expressed confidence in America's capacity to absorb the immigrants, or they invoked the concept of a vast melting pot in which all people contributed something to a novel American type. In addition, the doctrine of cultural pluralism—that each immigrant group should preserve its own heritage—gained a number of converts. Norman Hapgood, Randolph Bourne, and Horace Kallen, among others, envisioned the United States as a world federation in miniature. Asserting that diversity enriched American culture, Kallen held that each immigrant group could preserve its own language, religion, and culture yet share equally in American life. He favored "a democracy of nationalities, cooperating voluntarily and autonomously . . . an orchestration of mankind."

## RACISM AND REFORM

Black Americans occupied a more precarious political and economic position than did immigrants, yet attracted even less support from Progressives, few of whom saw any conflict between racial discrimination and social reform. In the South, woman suffragists promised that they would use the vote to maintain white supremacy. In the North, black women sometimes marched in a separate column at the rear of suffrage parades. Settlement houses often set aside segregated facilities, if they provided them at all, for blacks. New York social worker Mary White Ovington attempted but failed to found a settlement house for blacks; in 1911 she published a pioneer study about the problems of New York's black ghetto for the Greenwich Street Settlement. But few settlement workers shared Ovington's interests or sympathies. Most Progressives would surely have agreed with Theodore Roosevelt who, although he opposed the disfranchisement of blacks, held that "as a race and in the mass they are altogether inferior to the whites."

During the Progressive Era most southern blacks lost the right to vote. In the 1890s three states disfranchised blacks. After the Supreme Court ruled in favor of the literacy test in *Williams v. Mississippi* (1898), ten southern states deprived blacks of the franchise. Some set literacy and property qualifications for voting, but added "understanding" and "grandfather" clauses that in effect exempted whites. Persons without property and illiterates could vote if they demonstrated an understanding of the Constitution or if they were the lineal descendants of someone who had voted in 1867. Most southern states enacted poll taxes, which, although

W.E.B. DuBois, arguably the most notable political activist on behalf of African-Americans in the first half of the twentieth century. *(Library of Congress)*

not very high, deterred poor blacks and whites from voting. Poll taxes had to be paid well in advance (usually during the spring when farmers had little spare cash) and were cumulative, so as people fell into arrears it became more difficult to catch up. Finally, the South adopted the white primary. Given Democratic control of southern politics, exclusion from the primaries amounted to virtual exclusion from the political process. These measures had an awesome effect. From 1896 to 1904 the number of black voters in Alabama plunged from 180,000 to 3,000; the number in Louisiana from 130,000 to 5,000. Southern Progressives defended these measures in part on reform grounds: removing Negro voters, they said, would end political corruption and produce good government. Indeed, one way to stop the stealing of ballots, historian C. Vann Woodward has remarked, was to stop people from casting them.

If progressivism could serve as the basis for white supremacy, it also provided W.E.B. DuBois and other black leaders with a model for new strategies of protest. DuBois, who had studied in Berlin and received a doctorate from Harvard, taught at Atlanta University from 1897 to 1910. He served as a spokesman for black intellectuals who rejected Booker T. Washington's program of racial accommodation. DuBois also exhibited a characteristically Progressive faith in the redemptive powers of reason. He assumed that by presenting empirical data about black Americans' condition he could persuade white Americans to eliminate racial injustice. In *The Philadelphia Negro* (1899) and other books, DuBois offered a meticulous examination of the conditions under which blacks lived in the hope that his readers would recognize the need to end discrimination. For DuBois, as for other Progressive intellectuals, research was the first step on the road to reform.

But it was no more than a first step. As early as 1905 DuBois attempted to found an organization devoted to the defense of civil rights. Five years later he succeeded in creating the National Association for the Advancement of Colored People (NAACP), with the goals of abolishing segregation, restoring voting rights to blacks, achieving equal educational facilities, and enforcing the Fourteenth and Fifteenth Amendments. The NAACP had the support of such white reformers as Oswald Garrison Villard, Jane Addams, Lincoln Steffens, John Dewey, and Moorfield Storey, who became its first president. In 1915 the NAACP filed an amicus curiae brief in a Supreme Court test of Oklahoma's "grandfather" clause, which the Court found unconstitutional. With its emphasis on political and legal rights, its belief in educating the public, and its assumption that segregation hindered the free development of the individual, the NAACP accurately reflected the Progressive movement, of which it was part. Perhaps it did so in another way as well: during its first seven years, DuBois was the only black to serve in a policy-making position.

## THEODORE ROOSEVELT

Theodore Roosevelt's contribution to Progressivism, one historian has said, was "to infuse reform with respectability." Born in New York to a well-to-do family in 1858, Roosevelt graduated from Harvard in 1880 and then was elected a Republican state assemblyman. A profound personal tragedy struck in 1884 when his wife died of Bright's disease the day after giving birth to a child. Roosevelt sought refuge for a time in the Dakota Badlands, but returned to New York and began his climb up the political ladder. In 1889 he became a member of the Civil Service Commission, in 1895 president of the New York City Police Board, and in 1897 assistant secretary of the Navy. In 1898, after his service with the Rough Riders in Cuba, he was elected governor of New York. Two years later the Republican leaders decided to exile Roosevelt to the vice presidency. Political boss Thomas C. Platt said, "Roosevelt might as well stand under Niagara Falls and try to spit water back as to stop his nomination." Roosevelt complained that he would "a great deal rather be anything, say professor of history, than Vice-President," but, like the good party man he was, he went along. In September 1901, with the assassination of William McKinley, Theodore Roosevelt took over the presidency.

Roosevelt had much in common with the conservatives of his day. He believed in the essential goodness of American institutions, and he hated those who wanted to tear down what had taken so long to construct. He always considered the muckrakers overly concerned with the seamy side of life, and throughout his career he denounced Populists, trade unionists, and socialists who threatened the existing order of things. In the 1890s he had noted, "the sentiment now animating a large proportion of our people can only be suppressed as the Commune in Paris was suppressed, by taking ten or a dozen of their leaders out, standing . . . them against a wall, and shooting them dead." The realities of political life in 1901 nourished his conservative instincts. In the White House only by accident, Roosevelt faced a Republican Party and a Congress dominated by conservatives. Mark Hanna, a powerful party leader and senator from Ohio, warned the new president to "go slow."

What set Roosevelt apart from the stand patters and validated his Progressive credentials was his belief in orderly change. Reform, by perfecting the system, would help to preserve it. "The only true conservative," Roosevelt remarked, "is the man who resolutely sets his face toward the future." Not only did he welcome moderate change, but Roosevelt also thought that the national interest transcended the claims of any particular class, and he assumed that the president had an obligation to act as spokesman for that interest. These beliefs helped shape the response of his administration in four important areas: business, labor, reform legislation, and conservation.

## THE SQUARE DEAL

Despite his reputation, Roosevelt never believed in trust-busting. Combination seemed to him a natural process, but one that required federal supervision to protect consumers. Eventually Roosevelt came to a tacit understanding with some of the biggest businessmen: he would not enforce the antitrust law if they would open their books for inspection and keep their dealings aboveboard. But in some cases Roosevelt considered government intervention necessary. During his presidency the Justice Department instituted forty-four antitrust suits, the most famous of which involved the Northern Securities Company. J.P. Morgan had created this $400 million holding company through a merger of important northern railroad lines. In 1902 the Justice Department invoked the Sherman Antitrust Act, claiming that the Morgan firm unfairly restrained trade, and two years later the Supreme Court narrowly upheld the government. The significance of Roosevelt's move lay less in its impact on the railroad—the ruling merely banned one particular holding company—than in its clear assertion of his willingness to act in behalf of the public interest.

Roosevelt's action in the anthracite coal strike illustrated his skill as a mediator. In 1902, 50,000 Pennsylvania miners struck for higher wages, an eight-hour day, and union recognition. Management refused to negotiate. By October, when the fuel shortage threatened homes, hospitals, and schools, Roosevelt called both sides to the White House. Even then the owners refused to talk to the union leaders, whom they considered "outlaws" responsible for "anarchy" in the coalfields. Furious at what he termed their "arrogant stupidity," Roosevelt, without any clear constitutional authority, declared that he would send 10,000 soldiers to the mines, not to break the strike, but to dispossess the operators. The owners quickly agreed to the creation of an arbitration commission, which, in March 1903, proposed a 10 percent increase in wages (and the price of coal) and establishment of an eight- or nine-hour day, but did not recommend union recognition. Roosevelt did not consider himself a champion of labor—on other occasions he used troops against strikers in Colorado, Arizona, and Nevada—but a steward of the national interest. In his successful campaign against the Democrat Alton B. Parker in 1904, Roosevelt said that his mediation in the coal strike had afforded both sides a "square deal."

The Square Deal reached a culmination in Roosevelt's second term with the enactment of three major pieces of legislation. The Pure Food and Drug Act of 1905 made it a crime to sell

## BOXING
### BLACK CHAMPIONS AND WHITE HOPES

James Jeffries and Jack Johnson at the World Championship battle in Reno, Nevada, on July 4, 1910. *(Library of Congress)*

Boxing, in its modern form, originated in England in the nineteenth century. Efforts to civilize the sport ("All attempts to inflict injury by gouging or tearing the flesh with the fingers or nails, and biting shall be deemed foul.") culminated in 1867, when John Sholto Douglas, the Marquis of Queensberry, proposed new rules. They eliminated "wrestling or hugging," provided for three-minute rounds (rather than rounds lasting until a knockdown), established a sixty-second rest period between rounds, substituted padded gloves for bare fists, barred hitting a man who was down, and warned: "A man hanging on the ropes in a helpless state, with his toes off the ground, shall be considered down." For years, boxing in America was dominated by Irish immigrants, the most famous of whom was John L. Sullivan. But the era of Irish supremacy was interrupted in 1908 when Jack Johnson, a black fighter, won the heavyweight title.

During the seven years he held the championship, Johnson elicited a response from white America that reflected broad currents of racial tension in the Progressive Era. Johnson flouted social conventions, most importantly the injunction against interracial sex. He was often seen with white women, and three of his four wives were white. A black newspaper speculated that his behavior had led directly to the introduction of bills banning interracial

Joe Louis *(AP Photo)*

marriage in several state legislatures. In any event, a search rapidly began for a "white hope" who might defeat Johnson. It soon narrowed to Jim Jeffries, who had retired unbeaten in 1905. The fight was scheduled for July 1912. Jeffries's supporters were confident, believing him superior "in both breeding and education." But Johnson won easily and collected $120,000. An outcry then arose against showing films of the fight, for many believed that youths would be "tainted, corrupted, and brutalized by such scenes." Reformers claimed a victory when Congress made it a federal offense to transport motion pictures of prizefights across state lines.

It was another act of Congress, however, that proved Johnson's undoing. The Mann Act (1910) was aimed at the "white slave trade," that is, at those who transported women across state lines for purposes of prostitution. Given the existing prejudice, Johnson was a natural target. "In Chicago," thundered a southern congressman, "white girls are made the slaves of an African brute." Johnson, who had sent his white girlfriend a railroad ticket, was unfairly convicted of violating the law and in 1913, rather than serve a jail sentence, he fled to Canada and then to Europe. In 1915 he lost the title to Jess Willard in a match fought in Havana, Cuba. In July 1920 Johnson returned home, surrendered, and was sentenced to a year in the penitentiary. After his release he fought exhibition matches, worked in nightclubs, and developed a vaudeville routine. He died in an automobile crash in 1946.

The next black heavyweight champion, Joe Louis, aroused no such bitter antagonism. Louis held the title from 1937 until his retirement in 1949, and his victories became occasions for celebration in black communities. Novelist Richard Wright believed that Louis tapped the deepest springs of rebellion in the black community: "Joe was the concentrated essence of black triumph over white." Yet Louis was at the same time exceedingly popular among whites. He violated no racial taboos and he epitomized good sportsmanship in the ring. In 1938 his crushing first-round defeat of the German fighter Max Schmeling, who supposedly believed in Aryan supremacy, was hailed as a vindication of democracy. When the United States entered World War II, Louis enlisted and was frequently cited as a model of patriotism.

Attitudes toward military service affected the career of another black fighter in a much different way. In 1964 Cassius Clay won the heavyweight championship. He then announced his conversion to the religion of Islam and changed his name to Muhammad Ali. His commitment to black nationalism provoked anger among those who favored integration. Former champion Floyd Patterson challenged Ali ("just so I can bring the championship back to America"), thereby becoming what one critic termed "the first black 'white hope' in boxing history." In 1967, Ali refused induction into the army on the grounds of religious objection. He told reporters, "I ain't got no quarrel with them Viet Cong." Indicted for draft evasion, Ali was stripped of his title and denied a chance to fight until March 1971, when he lost a decision to Joe Frazier. Ali later regained his title, but his most significant victory came in June 1971 when the Supreme Court found that his religious convictions entitled him to a draft exemption.

In Ali's case, as in Jack Johnson's, the heavyweight championship had itself become a focal point of racial tension.

## Web Links

**www.ibhof.com**
The site of the International Boxing Hall of Fame in Canastota, New York.

**www.cyberboxingzone.com/boxing/jjohn.htm**
Website with many video clips of Johnson's boxing matches.

**www.cyberboxingzone.com/boxing/jlouis.htm**
The career of Joe Louis.

**www.ali.com**
The official Muhammad Ali website.

adulterated foods or medicines and provided for the correct labeling of ingredients. The Meat Inspection Act of 1906 led to more effective supervision of slaughterhouses, provided for the dating of canned meat, and prohibited the use of dangerous chemicals or preservatives. The Hepburn Act of 1906 authorized the Interstate Commerce Commission to set aside railroad rates upon the complaint of a shipper and to establish lower rates. The courts would then pass on the "reasonableness" of commission rulings. These new laws, which had attracted public backing as a result of muckraking exposures, broke new ground in regulating business practices.

Perhaps no cause was more closely linked to Roosevelt's name than that of conservation. Unlike aesthetic conservationists who wished to save the forests from commercial exploitation, Roosevelt preferred a utilitarian approach to natural-resource development. Roosevelt favored the commercial use of such resources in a controlled and scientific manner. He popularized conservation through several White House conferences and broadened its definition to include coalfields, mineral lands, and oil reserves as well as forests. And he supported the Newlands Reclamation Act (1902), which enabled the proceeds from the sale of western lands to be used for federal irrigation projects. Under Frederick H. Newell, the Bureau of Reclamation undertook work on twenty-five major projects within a few years. Roosevelt created the Forest Service in the Department of Agriculture and made Gifford Pinchot its chief. He appointed an Inland Waterways Commission, which in 1908 submitted a plan for multipurpose river development. Using executive authority, Roosevelt created five new national parks, established fifty-one wildlife refuges, restricted the uncontrolled development of coalfields and waterpower sites, and added 43 million acres to the national forests.

## THE NEW NATIONALISM

During his second term Roosevelt became a more ardent reformer. In his last two years in office, he called for increased federal controls, taxes on income and inheritances, stricter regulation of railroad rates, implementation of the eight-hour day and workmen's compensation, and limitations on the use of injunctions in labor disputes. Roosevelt spoke indignantly about "certain malefactors of great wealth" and condemned the conservatism of the courts. This posture may have reflected Roosevelt's concern over the strength shown at the polls by socialists, his resentment at the effort of businessmen to attribute the economic slump of 1907 to his policies, or his willingness to speak out more boldly since he did not expect to seek renomination. Whatever the reason, Roosevelt had gone far toward embracing the doctrine that came to be known as the "New Nationalism."

That doctrine received its fullest statement in Herbert Croly's *The Promise of American Life* (1909). A prominent Progressive who later helped found the *New Republic*, Croly believed that a "morally and socially desirable distribution of wealth" must replace the "indiscriminate individual scramble for wealth." A Jeffersonian fear of positive government, Croly said, had kept American reformers in a straitjacket. To achieve order and rationality, they must reject laissez-faire in favor of positive action, competition in favor of concentration, and equal rights in favor of aid to the underprivileged. Croly, who regarded labor as another selfish interest group and opposed the common ownership of property, was not a socialist. But he went as far toward accepting the welfare state as any Progressive when he said: "Every popular government should have, after deliberation, the power of taking any action which, in the opinion of a decisive majority of the people, is demanded by the public welfare."

## TAFT AND THE INSURGENTS

Theodore Roosevelt groomed William Howard Taft as his successor, and as president, Taft helped win important victories for progressivism. He proved to be a vigorous trust-buster. His attorney general brought twenty-two civil suits, and the courts returned forty-five criminal indictments, for violations of the Sherman Antitrust Act. In 1911, however, the Supreme Court crippled antitrust enforcement by accepting the "rule of reason." Asserting that the Sherman act was not intended to prohibit all combinations in restraint of trade, but only those that were unreasonable, the Court made it virtually impossible to prosecute monopolies successfully. In the field of conservation, Taft continued Roosevelt's program by safeguarding additional forest lands and oil reserves. Taft favored the Mann-Elkins Act (1910), which placed telephone and telegraph companies under the jurisdiction of the Interstate Commerce Commission and authorized it to examine railroad rates on its own initiative. He reformed government administration by creating the Department of Labor, establishing a Children's Bureau, and introducing the eight-hour day for federal employees. Two constitutional amendments ratified in 1913—the Sixteenth Amendment authorizing an income tax and the Seventeenth Amendment providing for the direct election of senators—obtained congressional approval during Taft's years in office.

Despite his record, however, Taft gradually lost the confidence of Progressives. Between 1909 and 1912, Taft's position on three major issues—legislative reform, trade, and conservation—alienated Progressives. In each case Taft sympathized with their position, but his political technique, or lack of one, brought him into the conservative camp.

For many years the Speaker of the House of Representatives had dominated that body. He served as chair of the Rules Committee, made all committee assignments, and granted or withheld recognition during debate. Progressive Republicans disliked this arrangement because they considered the power itself inordinate and believed that the Republican Speaker, Joseph Gurney "Uncle Joe" Cannon of Illinois, used his position to subvert reform. Taft was no admirer of Cannon either, but conservatives threatened to block other legislation if he sided with the insurgents. Taft backed away from the fight and in 1909, when the challenge to Cannon failed, Progressives attributed their defeat in part to Taft's desertion. The revolt later succeeded: in 1910 the Rules Committee was enlarged and the Speaker was removed from it, and in 1911 the Speaker lost the right to make committee assignments. But Taft took none of the credit; instead, insurgents regarded him as an ally of the old guard.

Controversies over the tariff drove yet another wedge between Taft and the reformers, both of whom, ironically, favored downward revision. Their differences first emerged over the Payne-Aldrich Tariff of 1909. The measure effected a modest reduction in the tariff. But it did not go as far as some Progressives would have liked, and they strongly resented Taft's claiming credit for the measure and heralding it as a major reform. Again, in 1911 Taft urged Congress to adopt a reciprocal trade agreement with Canada that would remove tariffs between the two nations. Many midwestern Progressives, who came from dairy and lumber states, feared competition from Canadian imports and opposed this particular form of tariff revision. It passed over their objections, but Canada refused to cooperate and the plan died. Republican insurgents and Democrats then enacted three low-tariff bills. Taft, claiming that they were politically motivated attempts to embarrass him, vetoed the measures.

A bitter dispute over the activities of Secretary of the Interior Richard Ballinger completed the rupture between Taft and the insurgents. In the summer of 1909 Louis Glavis, an investigator for the Interior Department, informed Gifford Pinchot that Ballinger had, shortly before taking office, apparently profited from aiding a Seattle group in its effort to deliver rich Alaskan coalfields to a large business syndicate. Pinchot brought the accusation to Taft who, after listening to both sides and asking Attorney General George W. Wickersham to investigate, exonerated Ballinger and fired Glavis. Pinchot leaked his side of the story to the press and in January 1910 publicly condemned Ballinger. Taft then dismissed Pinchot, the idol of conservationists, from his post as chief of the Forest Service. From January to June 1910, a joint congressional committee conducted an investigation. It found no proof that Ballinger was corrupt, but it turned up a damaging fact: Taft had asked Wickersham to pre-date his report so it would appear that the decision to fire Glavis resulted from it rather than from a preliminary verbal report. A generation of reformers convinced itself that Ballinger and Taft had betrayed the conservation movement.

Dissatisfaction with Taft led Senator Robert M. La Follette of Wisconsin, Governor Hiram Johnson of California, and others to create the National Progressive Republican League in January 1911. Designed to push La Follette's candidacy within the Republican Party, the league ended by endorsing Theodore Roosevelt's candidacy on a third-party ticket. At first it seemed doubtful that Roosevelt would make the race. He had returned from a hunting expedition to Africa in June 1910 with no thought of seeking renomination and with some hope that Taft could heal the wounds in the Republican Party. But in 1911, as his disenchantment with the president grew, Roosevelt changed his mind. Taft's remark that the War of 1812, the Mexican War, and the Spanish-American War "might have been settled without a fight and ought to have been" offended Roosevelt. Taft's decision to bring an antitrust suit against United States Steel for its acquisition of the Tennessee Coal and Iron Company in 1907, a merger to which Roosevelt had tacitly assented, infuriated the former president.

By the time the Republican convention met in June 1912, the two men, once good political friends, had become bitter personal enemies. If Roosevelt, who had done well in the primaries, was the people's choice, Taft was the convention's. His control of the Republican National Committee and of the party machinery in the South assured Taft's renomination on the first ballot. Reformers walked out in disgust, and in August Roosevelt agreed to run as the candidate of a new Progressive Party. His assertion that "every man holds his property subject to the general right of the community to regulate its use to whatever degree the public welfare may require it" summarized the party's platform. His cry to the convention—"We stand at Armageddon and we battle for the Lord"—captured the movement's religious fervor.

## WOODROW WILSON

Republican disunity, however, permitted the Democrats to capture the White House for the first time in twenty years. Their candidate, Thomas Woodrow Wilson, was born in Virginia in 1856, the son of a Presbyterian minister. After graduating from Princeton (1879), Wilson studied law at the University of Virginia but gave up his practice for graduate work in political science at Johns Hopkins University. His doctoral dissertation, *Congressional Government*, appeared in 1885. In it Wilson held that American politics, characterized by a powerful but irresponsible Congress and a weak president, was inferior to the cabinet system that linked the interests of the executive and legislative branches. He then taught at Bryn Mawr, Wesleyan, and finally at Princeton, which named him its president in 1902. There, Wilson encouraged the introduction of small seminars and tried unsuccessfully to abolish the exclusive "eating clubs," which he regarded as anti-intellectual. In 1910 the New Jersey Democratic leaders, considering Wilson a safe but attractive figure, invited him to run for the governorship. He did and, to the bosses' dismay, presided over a reform administration, enacting a direct primaries law, a corrupt practices act, and workmen's compensation. In 1912 Wilson won the Democratic presidential nomination on the forty-sixth ballot. That November, with Roosevelt and Taft dividing the normal Republican vote, Wilson, although he received only 41.8 percent of the popular vote, carried forty states and won an overwhelming electoral college victory.

His southern upbringing helped mold Wilson's political outlook. Wilson, whose father had owned slaves and served as a chaplain in the Confederate army, remarked, "The only place in the country, the only place in the world, where nothing has to be explained to me is the South." He later demonstrated his loyalties to section and party by rigidly segregating black and white officeholders in government agencies and by removing southern blacks from federal jobs. Like most white progressives, Wilson saw no contradiction between his political convictions and his racial practices.

In 1912 Wilson campaigned on the slogan of the "New Freedom," which he presented as an alternative to Roosevelt's New Nationalism. The New Freedom, which Wilson worked out in discussions with the prominent Boston attorney Louis D. Brandeis, held that government should intervene in the economy to the extent necessary to restore competition. Unlike Roosevelt, who now viewed antitrust actions as a throwback to the past, Wilson asserted that trusts were inefficient, the product of financial manipulation, and the cause of artificially inflated prices. He would not go on a rampage against trusts but believed that by stripping them of special privileges they would fall of their own weight. Unlike Roosevelt, who favored child-labor legislation and a minimum wage for women, Wilson denounced paternalism. He told a group of workers: "The old adage that God takes care of those who take care of themselves is not gone out of date. No federal legislation can change that thing. The minute you are taken care of by the government you are wards, not independent men." Whereas Roosevelt, in advocating welfare measures, implied that the condition of the poor did not necessarily reflect a failure on their part, Wilson placed the issue squarely on moral grounds: under the rules of free competition an individual's character—as measured by thrift, hard work, ingenuity—would determine the individual's reward.

## ENACTING THE NEW FREEDOM

Once elected, Wilson met with remarkable success in enacting his program. This resulted from a receptive legislative climate as well as from his creative use of presidential authority. In 1913 the Democrats controlled both houses of Congress. With Wilson only the second Democrat to occupy the White House since the Civil War, the party was determined to demonstrate its capacity for national leadership. Moreover, presidents usually receive wide support from newly elected congressmen, and of the 290 House Democrats, no fewer than 114 were first-termers. Wilson used every device at his disposal to corral supporters. He conferred regularly with legislative leaders, enforced party discipline by dispensing patronage, stressed loyalty to caucus decisions, and, when he thought it necessary, appealed directly to the people. His strategy reflected his admiration for English government and his belief that the president "must be prime minister, as much concerned with the guidance of legislation as with the just and orderly execution of law." Indeed, it was during Wilson's tenure that, for the first time since Jefferson abandoned the practice, a president delivered his messages to Congress in person.

Within a year and a half of Wilson's inauguration, Congress placed the New Freedom on the statute books. The Underwood Tariff (1913) substantially reduced import duties. During the debate Wilson had publicly denounced the lobbyists who were swarming into Washington to look after their clients' interests. He aroused such a furor that, before voting, senators felt obliged to reveal how the tariff affected their own financial holdings. The act also included the first income tax passed under the Sixteenth Amendment. The tax rose from 1 percent on personal and corporate income over $4,000 to 4 percent on incomes over $100,000. The Federal Reserve Act (1913), which reformed the banking and currency system, resulted in part from a congressional inquiry into the "money trust." The investigation revealed that Morgan and Rockefeller interests held a tight grip on credit institutions. The act provided for a more flexible currency and established a measure of public control over private bankers. It created twelve Federal Reserve Banks that, although privately controlled, also were responsible to a Federal Reserve Board. Finally, the Clayton Antitrust Act (1914) attempted to bolster the faltering attack on monopoly by prohibiting interlocking directorships and other devices that lessened competition. The Clayton act made a gesture toward exempting labor unions, but the wording remained ambiguous enough so that the Supreme Court could later rule certain kinds of strikes and boycotts illegal.

With the passage of this legislation, Wilson considered his work largely done. Convinced that reform had gone far enough, he wanted to go no further. The only important Progressive measure he endorsed in 1915, and grudgingly at that, was the La Follette Seamen's Act. It freed sailors on merchant ships from a contract system that, in practice, amounted to forced labor. In other areas Wilson drew the line. He opposed establishing federally financed credit institutions to provide long-term loans to farmers on the grounds that this would unduly favor one interest group. He continued to regard federal child-labor legislation as unconstitutional, and he refused to support woman suffrage. In February 1915 he nominated five men to serve on a newly created Federal Trade Commission. But Wilson, in the words of a cabinet member, regarded the commission as "a counsellor and friend to the business world" rather than as "a policeman to wield a club over the head of the business community." For the most part his appointees interpreted their task in the same way.

Yet by early 1916 Wilson began to modify his position, and he did so largely because he reassessed the political situation. The Democrats had done poorly in the 1914 elections, losing two dozen seats in the House and giving up the governorships of New York, New Jersey, Illinois, and Pennsylvania. Moreover, the Progressive Party had begun to disintegrate after Roosevelt's defeat. Lacking a formal grass-roots organization, beset by financial problems, torn by dissension over its policy toward business, the party met with disaster in 1914, losing virtually every contest it entered. Ironically, the demise of the Progressive Party, by raising the specter of a unified Republican opposition, helped move Wilson toward an accommodation with the Progressive platform. To win reelection, Wilson knew he must make inroads into Roosevelt's old constituency.

This he attempted to do in a number of ways. In January 1916 Wilson nominated Louis D. Brandeis to the Supreme Court, a move that infuriated conservatives and touched off a bitter four-month struggle for Senate confirmation. Wilson also reversed his position on several issues. He supported the Federal Farm Loan Act (1916), which created twelve regional banks to provide long-term, low-interest loans to farmers. Similarly, in July he asked the Senate to approve a child-labor bill that had already cleared the House. His efforts helped pass the Keating-

Owen Act (1916), which barred the products of firms employing child labor from interstate commerce. (In 1918 Wilson's earlier fears proved correct when the Supreme Court, in *Hammer v. Dagenhart*, found the measure unconstitutional.) Having made overtures to agrarians and social reformers, Wilson turned his attention to labor. He backed the Kern-McGillicuddy Act (1916), which provided workmen's compensation for federal employees. In September, to head off a railroad strike, Wilson urged Congress to pass a law giving the union essentially what it wanted: an eight-hour day for railroad workers in interstate commerce. Congress obliged by passing the Adamson Act (1916). Finally, Wilson moved still closer to the ground Roosevelt had once occupied by supporting the Webb-Pomerene bill (which did not pass until 1918), which exempted the overseas operations of business firms from the antitrust laws.

Wilson's strategy succeeded against a Republican opponent, Charles Evans Hughes, who had compiled a reform record as governor of New York and as a member of the Supreme Court. Campaigning not only on his record of Progressive achievement, but also on a pledge to keep America out of the European war, the president won a narrow victory. Wilson received 9.1 million votes to 8.5 million for Hughes and managed a twenty-three-vote margin in the electoral college. Nearly 3 million more people than in 1912 voted for Wilson, including many farmers, workers, and New Nationalist Progressives who approved of the direction his administration had taken in 1916. Also, the peace issue apparently helped Wilson among German Americans and socialists and among women in the eleven states—particularly California, Washington, and Kansas—that granted them the vote.

Early in 1917, therefore, most Americans expected Wilson's victory to keep the nation at peace and permit completion of the Progressive agenda. Few had any reason to suppose that, within a few months, Wilson would lead the nation into war. Indeed, World War I would expose many of the limitations of progressivism. In retrospect, the reformers' optimism would seem naive, their apparent dedication to serving the general interest merely a rationalization for preserving narrower class interests. Laws regulating morality would seem self-righteous attempts to impose conformity. The Progressive effort to throw the weight of government on the side of the less fortunate would, to a later generation, appear inadequate or paternalistic. Even the struggle for political democracy might be construed as emphasizing form over content. But during the Progressive Era only a handful of critics voiced such doubts. In the years before the war the Progressive faith burned brightly.

# CHAPTER THREE

# 1900–1917

## A Progressive Foreign Policy—From Peace to War

Theodore Roosevelt *(center)* inspects the construction of the Panama Canal in 1906.
*(Library of Congress)*

The ideals and policies that Americans have at home determine their ideals and policies around the globe. Between 1900 and 1917 the Progressive Party exemplified this rule of American history. As Progressives searched desperately for order and stability at home amid the industrial revolution, so overseas they used the new American economic and military power in an attempt to impose order in such areas as China, the Caribbean, Mexico, and western Europe. Many Progressives believed that only in orderly societies could the United States hope to find political cooperation and long-term markets for the glut of goods and capital produced by American corporations. Without such help from foreign friends, unemployment and radical movements could threaten Progressive programs at home.

## THEODORE ROOSEVELT

Theodore Roosevelt once remarked that a man's mission in life could be summed up by the admonition to "work, fight, and breed." He did all three rather well. Roosevelt (often called TR, but never Teddy—a name he hated) achieved particular success as a fighter in Cuba in 1898. Those wartime exploits associated his name with militant American expansionism and catapulted him into the vice presidency in 1900. After McKinley's assassination in September 1901, Roosevelt assumed personal control of American foreign policy.

The new president's alternatives were analyzed in an article published by his close friend Brooks Adams in the *Atlantic Monthly* in 1901. Adams observed that since 1860 the Republicans had helped create the nation's great industrial power by passing high tariffs that protected American producers from cheap foreign competition. Now the need was to find world markets for U.S. products. The president, Adams argued, would have to choose one of two paths. He could try to lower the tariff as part of a deal in which other nations would reduce their tariffs on American goods. This policy, however, could result in a violent struggle within the Republican Party between high-tariff and low-tariff advocates. The second alternative was to retain the high tariff, but then (1) to use the powers of the federal government to make American production and transportation so efficient that U.S. products could compete globally regardless of tariff policy, and (2) to develop a great military force, which would assure American producers and investors that their government could protect their interests in such vital potential markets as China, Latin America, and Africa. Unwilling to rock his own political boat and deeply committed to the idea that military force ultimately decided world affairs, Roosevelt enthusiastically chose the second alternative. In this way he hoped to achieve both political peace at home and expansion overseas.

Roosevelt was clear about the tactics for achieving these goals. He extolled the "strenuous life" of the military, continued the rapid building of the battleship fleet, and built an isthmian canal in Panama so that the fleet could more easily shift from the Atlantic to the Pacific theater. To ensure rapid decision making and to protect his foreign policy from what he believed to be the provincialism of American domestic politics, he concentrated the power to make decisions in the White House. This move drained the power from Congress, a body he believed was "not well fitted for the shaping of foreign policy."

In formulating his foreign policy strategies, TR distinguished sharply between friendly and potentially threatening nations. Although he had mistrusted the British during the 1890s, he now understood that they no longer threatened the United States in Latin America and that Great Britain and the United States had similar interests in Asia. Anglo-American cooperation, moreover, fit Roosevelt's views of the superiority of the Anglo-Saxon people, who were, in his eyes, destined to "civilize" the nonindustrialized areas of the world. Another partner would be Japan, which Roosevelt believed shared American open-door policies in Asia. Japan was certainly not Anglo-Saxon, but it was industrialized and efficient and thus, in the words of Captain Alfred Thayer Mahan (one of TR's close friends as well as a leading naval strategist), "Teutonic by adoption." On the other hand, Roosevelt feared Germany and Russia: the former because its rapidly growing navy threatened British dominion in Europe and Africa; the latter because it seemed to endanger Anglo-Japanese-American interests in Asia.

Roosevelt was willing to use the mushrooming American industrial and military power to expand the nation's interest. The president agreed not with Shakespeare's "Twice is he armed that has his quarrel just," but with the version of American humorist Josh Billings: "And four times he who gets his fist in fust."

## "I TOOK THE CANAL" . . .

Roosevelt followed Billings's admonition in regard to Latin America. Throughout the late nineteenth century the United States had tried to escape from an 1850 treaty made with Great Britain that pledged each nation to construct an isthmian canal only in cooperation with the other. Beset by problems in Africa and Europe, the British finally agreed to negotiate the point. In the Hay-Pauncefote Treaty of November 1901, Britain gave the United States the power to build and to fortify a canal.

As late as 1902, it seemed that the least expensive passageway could be built in Nicaragua. But a group of lobbyists who had interests in Panama used political pressure and bribes to win congressional support of the Panamanian site then ruled by Colombia. A treaty of January 1903 (the Hay-Herrán pact) gave the United States rights over a six-mile-wide strip in Panama in return for $10 million and a $250,000 annual payment to Colombia. The Colombian senate, however, then demanded $25 million. Roosevelt angrily—and ingeniously—announced that if the Panamanians revolted against Colombia, he would prevent Colombian troops from entering Panama by invoking an 1846 treaty in which the United States had promised Colombia to help keep Panama "free and open." The lobbyists gratefully arranged the revolution in November 1903. TR sent a warship to make sure that Colombia would not interfere. He then recognized the new government, gave it $10 million, and made the new country an American protectorate by guaranteeing its independence. In return, the lobbyists gave him a ten-mile-wide strip across Panama where he could build the canal. Later Roosevelt bragged, "I took the Canal Zone and let Congress debate."

## . . . AND ALSO SANTO DOMINGO

Fomenting revolutions was quite out of character for one as strongly antirevolutionary as Roosevelt. More characteristic was his policy in the Caribbean nation of Santo Domingo. The stage was set in 1903 when Great Britain and Germany temporarily landed troops in Venezuela in order to protect the property of their citizens. The resulting uproar in the United States and the threat that in the future such temporary landings might become a permanent occupation led Roosevelt to conclude that he could not allow an open door for European forces in Latin America. The Europeans announced that they did not like sending military personnel to Latin

America, but would have to do so unless the United States policed the region in order to prevent the recurrence of revolutionary disturbances and resulting dangers to foreign investors.

Roosevelt's opportunity soon appeared in Santo Domingo, a country plagued by dictatorial governments as well as by struggles between German and American business interests. The president initially moved into Santo Domingo not to check European threats to American security, but to fight the inroads that German shipping lines were making on American shippers. State Department officials on the scene told Roosevelt that the immediate threat was a revolution that the Germans might use as an excuse to land troops for the enforcement of their business claims.

The president responded by announcing a formula in December 1904 that has become known as the Roosevelt Corollary to the Monroe Doctrine. Any "chronic wrong-doing" might "require intervention by some civilized power," he warned. In the Western Hemisphere the United States would act as this "civilized power" by exercising "international police power" to correct "flagrant cases of such wrong-doing or impotence." In early 1905 Roosevelt displayed American strength by sending warships to Santo Domingo. He then made a pact with that country giving the United States control of the customs houses through which the Dominicans collected most of their revenue. In return Roosevelt promised to use the receipts from the customs to pay off the Dominican debts and the foreigners' claims. Although the American Senate refused to consent to this agreement, Roosevelt enforced it by calling it an "executive agreement" (that is, an agreement that would last at least through his presidency, but not necessarily be binding on the next president). He had again circumvented the constitutional restraints on his actions, and in 1907 the Senate reluctantly ratified the treaty. The president meanwhile kept warships in control of the waters around Santo Domingo. He instructed the naval commander "to stop any revolution." TR hardly solved the Dominican problem. In order to stop recurring revolutions, U.S. troops were periodically stationed in that country through the administrations of the next five American presidents.

The Roosevelt Corollary is important primarily because it committed American power to maintain stability in the Caribbean area. With that commitment, Roosevelt finally destroyed the ideal of the Monroe Doctrine of 1823, which had aimed at preventing outside forces from controlling sovereign nations in Latin America. Contrary to the principles of 1823—and 1776—New World revolutionaries were no longer necessarily allowed to work out their own nations' destinies. Roosevelt best summarized the results when he claimed that the American intervention would free the people of Santo Domingo "from the curse of interminable revolutionary disturbance" and give them "the same chance to move onward which we have already given the people of Cuba."

Cuba, however, was hardly a good example. In 1906 infighting between Cuba's two major political parties threatened to paralyze the island's government. Anti-American factions again surfaced in Havana. Roosevelt thereupon ordered U.S. troops to land and restore a government acceptable to Washington.

**ROOSEVELT LOSES HIS BALANCE**

Outside the Caribbean, the president faced a tougher job. In Europe and Asia he had to expand American interests not by unilateral military power but by the delicate game of balance-of-power politics.

During 1905, for instance, Germany challenged France's protectorate over Morocco, and the German kaiser asked his good friend Theodore Roosevelt to mediate the crisis. Despite their personal friendship, Roosevelt was alarmed by the rapid rise of German naval power, and he was not anxious to help Germany gain an important foothold in northern Africa. After TR finally arranged a conference at Algeciras, Spain, in January 1906, France's claims were upheld by nearly every European power in attendance. The president meanwhile worked through the two American delegates at the conference to ensure that the United States did not come away empty-handed. He gained a pledge from the powers for an open door in Morocco for American and other interests. After World Wars I and II the State Department used this 1906 pledge as an entering wedge to gain oil and trade concessions in northern Africa for American entrepreneurs.

Roosevelt did not, however, display such sure-footedness in the Far East. The focus in that area was on the struggle between Japan and Russia over the rich and strategic Chinese province of Manchuria. In that confrontation, TR much preferred the Japanese. As for China, the victim in the struggle, he observed that it was able neither to industrialize nor to militarize; when he wished to condemn an incompetent person, Roosevelt would call him "a Chinese." His racism, combined with his Progressive enchantment with efficiency, led him to view the Chinese less as actors on the world scene than as a people to be acted upon.

American missionaries and exporters viewed China from the same perspective. Businessmen particularly were watching the development of China. In 1900 they sent $15 million worth of products to the area; in 1902, $25 million; and by 1905, $53 million. The great China market was apparently being realized at last. Most of these U.S. goods went into Manchuria and northern China, precisely the area over which the Japanese and Russians were struggling. When Japan suddenly struck the Russians with a devastating sneak attack on February 9, 1904, Roosevelt happily wrote to his son that the Japanese were "playing our game."

But as Japan destroyed the Russian fleet, consolidated its control over Korea and Manchuria, then threatened to invade Siberia, the president had second thoughts. Fearing that a precarious Russian-Japanese balance was being replaced by an aggressive Japanese empire, Roosevelt moved to stop the war by calling on the two belligerents to meet at Portsmouth, New Hampshire, in mid-1905. TR was delighted with the conference's work. Japan received control over Korea and in return promised an open door in Manchuria for the United States and the other powers. The Japanese also obtained key Russian bases in Manchuria. The Russians received a badly needed peace.

Japan's promise of the open door, however, soon proved empty. Such major American exporters as Standard Oil, Swift meatpacking, and the British-American Tobacco Company were eventually driven out of Manchuria by Japan. Tokyo's policy was capped in 1907 when Japan and Russia, bloody enemies just twenty-four months before, agreed to divide Manchuria, with the Japanese exploiting the south and the Russians the north. Roosevelt's first attempt to form a profitable partnership with the Japanese had ended badly.

In 1907 another threat arose to endanger TR's dream of Japanese-American cooperation in developing Asia. Since the 1890s the number of Japanese living in California had leaped from 2,000 to nearly 30,000. Many of them were laborers who were willing to work more cheaply than Americans. Threatened by what California's governor, George Pardee, called a "Japanese menace," the state's legislature tried to pass an exclusion bill. Anti-Asian riots erupted. Having just defeated a major white power, Japan was in no mood to back down

Negotiating the Treaty of Portsmouth, 1905. *(Library of Congress)*

before laws that restricted the rights of its citizens to travel, either to Manchuria or to California. Roosevelt temporarily quieted the tumult by working out a deal: California dropped the impending exclusion act and the Japanese promised that they would voluntarily restrict passports issued to laborers wishing to move to the United States.

## THE FAILURE OF BIG-STICK DIPLOMACY

Roosevelt's hope that Japan would manhandle Russia in 1904 had produced not an open door but a one-way street for the movement of the Japanese empire. "I am more concerned over this Japanese situation than almost any other," TR admitted privately. So the man who gave his countrymen the phrase "Speak softly and carry a big stick" decided to send sixteen American battleships on a goodwill cruise to the western Pacific. Congress blanched when it heard of the plan, for it feared that Japan would destroy the fleet with a sudden attack like that launched against the Russians in 1904. Some congressional leaders announced that they would not appropriate money to send the fleet. Roosevelt thereupon bellowed that he had enough money to send the ships to Japan; if Congress wished to leave them there it was Congress's responsibility. Again outmaneuvered—even humiliated—by the president, Congress approved the funds. The visit of the Great White Fleet to Japan in 1907 produced effusions of friendship on both sides, but it failed resoundingly to persuade Tokyo officials to retreat in Manchuria.

On the eve of his departure from the presidency, TR made one last attempt to bring the Japanese into line. In the Root-Takahira agreement of November 1908 (negotiated for Roosevelt by his secretary of state, Elihu Root), the United States and Japan reaffirmed their meaningless pledge to maintain the open door, but in the wording of the agreement, Root accepted Japan's control of South Manchuria.

The president's gentle encouragement to Japan in 1904 had resulted in cruel policy dilemmas for Roosevelt. But perhaps the greatest irony of the Russo-Japanese War was that, although American Progressives wanted to avoid revolution at all costs, the conflict ignited the Russian Revolution in 1905. The victory of yellow over white also set off unrest in the French empire in Indochina, helped trigger revolts in Persia and Turkey, and fueled the Chinese revolutionary outbreak of 1911.

Roosevelt never understood that force determines not who is right, but who is strong. He therefore had been initially pleased with the Russo-Japanese War. TR failed to understand how the chaos and disruption of such a conflict could produce the revolutionary outbreaks that he and most Americans so dreaded.

## REPLACING BULLETS WITH DOLLARS

Roosevelt's successor, William Howard Taft, was too conservative for most Progressives, but his experience as governor-general in the Philippines and as TR's diplomatic troubleshooter in Cuba and Asia had made him a practitioner of the Progressives' ardent search for order and stability. He had learned from these experiences that military force had only a limited capacity for solving problems. Taft consequently hoped to use America's burgeoning financial power, instead of the army, as his main foreign policy instrument. He could point to the expansion of U.S. overseas investment from about $800 million at the time of the 1898 war to more than $2.5 billion in 1909 as proof that his countrymen were obtaining the power to achieve the economic reordering of the world.

Taft advocated dollar diplomacy, but not because of any special ties to American bankers. He appointed leading New York corporation lawyers Philander C. Knox as secretary of state and Henry Stimson as secretary of war, but Taft also thought "Wall Street, as an aggregation, is the biggest ass that I have ever run across." For this reason, Taft believed that private interests often needed direction from Washington.

## REPLACING DOLLARS WITH BULLETS

Roosevelt's actions in the Caribbean had spread ill will and fear throughout Latin America. Taft wanted a quieter policy, but the full force of dollar diplomacy was quickly made apparent in Nicaragua. That nation, the alternate site for an isthmian canal, was of particular interest to Secretary of State Knox because of his past associations with extensive American mining interests there. Events began to unfold in 1909 when a long-term dictatorship was overthrown by revolutionaries, including numerous Americans. Knox immediately sided with the revolution. He moved in to control the situation by seizing the customs houses, which were the country's main source of revenue. The secretary of state urged the new government to pay off long-standing claims to Great Britain by borrowing large sums from American bankers. When the Nicaraguans balked at Knox's demands, he dispatched a warship. The agreement was then quickly signed. But the fires of Nicaraguan nationalism had been lit, and the American-controlled government could not maintain order. In 1912 Taft took the logical step required by his dollar diplomacy, sending more than 2,000 Marines to protect American lives and property and to prevent European powers from intervening to shield the interests of their own citizens. The U.S. troops remained in Nicaragua for most of the next twenty years.

While the president dispatched troops to Central America, the U.S. Senate also tried to protect American interests in the area. In 1912 the Senate added the so-called Lodge Corollary to the Monroe Doctrine in reaction to the threat of a private Japanese company obtaining land on Magdalena Bay in lower California. (The corollary was proposed by the powerful Republican senator from Massachusetts, Henry Cabot Lodge.) The Lodge resolution stated that no "corporation or association which has such a relation to another government, not American," could obtain strategic areas in the hemisphere. This provision greatly extended the compass of the Monroe Doctrine, which had previously applied only to foreign governments, not to companies. The State Department used the resolution during the next quarter-century to stop the transfer of lands, particularly in Mexico, to Japanese concerns.

## CANADA

The giant neighbor to the north could not be dealt with in such summary fashion. Americans and Canadians had last warred against each other in 1814, but during the 1830s, 1860s, and 1870s conflict had threatened over border incidents. Canada was extremely sensitive to growing American power, particularly since discovering that, although it was a member of the British Empire, London officials were anxious to please the United States even when the matter involved conflicting Canadian-American claims. In 1903, for example, Canada had protested Roosevelt's demand that a disputed part of the Alaskan-Canadian boundary be settled in favor of the United States. When both parties agreed to submit the dispute to a jury of "six impartial jurists of repute," Roosevelt loaded the jury with his own type of expansionists and threatened to deploy the army if he did not get his way. The British jurist, casting the deciding vote, ruled in favor of Roosevelt and against the Canadians.

The Canadian government had scarcely recovered from this humiliation when in 1911 it signed a long-sought reciprocity trade agreement with the Taft administration. Canadian officials were initially pleased, believing that the pact opened the mammoth American market to their country's raw material producers. But the agreement could also make these producers an integral part of the U.S. industrial complex, a fact noted publicly when a congressional report in Washington likened the treaty to "another Louisiana Purchase." When the Speaker of the House of Representatives added that it would not be long before the American flag would be flying over all the territory to the North Pole, the ensuing uproar forced the Canadian government to call a national election. A new administration came to power, repudiated the reciprocity pact, and set higher tariffs on U.S. goods. The annexationist movement was dead. During Taft's presidency, dollar diplomacy worked no better in the north than in the south.

## CHINA ONCE AGAIN

The results were even worse in China, although in this labyrinth of revolution, power politics, and diplomatic double-dealing, Taft and Knox were not wholly to blame. But they certainly made a bad situation worse.

In late 1909 Knox feared that the Chinese would be unable to prevent Manchuria from being carved into Japanese and Russian protectorates that would exclude American products. Citing the open-door principle and insisting that the United States must share in the investment opportunities, the secretary of state proposed a "neutralization" scheme whereby Americans and Europeans would pool their money to help China buy back the key railroads in Manchuria from the Russians and Japanese. This would effectively "neutralize" the area, reopening it to American traders and investors. But Knox had made a blunder of the first magnitude, for when he tried to push his way into Manchuria, he only further united Russia and Japan against all outsiders. The neutralization plan was stillborn.

Apparently learning nothing from the experience, Knox made a second attempt to retain China as a frontier for Americans. In 1910 he insisted that the United States be allowed to participate in an international banking consortium organized by the British, French, and Germans to build railroads in the province of Hukuang. The Europeans allowed American financiers into the scheme reluctantly, realizing that once outsiders like the Americans entered, Russia and Japan would also demand entrance. This indeed occurred, and the Russians and Japanese proceeded to paralyze the Chinese consortium so it could not endanger their own private spheres of interest.

Now that he was faced with the utter failure of dollar diplomacy in the Far East, the only remaining tactic left to Taft seemed to be the use of American military force to prop open the gates of Manchuria. But the president knew the United States did not have the military power to scare either Russia or Japan. Theodore Roosevelt had finally realized this when he wrote privately to Taft in 1910: "Our vital interest is to keep the Japanese out of [the United States] and at the same time to preserve the good will of Japan." The Japanese, TR continued, must therefore be allowed to exploit Manchuria and Korea unless Taft was prepared to go to war. "I utterly disbelieve in the policy of bluff, . . ." Roosevelt railed, "or in any violation of the old frontier maxim, 'Never draw unless you mean to shoot!'" The mess was left for Woodrow Wilson.

## THE ULTIMATE PROGRESSIVE DIPLOMAT

Woodrow Wilson exerted extraordinary influence on twentieth- and early twenty-first-century American foreign policy. Richard Nixon, for example, privately remarked in 1968, "Wilson was our greatest President of this century. . . . Wilson had the greatest vision of America's role." Highly complex, insecure, and driven by ambition, Wilson once recalled that a classmate asked him, "'Why, man, can't you let anything alone?' I said, 'I let everything alone that you can show me is not itself moving in the wrong direction, but I am not going to let those things alone that I see are going downhill.'"

He wanted to move the world uphill—uphill, Wilson believed, to the political and economic systems of the United States. The touchstone of Wilson's dealings with other nations was whether they were moving rapidly enough in the direction of a democratic, capitalist system. "When properly directed," Wilson observed, "there is no people not fitted for self-government." He determined to provide the direction, not merely with self-righteousness, but within a framework in which morality, politics, and economics were closely integrated.

Since his objectives were so exalted, Wilson, like Roosevelt, did not worry often enough about the means he used to achieve them. He even told his closest friend and adviser, Colonel

**ASHCANS AND THE ARMORY SHOW**

Sculpture of a couple kissing by Constantine Brancusi, exhibited at the Armory Show of the Association of American Painters and Sculptors in New York, 1913. *(Library of Congress)*

For nearly a century American artists had painted idealized scenes of canyons, rivers, and people. The canyons and rivers had become polluted, and the people changed by industrialism, but the painters nevertheless had continued to draw the old, reassuring scenes.

In 1900 a few artists determined to change this. They shared a Progressive faith that by stripping away corruption and hypocrisy, they could make Americans see clearly and then save their republic. Some of these artists, such as John Sloan and George Luks, worked as illustrators or cartoonists for newspapers and so were outside the dominant art traditions but in positions to witness the social problems. When art organizations refused to show the works of these new artists, eight of them presented their own exhibition in 1908. As the titles demonstrated, these works depicted striking new subjects: Sloan's *Sunday, Women Drying Their Hair* and Luks's *The Wrestlers.* Some critics condemned them for "exhibiting our sores," denounced them as the "Ashcan School," and excluded them from polite art exhibitions.

Members of the Ashcan School and others excluded by art associations decided to hold an exhibition at the New York City Armory in 1913. This time they accompanied their work with recent European paintings by cubists, expressionists, and neo-impressionists. These new artists included Van Gogh, Cézanne, and Picasso, the fathers of twentieth-century

The oil painting *Nude Descending a Staircase, No. 2*, by French Dada and surrealist artist Marcel Duchamp. *(Lee Boltin/Time & Life Pictures/Getty Images)*

art, whose works often exhibited unrecognizable or weirdly distorted forms and violent, clashing colors. They differed as much from earlier paintings as the New York City tenements differed from the seventeenth-century English countryside. Marcel Duchamp's *Nude Descending a Staircase, No. 2* symbolized the Armory show, for the figure was dynamic and flowing but unrecognizable (newspapers ran "Find the Nude" contests). One critic called it "Explosion in a Shingle Factory."

Theodore Roosevelt stormed through the exhibition, according to a witness, "waving his arms, pointing at pictures and saying 'That's not art! That's not art!'" But he wrote a moderate review for a periodical praising the more traditional American works. That was a misjudgment for the Europeans overpowered the American painters. American audiences were particularly frightened by the European claim that art was not decoration, but a judgment on Western society and especially the fragmentation of the human spirit resulting from the industrial revolution. The artist now claimed total freedom to show this new world. If the machine had created a modern environment and if psychiatrists were discovering hidden motivations, then artists had to be free to show these new worlds in new ways.

Such radical art has never been welcome in traditional societies. Nearly 300,000 Americans saw the 1,300 paintings in New York, Chicago, and Boston, but in Chicago art students burned in effigy the show's organizer as well as a copy of Matisse's *Blue Nude*. The exhibition, however, was applauded by others, especially women, whose own drive for equality made them sensitive to the new art's demands for freedom. The Armory show shocked the United States into twentieth-century culture, while warning of a breakdown in Western culture itself, a breakdown made real in the horrors of World War I.

## Web Links

**www.artlex.com/ArtLex/a/armoryshow.html**
The story of the 1911 Armory Show.

**www.marcelduchamp.net**
The career of the famous artist.

Edward House, that lying was perhaps justified if it involved a woman's honor or a matter of public policy. Those categories gave Wilson ample room for maneuver. Even as a young professor of political science he had advocated strong presidential rule that would circumvent the often-messy pluralistic politics of the American congressional system. During an explosive crisis with Germany in 1915, he refused to see not only congressmen but also his closest advisers and communed only with himself for several days. Wilson also exemplified how such self-isolation often ends in disaster.

His policies rested on a crucial belief: the world must look to the United States for its example and, in turn, Americans depended on the rest of the world for their survival. Wilson had been deeply affected by the depression and threats of revolution within the United States during the 1890s. He was therefore open to the influence of Frederick Jackson Turner's frontier thesis, which argued that the 1890s crisis could be understood as the terrible result of the closing of America's land frontier. After 400 years, Turner had warned in 1893, the United States had lost that frontier. Wilson, who knew Turner personally, paraphrased the frontier thesis several years later: "The westward march has stopped upon the final slopes of the Pacific; and now the plot thickens." The world market must act as the new frontier for the American system, Wilson warned during the 1912 presidential campaign, or disaster threatened: "Our industries have expanded to such a point that they will burst their jackets if they cannot find free outlets in the markets of the world."

He believed that open markets and capitalism were necessary for democratic political systems. His famous remark "Without freedom of enterprise there can be no freedom whatsoever" applied, in his mind, at home and overseas. So Wilson felt justified in intervening in revolutions in Mexico or Russia because such upheavals threatened to become both antidemocratic and anticapitalist. The meshing of his economic, political, and moral beliefs was perhaps most strikingly phrased by Wilson during his first presidential term:

> Lift your eyes to the horizons of business . . . let your thoughts and your imagination run abroad throughout the whole world, and with the inspiration of the thought that you are Americans and are meant to carry liberty and justice and the principles of humanity wherever you go, go out and sell goods that will make the world more comfortable and more happy, and convert them to the principles of America.

Wilson tied the American need to export its goods, its political system, and its morality in a single package of red, white, and blue.

In encouraging such expansion, he went beyond the acts of previous presidents in two respects. First, he used military force not only to a greater degree, but also in an attempt to reform entire societies (see Marine Corps Progressivism below). Second, he used the powers of the federal government to a greater extent in capturing markets. The Federal Reserve Banking Act of 1913, for example, created new powers that American bankers and industrialists could use in competing for credit and money in foreign money markets. In 1914 Wilson sponsored the creation of a Bureau of Foreign and Domestic Commerce within the Department of Commerce. This bureau sent government agents abroad to be, in the president's words, the "eyes for the whole business community." The Webb-Pomerene Act of 1918 allowed exporters to organize associations for the development of overseas trade, associations that previously had been outlawed by antitrust laws. The Edge Act of 1919 provided similar privileges for American bankers, and for the same reasons.

In all, it was a beautifully integrated program. They key was restoring vitality and competition at home by exporting goods, political ideals, and morality abroad. The government was to play a central role by creating new agencies and laws for the benefit of various exporters. This was hardly traditional "free enterprise" capitalism. And if Progressive agencies did not do the job, there was always the Marine Corps.

## THE FAR EASTERN MERRY-GO-ROUND

Shortly after entering the White House, Wilson destroyed the China consortium, which had been established by Taft and Knox, by allowing American bankers to leave the group. This did not signify an American retreat from Asia, however. Realizing that the consortium was useless in maintaining the open door, Wilson attempted to devise an independent, go-it-alone approach to China that would provide American financial support unfettered by any European or Japanese controls. The president believed that this unilateral approach would build China to the point where Japan and Russia could no longer exploit it at will.

Wilson's first attempt at making his progressivism work abroad never had a chance to succeed. The Chinese Revolution, erupting in 1911, wrecked his policies, and the approach collapsed entirely when World War I began in August 1914. Japan took advantage of the European struggle to seize German possessions in China (including the strategic Shantung Peninsula), and then tried to impose the so-called Twenty-one Demands on the Chinese. If China had acquiesced, these demands would have not only consolidated the Japanese hold on Manchuria, but also given Japan economic and political concessions in China proper. Wilson strongly protested the demands, but it was British pressure and Chinese resistance that finally forced the Japanese to retreat. By 1917, as he prepared to go to war in Europe, Wilson had been ineffective in trying to roll back the Japanese.

## MARINE CORPS PROGRESSIVISM

The open door was also closing in the Caribbean area, but here it was Wilson and Secretary of State William Jennings Bryan who vigorously excluded European powers. Wilson sought stability and control in the Caribbean, especially after the Panama Canal opened in 1914 and war broke out in Europe.

In 1914, for instance, Bryan signed a treaty with Nicaragua giving the United States rights to a future isthmian canal, bases on the Pacific, and the right to intervene in Nicaragua to protect these new interests. In Santo Domingo, Wilson mistakenly thought he had averted a revolution by holding an election in 1914. When the new government failed to show its friendship by extending financial favors to Americans, however, chaos developed, and Wilson finally sent the Marines in 1916 to control the country. The following year U.S. troops entered Cuba once again, remaining until 1921 in order to protect American-controlled sugar plantations, particularly from attacks by armed Cubans.

But it is Haiti that provides a case study of the tragedy of Wilsonian Progressive diplomacy. Black slaves had successfully revolted against France in 1801, making Haiti the oldest independent nation in the hemisphere except for the United States. In a population of 2 million, the vast majority were small independent farmers and more than 95 percent were illiterate. Politics were controlled by and for the elite. Presidential political life in Haiti was about as

A guide *(right, front)* leads U.S. Marines searching for bandits in Haiti, 1919. *(Time Life/Getty Images)*

violent as in America—between 1862 and 1914 three presidents were assassinated in each nation. Until 1910 the United States had displayed relatively little interest in Haiti. But then the harbor of Môle-Saint-Nicolas became attractive to the growing American navy, and the Banque Nationale (the major financial institution in the country, controlled by French-German interests) fell into the hands of New York City bankers after a slight push by the State Department.

The American bankers next sought to control the customs houses. Since these provided the government's main source of income, however, Haiti refused. The bankers went to Bryan, giving him false information about the impending dangers of revolution and European control if they did not have their way. The secretary of state was hardly capable of making his own estimate. Both he and Wilson were largely ignorant of Latin American affairs, and both shared the racism that had influenced Roosevelt's diplomacy. When a New York banker tried to inform the secretary of state about the language and culture of Haiti, Bryan could only utter with amazement, "Dear me, think of it! Niggers speaking French."

In 1915 the Haitian president was killed by a mob because of his supposed involvement with a mass murder of political opponents. Wilson seized on this disruption as an excuse for landing more than 300 Marines and sailors in Haiti. The Haitian treasury was given to the bankers, while the United States gained control of the customs houses. The State Department succeeded in finding an acceptable president only after promising to use the Marines to protect him from his own countrymen. But still the Haitians fought back with guerrilla warfare in 1915 and again more massively in 1918 and 1919. After Wilson imposed martial law, the American military killed more than 2,000 Haitians while losing sixteen Marines. In several major actions, Americans slaughtered their opponents rather than take prisoners.

Progressive diplomacy succeeded in tearing up Haiti's society by its roots. A 1918 constitution (written largely by Assistant Secretary of the Navy Franklin D. Roosevelt) legalized American economic interests and the military occupation. Years later Americans had difficulty understanding why Haitians were impoverished and endured repressive dictators who received support from Washington.

## THE FIRST TWENTIETH-CENTURY REVOLUTION: MEXICO

Wilson's attempts to apply some of these methods to Mexico ended in failure. In that nation the president encountered his first twentieth-century revolution, one of those upheavals that, because of their turmoil and radical redistribution of power, gravely endangered the American hope for orderly change. American interests in Mexico were large. With the help of dictator Porfirio Díaz, Americans had amassed holdings amounting to between $1 and $2 billion. Most of this investment was in railroads, oil, and mines. In 1911 the aged Díaz surrendered to the superior force of Francisco Madero, who, after threatening foreign economic holdings, was himself overthrown by opposing forces under the control of General Victoriano Huerta. Huerta was strongly supported by the American ambassador in Mexico City. Then, to the horror of the world, Madero was murdered by Huerta's forces.

Entering the White House at this point, Wilson refused to accept Huerta's methods, and his refusal became adamant as it appeared that British oil interests were supporting Huerta. In fact, Wilson would not recognize the new government, thereby marking a historic shift in American recognition policy. Before 1913 the United States had recognized any government that controlled its country and agreed to meet its international obligations. Wilson now insisted that the government also be politically acceptable, that is, that it be elected through democratic procedures. The president threw his support to Venustiano Carranza, a military leader enjoying successes in northern Mexico. Huerta did hold elections in late 1913; not surprisingly, he won the presidency.

Deeply angry, Wilson redoubled his efforts to support Carranza and cut off aid to Huerta. In April 1914, on learning that a German ship was taking supplies to Huerta at Vera Cruz, Wilson landed troops to occupy the port. Mexican cadets opened fire. More than 300 Mexicans and 19 Americans were killed. Wilson's display of force and Carranza's steadily successful military campaigns finally forced Huerta to flee to Europe in August 1914. When Carranza assumed power in Mexico City, however, Wilson discovered that, like his predecessors, the new ruler would make no deals with the United States.

Searching for an alternative to Carranza, Wilson briefly thought that he had found his man in the notorious bandit Pancho Villa. But Carranza succeeded in isolating Villa, and then began preparations for a convention that would issue a revolutionary constitution promising agrarian reform and the placing of all subsoil mineral rights (such as oil and mines) in

Mexican hands. Outmaneuvered by Carranza and spurned by Wilson, Villa retaliated with attacks against American citizens, including killing seventeen Americans in Columbus, New Mexico. In March 1916 Wilson insisted that U.S. troops be allowed into Mexico to capture Villa. Carranza agreed reluctantly and then was horrified to discover that an army of 6,000 troops under the command of General John J. ("Blackjack") Pershing was marching into his country. As the American troops penetrated farther south, Carranza finally tried to stop them with force. Forty Mexicans and twelve Americans lost their lives. Carranza steadily refused to listen to Wilson's demands for new elections and the protection of foreign holdings. The president, moreover, now faced the much greater problem of American involvement in Europe.

In early 1917 the last American troops left Mexico. Carranza issued his constitution several months later. Wilson had utterly failed to control the Mexican revolution.

## FIRST PHASE: AMERICAN ENTRY INTO WORLD WAR I

Wilson's immersion in the revolutions of China and Mexico was unfortunate, particularly since he had little experience in foreign policy before becoming president. His policies tended to emerge from an understanding of the marketplace requirements of the American industrial complex and his personal preferences for the order, stability, and gentlemanly processes that he associated with Anglo-Saxon institutions. As a young professor, he had venerated the British political system. When World War I exploded in August 1914, therefore, Wilson asked the impossible even of himself when he pleaded that the American people be "neutral in fact as well as in name" and "impartial in thought as well as in action." Within a year, however, Wilson told Colonel House that he "had never been sure that we ought not to take part in the conflict," especially if Germany appeared to be growing stronger. By that time, the United States was well down the road to war. The American approach to the conflict evolved through three phases.

The first occurred in 1914 and early 1915 when the Allies (Great Britain, France, and Russia) seriously discriminated against American and other neutral shipping by blockading the Central Powers (Germany and Austro-Hungary). The Allies mined shipping routes through the North Sea and forbade neutrals even from trading with other neutrals if the goods traded appeared to be heading ultimately for Germany. After extended negotiations the United States accepted these Allied policies.

Several factors shaped the American surrender. Since 1900 American officials had viewed Germany, and not Great Britain, as the gravest military threat to U.S. interests in the Western Hemisphere. Once war broke out, moreover, London played on such fears by flooding the American press with stories of supposed German atrocities. The effect of this propaganda has probably been overestimated, but it intensified the sympathy most Americans already felt for the British. On the official level, Washington's responses to London were written not by Wilson (who was grieving over the death of his first wife), but by Robert Lansing, counselor to Bryan in the State Department. A former member of the New York City mercantile community, which had strong economic and social ties with Great Britain, Lansing did not even pretend to be neutral. He later bragged that he weighted down the American protests with complex legal language that would prolong the dispute until Americans perceived that "German absolutism was a menace to their liberties and to democratic institutions everywhere. Fortunately this hope and effort were not in vain." But Lansing did not wholly have to fabricate a case for Great Britain. Judged by traditional international law, most of the British actions were not illegal.

Most important, however, the ultimate recourse against the British acts, short of war, would have been an American embargo on exports to Great Britain. This alternative was never seriously considered because, Wilson admitted, an embargo would be "a foolish one as it would restrict our plants." During the summer of 1914 the economy was already depressed. An embargo on exports, even on ammunition and other articles related to war, could gravely affect the American system. When Wilson made this assumption—that is, that the United States had to be able to carry on its large international trade with all the markets the British navy would allow—he had ceased being neutral. The *Literary Digest* phrased this perfectly: "The idea generally held is that we are not our brother's keeper. We can make and sell what any nation wishes to order. . . . If it happens that only certain nations control the Atlantic, . . . that is not our fault or concern."

By early 1915 Great Britain and France were running short of money to pay for these American goods. During the early days of the war Wilson and Bryan had determined that no loans or credits could be issued by American bankers to either side, for "money was the worst of all contraband" in that it determined all other trade. That policy, however, was completely undercut by the president's determination to keep overseas markets open. By late autumn of 1914 the administration agreed to turn its head while U.S. bankers gave both Germany and the Allies credits, that is, money tagged for specific purchases in the United States. A year later, in August 1915, an intense debate within the Wilson cabinet ended in permission for American bankers to float a $500 million loan to the Allies. The lid was completely off. By early 1917 Americans had provided $2.5 billion in credits or loans to the Allies and less than $300 million to the Central Powers. Wilson explained the necessity for this policy in 1916: "There is a moral obligation laid upon us to keep out of this war if possible. But by the same token there is a moral obligation laid upon us to keep free the courses of our commerce and of our finance."

## SECOND PHASE: SUBMARINES

Once Wilson accepted the British blockade, another major obstacle to American trade— German submarine warfare—arose. Unable to compete with British surface naval power by February 1915, the Germans launched a submarine campaign that hardly distinguished among armed ships of war, unarmed merchant ships, and transports carrying civilians. Americans found this relatively new kind of warfare full of horrors. They sharply distinguished between British blockades, in which the English could leisurely search suspected merchant ships, and German submarines, which (because their thin plates and light arms rendered them an easy target) could not surface to ask a ship to identify itself or evacuate civilians before sinking it. Nor did the British make Wilson's situation easier when they illegally flew American flags from some of their vessels.

The president warned that he would hold Germany to "strict accountability" for any underwater attacks on American shipping. On May 15, 1915, the British liner *Lusitania* went down with the loss of 1,198 lives, including 128 Americans. Historians later discovered that the ship was carrying a large amount of ammunition from New York to London. Even had that been known at the time (and there is evidence the president did indeed know the *Lusitania* was carrying war materiel), Wilson doubtless would have sent the same strong protest to Berlin. When Germany seemed to snub this note, he sent one that threatened war. Secretary of State

German submarines in harbor, including the U-20 *(front row, second from left),* which sank the *Lusitania. (Library of Congress)*

Bryan resigned over the dispatching of this second note. The secretary of state insisted that if Wilson protested so strongly against submarines, he should also wage a stronger fight against the British blockade, which threatened the Central Powers with starvation. Wilson refused to take that position. A leading Democratic newspaper editor wrote of Bryan's resignation, "Men have been shot and beheaded, even hanged, drawn and quartered, for treason less heinous." Bryan's departure removed the only relatively neutral member of Wilson's cabinet. Lansing became secretary of state.

Although the Germans finally promised not to attack passenger liners, they stepped up their attacks on merchant vessels. In February 1916 many Americans feared that the sinkings would soon pull the United States into war. Congress threatened to pass the McLemore Resolution warning Americans not to travel on belligerent ships, that is, ships owned by nations fighting in the war; but Wilson waged an all-out effort to kill the measure, vowing that he would never "consent to any abridgement of the rights of American citizens in any respect." It was a brave statement, but his refusal to restrict the rights of Americans to trade or travel in wartime meant that he would have to protect those rights.

Then, on March 24, 1916, several Americans suffered injuries when an unarmed French passenger liner, the *Sussex,* was torpedoed. This sinking marked a turning point in Wilson's diplomacy. He demanded that underwater attacks on both passenger and unarmed merchant vessels cease or the United States would have to go to war. Germany responded with the so-called *Sussex* pledge: Germany would sink no more such vessels unless adequate search and safety procedures were carried out. But Germany asked that Wilson also issue a strong protest against the British blockade of central Europe. The president ignored the German request. In obtaining the pledge, Wilson believed he had scored a significant diplomatic victory.

## THIRD PHASE: MAKING THE WORLD SAFE FOR DEMOCRACY

After receiving the *Sussex* pledge, Wilson pushed the submarine problem to the background and concentrated on devising a method of intervening in the war. He hoped to act as a mediator trusted by both sides. As early as 1915, he saw himself as the central figure in reconstructing a postwar world in accord with Progressive principles.

During the early months of the war, Colonel House journeyed twice to Europe in attempts to prepare the ground. House got nowhere with the Germans, who clearly perceived the Americans' pro-Allied bias; the British and French refused to cooperate because they believed they could win a military victory. In any event, the Allies' and Central Powers' peace terms were irreconcilable by late 1915. So much blood had already been shed that a compromise peace was not possible. The president's situation worsened in 1916. The British not only refused to ask for his mediation, but angered Americans by further restricting U.S. mail, goods, and passengers that had to travel through the war zones.

In 1916 Wilson started out on a course to try to be more independent of the Allies. He had carefully laid the groundwork the year before with his "preparedness" program that started the construction of new warships and armed additional men. In July 1916 he supported legislation for more warships and submarines. As he told House, "Let us build a navy bigger [than Great Britain's] and do what we please." This remark was not in the same spirit as the slogan "He kept us out of war," which Democrats were then spreading across the country to urge Wilson's reelection. But the president did not care for that slogan. During the presidential campaign he warned that Americans must help in the search for peace, for they could not "any longer remain neutral against any willful disturbance of the peace of the world." Throughout the year he elaborated on his idea, first revealed in May 1916, when he called for a "universal association of nations" that would carry out worldwide progressivism by creating global free trade, freedom of the seas, and stability through territorial guarantees.

Wilson's hope for the postwar world became more urgent in June 1916 when the French, British, and Russians met secretly at the Paris Economic Conference to make plans for economic warfare against the United States. The Allies agreed on schemes for government-subsidized industries that would be able to compete against such American giants as United States Steel and Standard Oil. When Wilson and Lansing learned of these agreements, they drew up their own economic plans, but equally important, the president increasingly feared what might happen to American interests if the Allied nations won a total victory and then dictated a peace without his mediation. Such a victory could produce an overwhelmingly dominant power (such as Great Britain or Russia), which could dictate a peace that threatened American global interests.

But the president was given little choice. A month after his reelection in November 1916, Germany decided to wage all-out submarine warfare, even if such a policy brought the United States into the war. German war aims had escalated during the war until only a quick military victory could obtain those prizes—neutralization of Belgium, annexation of French territory, naval bases in the Atlantic and Pacific, perhaps even economic reparations from the Allies. The German naval command confidently told the kaiser, "England will lie on the ground in six months, before a single American has set foot on the continent."

Learning of this decision, Wilson went before Congress on January 22, 1917, in a last dramatic attempt to preserve his role as a neutral broker in a postwar peace. He demanded a "peace without victory." The Allies responded with cynicism, and on January 31 German underwater warfare began.

But Wilson, continuing to stall, did not move to declare war for two months. He feared above all that taking the United States into the conflict would guarantee an overwhelming Allied victory, ruin his own hopes of acting as mediator, and ensure the carrying out of the Paris Economic Conference's plans. Wilson worried, moreover, that American entry would decimate the "white civilization" needed to rebuild the postwar world, while allowing a "yellow race—Japan, for instance, in alliance with Russia," to exclude the United States from China. That was an exclusion Wilson swore he would never allow.

The president also encountered determined antiwar opposition led by Republican Progressive senators Robert La Follette of Wisconsin and William Borah of Idaho. Since 1900 a small band of Progressives had vigorously opposed the use of military intervention by Roosevelt, Taft, and Wilson, particularly since foreign involvements could take the nation's attention away from domestic reforms. They now also feared that entry into war could tie Americans into a power structure that would force the United States to support European empires and to fight wars for European, not American, interests.

On March 1, 1917, the antiwar group suffered a severe defeat with the publication of the Zimmermann telegram. British agents had intercepted and given to Wilson a note written by the German foreign minister, Arthur Zimmermann, which proposed to Mexico a Mexican-German alliance. If Mexico cooperated, Germany would help it retrieve the "lost provinces" of Texas, New Mexico, and Arizona, taken from Mexico in the 1840s. Newspapers headlined the telegram, and prowar sentiment flashed to new heights—especially in the Southwest. But despite this sensation, antiwar voices were not stilled. When the president asked Congress in April 1917 for a declaration of war, six senators and fifty representatives voted against entering the conflict, while eighty-two senators and 373 representatives supported Wilson's request. American men and women prepared to fight and die in the first modern global conflict.

As his nation finally entered the struggle, Wilson tried to preserve part of his status as a neutral by designating the United States an "Associated" power rather than a full-fledged Allied partner, but this was equivalent to a hope of losing only part of one's virginity. The president went to war because Germany declared submarine warfare against the United States, but equally important, because American economic requirements developed since 1914 left no alternative but to work with the Allies. Wilson especially believed that only by becoming a belligerent could he force Britain and France to open the world to the stabilizing influences of American progressivism. As he explained privately, he had to participate in the war if he hoped to have a seat at the peace table rather than "shout through a crack in the door." So he asked Americans to go to war to "make the world safe for democracy." Progressive diplomacy had once again ended in the use of military force, this time on a level never before seen in world history. Given the record of 1900 to 1917, too few Americans were asking whether progressivism was safe for the world.

# CHAPTER FOUR

# 1917–1920
## The Failure of World War I

American soldiers demonstrating the different types of gas masks worn by *(left to right)* U.S., British, French, and German troops. *(The Granger Collection, NYC)*

When Woodrow Wilson addressed Congress in April 1917, he proclaimed that World War I would be fought for the cause of humanity, not for mere conquest. The president and his supporters justified U.S. intervention on the ground that while Germany stood for reaction, that is, extreme political conservatism, the United States and its allies fought for liberalism. Confident that an American victory would make the world safe for their brand of democracy, Progressives also assumed that at home the war could be conducted in accord with their principles. Progressives had always valued efficiency, harmony, and the search for a "constructive social ideal." Now, many reasoned, wartime mobilization would be entrusted to the very experts in whom they had such confidence. Nagging social conflicts would be swept away in a wave of patriotic unity. The terrible realities of war soon shattered these expectations. Far from making the world safe for anything at all, the war undermined progressivism and unleashed revolutionary forces on an unparalleled scale.

## MOBILIZATION AND REFORM

A month after Wilson's war message, Walter Lippmann (an influential Progressive journalist) remarked that the nation stood "at the threshold of a collectivism which is greater than any as yet planned by the Socialist party." In fact, the war did enable Progressives to push through much of their remaining program in the fields of economic policy, moral uplift, and political reform. For a brief, euphoric moment Progressives imagined that the war served their own purposes. "Into a year has been packed the progress of a decade," one reformer exulted in 1918. Only gradually did it become apparent that, whatever the immediate accomplishments, World War I had exacted a frightful toll.

The War Industries Board served as the chief vehicle for directing the production and distribution of war materials. Created in July 1917 and headed after March 1918 by financier Bernard Baruch, the board embodied several features of the business-government partnership envisioned by New Nationalist Progressives. Under Baruch's guidance the board performed a variety of functions: it allocated scarce materials, coordinated purchasing, determined priorities, encouraged the development of new facilities, fixed prices, and occasionally granted exemption from the antitrust laws to promote efficiency. All these functions usually gained the approval of businessmen who cooperated because they respected Baruch (a highly successful Wall Street operator), were given a large role in deciding board policy, and could usually count on making a handsome profit from war orders.

The Wilson administration experimented with new policies to increase wartime food production. Because European nations relied heavily on American wheat and sugar exports, food administrator Herbert Hoover got farmers to bring additional land under cultivation by offering to purchase agricultural commodities at high prices. At the same time Hoover urged consumers to observe "wheatless," "meatless," and "porkless" days, and he also asked grocers to restrict each person's sugar ration to two pounds per month. Hoover ruled that restaurants could not serve bread until after the first course, and he insisted that they serve small cubes of sugar rather than sugar bowls. Posters and billboards appeared everywhere with such slogans as "Food Will Win the War," "Serve Just Enough," and "Use All Left-Overs." Conserving food itself came to be known as "Hooverizing." Meanwhile, food exports nearly tripled during the war.

In two additional areas—fuel and transportation—the Wilson administration assumed far-reaching power. The Fuel Administration under Harry A. Garfield fostered a substantial increase in coal and oil production, in part by increasing the mechanization of mines. When a coal shortage threatened, Garfield ordered many factories producing civilian goods to close down for a few days and to observe subsequent "heatless" days as a conservation measure. In December 1917, faced with a massive transportation tie-up, the administration took over the railroads. William G. McAdoo, who headed the Railroad Administration, proceeded to integrate rail schedules, limit passenger traffic, modernize equipment, and increase the amount of uniform track gauge. Private owners took directions from the Railroad Administration, but received a rental fee that guaranteed them a substantial return on their investment.

Besides encouraging these new techniques of industrial control, the war also paved the way for other reforms that Progressives had been demanding for years. For the first time the government interceded on behalf of trade unions. The War Labor Board supported the right of workers to unionize and bargain collectively, and it succeeded in obtaining the eight-hour day in many places. A newly created U.S. Employment Service helped workers find war jobs. In 1919 the Labor Department established a Women's Bureau to protect the interests of women workers, a major goal of Progressive reformers. The government, in addition, took pioneering steps in the field of social insurance and public housing. The Military and Naval Insurance Act (1917) provided for the retraining of disabled veterans and established a voluntary insurance system under which families of servicemen received federal aid. Finally, a dream of reformers seemed to come true with the initiation of a public housing program for workers who had gone to cities in search of defense jobs in shipyards and munitions plants.

## PROHIBITION AND WOMAN SUFFRAGE

Progressives had always exhibited a keen concern with moral questions, and World War I gave the moral uplift forces a golden opportunity. Starting with the premise that men in uniform must be protected against venereal disease, social hygienists, with the support of the War Department, launched a successful campaign to shut down brothels near military bases. They adopted the motto "Men must live straight if they would shoot straight." The government's Committee on Women's Defense Work created a department for "Safeguarding Moral and Spiritual Forces" to preserve American purity. Lecturers from the Young Women's Christian Association traveled across the country, warning young women against the hazards of illicit love, fostering "a higher standard of personal conduct and civil cleanliness," and exhorting their listeners to "Do Your Bit to Keep Him Fit." The obsession with cleanliness was sometimes carried quite far. One crusader noted that a boy who joined the army was "swept into a machine that requires cleanliness first, last, and all the time" and consequently became a person with "clean motives and higher desires."

The forces of moral uplift won by far their most important victory with the enactment of Prohibition. Although prohibitionists had always relied on a variety of medical, moral, and social arguments, the war provided them with just the ammunition they needed. Since the manufacture of beer required barley, temperance became a means of food conservation. Since many brewers were German-Americans, temperance could be equated with Americanism. Since drunkenness lowered the efficiency of defense workers and the potential fighting ability of soldiers, temperance achieved the status of a patriotic necessity. Liquor manufacturers, said William Jennings Bryan, "would, if they could, make drunkards of the entire army and leave us defenseless before a foreign foe." The year 1917 saw a form of creeping prohibitionism.

In May the sale of liquor around military camps was forbidden. In December the alcoholic content of beer was reduced, and Congress passed the Eighteenth Amendment. Even before the amendment was ratified in January 1919, a Prohibition Act (1918) outlawed the sale of all intoxicating beverages. Elated by their success, some reformers believed that World War I might yet make the world safe for teetotalers. A speaker at an Anti-Saloon League Convention proclaimed, "With America leading the way, with faith in Omnipotent God, and bearing with patriotic hands our stainless flag, . . . we will soon . . . bestow upon mankind the priceless gift of world Prohibition."

Finally, the war helped Progressives win the battle for woman suffrage. By the time the United States entered the war, women had gained the vote in eleven states. However, the House had defeated a constitutional amendment that would have given women the vote, and the suffrage movement seemed stalled. A dissident wing, inspired by British suffragists and led by Quaker Alice Paul had broken off to form the Woman's Party. Attacking the party in power, as British suffragists did, the Woman's Party adopted militant tactics such as picketing the White House, to the dismay of other suffragists. But war enabled the suffrage movement to gain the momentum it had sought for half a century. The incongruity of fighting a war for democracy while denying the vote to half the population—at the very time that women were playing an increasingly essential part in industry—suddenly became too painful. Besides, many claimed that women possessed nurturing qualities of tenderness and mercy that a war-ravaged world desperately required. Suffrage leader Carrie Chapman Catt was more pragmatic. In 1917 she announced that she did not know whether the vote was a right, a duty, or a privilege, but "whatever it is, women want it."

In 1917 six states—including New York, the key political battleground where women's suffrage had been rejected in 1915—enfranchised women; in January 1918 the House adopted the suffrage amendment, but the Senate rejected it. By then Woodrow Wilson had finally come over to the side of suffrage. He began to define it as a war measure, "an essential psychological element in the conduct of the war for democracy." For a time southern Democrats, who apparently feared that enfranchising women might set a precedent for protecting the right of blacks to vote, helped block action by the Senate. But in 1919 the Nineteenth Amendment obtained the needed congressional majority in both the House and Senate, and a year later, after ratification by three-fourths of the states, it became law.

## PROPAGANDA AND POLITICS

Although the war smoothed the passage of political, moral, and economic reforms long sought by Progressives, it also led to government actions that conflicted sharply with Progressive values. In its search for wartime unity, the Wilson administration conducted a massive propaganda campaign, one designed to inspire rather than to instruct. The Committee on Public Information under George Creel published millions of pamphlets, all hammering home the same message: the forces of a peace-loving democracy were pitted against those of a war-crazed autocracy. The Creel committee recruited 75,000 "Four Minute Men" who, in some 7.5 million speeches at theaters, clubs, and churches, described German atrocities and urged people to buy Liberty Bonds. One pamphlet predicted the consequences of a hypothetical enemy invasion: German soldiers would "pillage and burn," demand huge sums of money, execute anyone who refused to cooperate, and then "look on and laugh" while a priest and a minister were "thrown into a pig-sty."

Supreme Court Justice Oliver Wendell Holmes. *(Library of Congress)*

The war injected into politics new issues that badly shook Wilson's electoral coalition. Because the administration imposed controls on wheat but not on cotton prices, Democrats representing midwestern wheat growers charged that Wilson unfairly favored the South. Democrats from the South and West called for stiffer corporation taxes and complained that the administration, under the influence of the party's eastern wing, was coddling war profiteers. Many southern Democrats opposed Wilson on the issue of conscription. They asserted that volunteers would make better soldiers and that a draft would militarize the nation. Although conscription bills passed in 1917 and 1918, with the result that 24 million men registered and 3 million were drafted (and 1.8 million volunteered), Democrats in Congress were sharply divided.

Not only did the war distort certain Progressive principles and disrupt Wilson's coalition, but also it gradually eroded the reformers' confidence in progress, rationality, and order. With the Western world in flames, with senseless slaughter occurring daily and national passions aroused beyond all reason, it became increasingly difficult to sustain the old faith in the perfectibility of either people or institutions. If this disillusionment were not serious enough, Progressives' confidence in Wilson's policies and in their own ability to control events was badly shaken by the administration's response to wartime dissent and to the Russian Revolution.

## CURBING DISSENT: WHY

In November 1917 the motion picture *The Spirit of '76*, which depicted various atrocities committed by British soldiers during the American Revolution, played in Los Angeles. The film was seized and the producer indicted under the Espionage Act, for in 1917 the British were allies. The judge in the case *United States v. The Spirit of '76* sentenced the producer to a $10,000 fine and a ten-year prison term (later commuted to three years). Although extreme, this was not an atypical case. During World War I the government imposed harsh restrictions on the expression of antiwar opinion, and when official action was not swift enough to suit the public, vigilante groups took matters into their own hands. The targets of repression were radicals who opposed the war, pacifists who opposed all wars, and German-Americans and other immigrant groups who were suspected of having a divided allegiance.

The amount of dissent a nation tolerates in wartime is usually proportional to the internal threat it perceives. In 1917 many Americans felt a keen sense of peril from within because of the nation's very heterogeneity. In the preceding twenty-five years nearly 18 million immigrants had come to the United States, most of them from countries involved in the war. One of every three Americans at the time was either an immigrant or the child of an immigrant. Many people, who imagined that the newcomers retained Old World loyalties, feared that entering the war with a divided populace would destroy the bonds of social cohesion. Wilson himself had once warned of the danger that Americans might be divided into "camps of hostile opinion, hot against each other." For those plagued by fears of disunity, the war created a grave threat.

Such fears led to different sorts of defensive reactions. Some Americans tried to extinguish manifestations of German culture: several state legislatures eliminated the "kaiser's tongue" from school curricula, a few universities revoked honorary degrees bestowed in the past on noted Germans, and a town in Oklahoma even burned German-language books as part of a Fourth of July celebration. Others revealed their fears by insisting on a formal observance of patriotic ritual. Mobs often forced people who had criticized the war to buy Liberty Bonds, to sing the national anthem in public, or even to kiss the American flag, presumably with the proper ardor.

For those who were not satisfied with symbolic acts of conformity there remained yet another possibility—joining a patriotic organization. By far the largest was the American Protective League. With a membership that eventually climbed to 250,000, the league pried into people's opinions and checked on who was buying war bonds. To uncover "slackers," the league stopped men on the street and demanded that they produce their draft cards. The league even enjoyed quasi-official status. Its stationery read "Organized With the Approval and Operating Under the Department of Justice of the U.S."; its members received cards identifying them as federal agents; and in May 1918 the attorney general named the league an "Auxiliary to the Justice Department."

In addition to this widespread feeling of insecurity, the behavior of government officials fanned the flames of repression. Woodrow Wilson considered dissent dangerously disruptive, and he regarded the socialist leader Eugene V. Debs and other antiwar spokesmen as little better than traitors. Unable to give personal attention to each civil liberties case, Wilson delegated broad responsibility to members of his cabinet and usually stood by their decisions. Postmaster General Albert Burleson wanted to bar from the mails any publication that criticized the reasons for American entry into the conflict or said anything "to hamper and obstruct the Government in the prosecution of the war." Attorney General Thomas Gregory advised opponents of the war to seek mercy from God "for they need expect none from an outraged people and an avenging government." On occasion Wilson would overrule his subordinates, as when Burleson barred an issue of the liberal journal *The Nation* from the mails. Also, such officials as Secretary of Labor William Wilson and Secretary of War Newton D. Baker held more libertarian views. But usually the Wilson administration cracked down on dissenters with little hesitation.

## SOCIALISTS AND PACIFISTS

It could do so in part because of the nature of the opposition to the war. Not only were there relatively few war critics, but also most were socialists, anarchists, or members of the Industrial Workers of the World (IWW), people on the margins of society who had little political or economic weight and therefore made convenient targets. The war, in fact, proved disastrous for the Socialist Party, which had until then achieved a modest degree of success. In 1912 Debs had polled 900,000 votes—6 percent of the total—in the presidential election. Even in 1916 the party received 600,000 votes, elected candidates to office in scores of cities and towns, and reached a wide audience through its press. But when the United States entered the war, the Socialist Party, declaring that the war benefited only the ruling classes, called on American workers to repudiate the government. It branded the declaration of war "a crime against the people of the United States and against the nations of the world. In all modern history there has been no war more unjustifiable."

This posture weakened the socialist movement for several reasons. Although most socialists opposed the war, not all party leaders did. A small but influential segment, including Upton Sinclair, Charles Edward Russell, and Jack London, supported Wilson. Not only did the war split socialists into warring camps, but it linked the party in the public mind with treason and thereby robbed it of a good deal of its respectability. Finally, suppression broke the back of the party in some areas. Socialists found their literature barred from the mails, their headquarters wrecked, and their leaders indicted for sedition.

Like the Socialist Party, the women's movement also divided on the issue of war. Women reformers had long been committed to pacifism. In 1915, a coalition of delegates from women's organizations formed the Woman's Peace Party, led by Jane Addams and Carrie Chapman Catt. Once the United States entered World War I, the party splintered and women's pacifist efforts disintegrated. The woman suffrage movement, which supported the war, took the opportunity to prove its patriotic fervor. Clubwomen similarly joined the war effort by selling war bonds and running canteens. But there were dissidents. Some women socialists maintained their opposition to the war. Members of the Woman's Peace Party continued to demonstrate against "Kaiser Wilson" and, when arrested, went on hunger strikes. Pacifist and feminist Crystal Eastman led a remnant of the Woman's Peace Party that campaigned against American policy.

For pacifists, the war produced a crisis of conscience. In an atmosphere in which an ordinarily tolerant man like attorney Clarence Darrow could remark that "the pacifist speaks with the German accent" and in which conscientious objectors were labeled parasites whose liberties were being preserved by others on the battlefield, it is not surprising that many pacifists recanted. In 1916 the American Peace Society declared that Jesus Christ was a pacifist; in 1917 it backed the war. More than one hundred prominent Quakers announced their "loyalty to the Cause of Civilization, and to the President of the United States."

For those conscientious objectors who stood by their convictions, the government made provisions of a sort. The Selective Service Act of 1917 exempted from combat duty members of recognized religious sects whose teachings forbade participation in war. These men had to register for the draft and accept induction as noncombatants in the medical, engineering, or quartermaster corps. Of the 24 million registrants, 65,000 requested this classification. Only 21,000 were actually inducted, but fewer than 4,000 of them made use of their noncombatant status. The rest apparently took up arms. About 500 men who refused to cooperate in any way, or whose opposition to the war rested on political grounds and did not qualify them for consideration, were sent to jail; the last was not freed until 1933. In all, the number of conscientious objectors never approached the number of draft dodgers, which the War Department estimated at 171,000.

## CURBING DISSENT: HOW

The Wilson administration launched a three-pronged assault on dissenters. First, it attempted to deport radical aliens. Existing laws already excluded immigrants who favored the forcible overthrow of the government. Immigration legislation in 1917 and 1918 tightened these provisions and gave the government additional power to deport aliens who advocated the destruction of private property or who belonged to organizations that worked for revolution. No trial was needed. Deportation could be accomplished through an administrative proceeding. Second, the government dispatched troops to break strikes led by the IWW in lumber camps in Washington and in copper mines in Montana. Claiming that the IWW engaged in sabotage and that it instigated strikes not to improve working conditions but to cripple war production, the government threw union leaders into jail and held them for months on the flimsiest of evidence or on no charge at all.

The third and most widely used weapon to curb dissent was prosecution under the Espionage Act (1917) and the Sedition Act (1918). The Espionage Act made it a crime to obstruct military recruitment, and it authorized the postmaster general to deny mailing privileges for any materials he considered treasonous. Under its terms Burleson barred dozens of periodicals, including an issue of *The Masses*, which had a cartoon captioned "Making the World Safe for Capitalism." Eugene Debs was convicted under the Espionage Act for making a speech that condemned the administration's war policies and its violations of civil liberties. When the Supreme Court upheld his conviction, Debs spent two and a half years in jail. His comrade, Kate Richards O'Hare, was indicted for allegedly saying that any man who enlisted in the army "would be used for fertilizer" and that women who allowed their sons to enlist were "nothing more nor less than brood-sows." Although she denied having made the statements, O'Hare, a victim of wartime hysteria, served fourteen months in the penitentiary.

In the spring of 1918, as reports of mob violence against radicals reached Washington, the Wilson administration decided to support a sedition act in the hope that such a measure would calm public apprehension. The Sedition Act made it illegal to "utter, print, write, or publish

any disloyal, profane, scurrilous, or abusive language" about the government, the Constitution, the flag, the armed forces, or even the "uniform of the Army or Navy." Ultimately, more
than 1,000 persons were convicted under the Espionage and Sedition acts, including more
than a hundred members of the IWW who, President Wilson noted privately, "certainly are
worthy of being suppressed."

The Supreme Court ultimately approved these wartime prosecutions. In *Schenck v. United
States* (1919), a unanimous Court found that a socialist who had mailed circulars to men
eligible for the draft, circulars stating that conscription was unconstitutional and should
be resisted, had violated the Espionage Act by interfering with the legitimate power of the
government to raise an army. Oliver Wendell Holmes Jr., who delivered the opinion, tried
to define the boundaries of permissible speech. The question, Holmes said, "is whether the
words used are used in such circumstances and are of such a nature as to create a clear and
present danger that they will bring about the substantive evils that Congress has a right to
prevent. It is a question of proximity and degree." In *Abrams v. United States* (1919), the Court
found the Sedition Act constitutional. Jacob Abrams, an anarchist, and several of his friends
had distributed leaflets in August 1918 condemning American intervention in Soviet Russia
and calling on munitions workers to strike in protest. The government contended that such a
strike would also interfere with the conduct of the war against Germany. The Court upheld
the convictions, but Holmes now dissented, asserting that "the best test of truth is the power
of the thought to get itself accepted in the competition of the market."

The suppression of free speech had both predictable and unforeseen consequences. It
seriously weakened the radical movement. Indeed, groups were sometimes singled out not
only for their antiwar stand but also precisely because of their radicalism. For example, the
war furnished to employers who had always hated the IWW a patriotic pretext for attacking it. But restrictions on civil liberties also dismayed many Progressives who, though they
supported the war, believed that the Wilson administration had gone overboard in curbing
individual rights. The crusade for conformity also substantiated the argument of intellectuals,
like Randolph Bourne, who rejected all along the notion that war could be directed toward
humane ends. War was an inexorable situation, Bourne reasoned, in which the government
would do anything it thought necessary to achieve victory. Intellectuals who believed that
war could be "moulded toward liberal purposes" were therefore deceiving themselves. The
attack on civil liberties, as much as anything else, proved Bourne correct.

## ANOTHER REVOLUTION

If the war profoundly affected Americans, it was because, as Bourne observed, they expected
too much from the conflict, not because—as compared with the other belligerents—they
sacrificed too much for it. The growing American disillusionment with Russia was an excel-
lent example. In March 1917 the Russian people, bankrupt and bled to the breaking point,
overthrew the hollow, corrupt regime of Czar Nicholas II. The czar was replaced with a liberal
republic headed by Prince Georgy Lvov. President Wilson welcomed the new government,
particularly after Lvov promised to keep Russia in the war whatever the cost. The change of
government confirmed Wilson's faith that democracy, not authoritarianism, would shape the
future. By summer 1917, however, the war was still taking its murderous toll of the dispirited,
inefficient Russian army. The slow collapse of Lvov's regime allowed a corresponding rise

in the power of V.I. Lenin, a communist leader who had recently returned to Russia from Switzerland. Disillusionment with Lvov's inept policies resulted in July in a new, more conservative regime headed by Alexander Kerensky. The Kerensky government refused to listen to Lenin's demands for withdrawing Russia from the war.

Wilson appointed a special commission to visit Russia during the summer. The commission's report was optimistic, a mood not shared by Wilson or by Secretary of State Robert Lansing, who was convinced the Russians were sailing straight into another bloody French Revolution. This view was confirmed on November 7, 1917, when Lenin's Bolsheviks overthrew the Kerensky regime. Wilson's and Lansing's pessimism turned to hatred as Lenin began confiscating private property, radically redistributing political power, proclaiming the need for worldwide revolution, and in March 1918 making peace with Germany. The Bolsheviks "are avowedly opposed to every government on earth," Lansing privately exclaimed. He hoped they would "go to pieces," but doubted this would occur, for "their cry of 'Peace and Land' is popular with the ignorant Russians who have suffered grievously in the past." Wilson's and Lansing's fear of Lenin, however, did not get in the way of their understanding that the Bolsheviks fundamentally challenged Western "political institutions as they now exist . . . based on nationality and private property," in Lansing's words. Lenin threatened Wilson's entire postwar program.

The president's Fourteen Points speech of January 1918, one of the most famous speeches in American history, was Wilson's first response to Lenin. Two motives, the fear of bolshevism and the desire for American postwar economic expansion, explained why the Fourteen Points speech demanded covenants openly arrived at: freedom of the seas in peace and for neutrals in war; the removal of tariffs, trade preferences, and other economic barriers; reduction of armaments; self-determination as a political principle; recognition of a Russia that would be a reasonable neighbor (to Wilson this obviously meant a noncommunist neighbor); and, finally, "a general Association of Nations" that would uphold all these principles.

Not even Wilson's allies would accept the entire program. At the Paris Economic Conference of 1916, for example, they had planned to keep ambitious Americans out of British, French, and Italian markets. Great Britain, France, and czarist Russia, moreover, had signed secret agreements with Japan and Italy that promised territorial gains and economic booty from the war if they maintained a common front against Germany. Wilson knew about these treaties because Lenin had gleefully published them. The president understood that they ran directly against his principle of self-determination. To keep Japan away from China while American attention was on Europe, Wilson had even ignored several of his own points by negotiating a secret deal with Japan in which the United States agreed to recognize Japan's "special" interests in China. Tokyo officials in turn promised not to use the war as a cover for seizing "special rights or privileges in China." The president knew that this pact (the Lansing-Ishii agreement of November 1917) might later be used by Japan to claim special interests in Manchuria, but Wilson believed that at a postwar conference his own moral stature and his nation's mushrooming economic power would overcome the Allied and Japanese plans. The Bolsheviks, however, were another matter.

## INTERVENING IN THE RUSSIAN REVOLUTION

Lenin's government seemed to be beyond Wilson's control. As the American humorist Finley Peter Dunne once observed, a revolution could not be bound by the rules of the

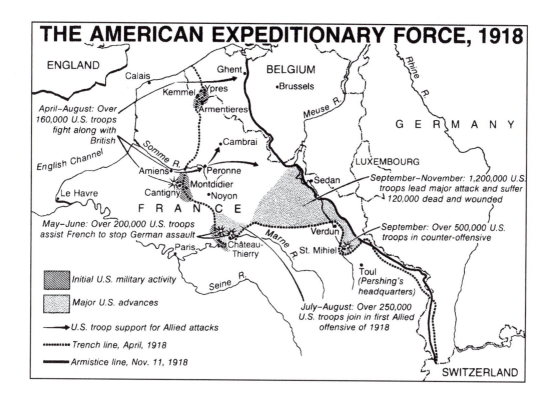

THE AMERICAN EXPEDITIONARY FORCE, 1918

ENGLAND

Calais

Ghent

BELGIUM
•Brussels

Kemmel Ypres

Armentieres

Rhine R.

GERMANY

*April–August: Over 160,000 U.S. troops fight along with British*

Somme R.

English Channel

Meuse R.

LUXEMBOURG

•Cambrai

Amiens Peronne

Le Havre

Montdidier

Cantigny •Noyon

FRANCE

Sedan

*September–November: 1,200,000 U.S. troops lead major attack and suffer 120,000 dead and wounded*

*May–June: Over 200,000 U.S. troops assist French to stop German assault*

Marne R.

Verdun

St. Mihiel

*September: Over 500,000 U.S. troops in counter-offensive*

Paris Château-Thierry

Seine R.

Initial U.S. military activity

Toul
(Pershing's headquarters)

Major U.S. advances

*July–August: Over 250,000 U.S. troops join in first Allied offensive of 1918*

U.S. troop support for Allied attacks

Trench line, April, 1918

Armistice line, Nov. 11, 1918

SWITZERLAND

game, for it is rebelling against those rules. The president was therefore open to demands by the British and French that he join them in intervening militarily in Russia to overthrow the Bolsheviks and reopen the eastern front. At first Wilson refused, in part because of opposition from young liberals in the State Department who were led by William Bullitt. A handsome, ambitious, aristocratic Philadelphian, Bullitt argued that Leninism could be destroyed only if Wilson moved farther to the left politically and undercut the attractiveness of the Bolshevik program.

The president rejected such advice. In June 1918 he agreed to land Americans at Murmansk in northern Russia. The landing was made in cooperation with French and British troops. The Japanese meanwhile moved into Siberia, threatening to control the vital Trans-Siberian railway system while disguising their takeover as "anti-Bolshevism." In July Wilson sent 10,000 troops to Vladivostok in Siberia, then established an American-controlled group to run the railways. He thus assumed responsibility in that far-off part of the world to stand guard against both Japanese and Bolsheviks. Making the world safe for democracy obviously was becoming a big job.

Wilson publicly justified the intervention in Murmansk on military-strategic grounds, but within days the Allied forces were fighting Bolsheviks, not Germans. The American force remained there, moreover, until June 1919, nearly eight months after the war against Germany ended. The president excused the Vladivostok operation by arguing that he hoped to help some 60,000 Czech soldiers who had been fighting Germany and now apparently wanted to escape through Vladivostok to fight on the western front. When the Americans landed, however, the Czechs were fighting Bolsheviks. The United States protected the rear of the Czech forces and supported White Russian troops that were trying to overthrow Lenin. The American soldiers remained in Siberia until April 1920.

The interventions made little sense in the overall war effort. They were crucial, however, if Wilson hoped to destroy the communist regime and keep Siberia out of Japanese hands. As Secretary of War Newton D. Baker candidly remarked in September 1919, American troops remained in Siberia because withdrawal would leave the area "open to anarchy, bloodshed and Bolshevism." But Wilson failed to overthrow Lenin. He only worsened an already poisonous relationship between Russia and the West. The president fully realized the dilemma. In 1919 he declared that using troops to stop a revolution was "like using a broom to hold back a great ocean." He nonetheless tried to use the broom.

## THE YANKS IN EUROPE

A central problem for Wilson was that he had to watch closely not only Germans, Bolsheviks, and Japanese but also his European allies. The political relationship with London and Paris, already strained by the Fourteen Points speech, was not improved by the timing and nature of the American military effort.

No major U.S. force landed in France until eight months after Wilson's war message of April 1917. Not until the spring of 1918 did Americans decisively affect the fighting. But they were then pivotal in turning back a large German offensive just forty miles from Paris. The Americans won a major victory at Château-Thierry, a triumph that Wilson mistakenly thought would put the French in his debt at the postwar peace conference, and then drove the Germans back along the southern front until Berlin asked for peace in November 1918. The war ended on November 11.

The Yanks had arrived none too early, for throughout 1917 and early 1918 the Allies nearly bled themselves to death. In one offensive alone they expended more than a half million lives to move the battle line several miles. An entire generation of Europeans was being extermi-nated. Nearly 3 million Allied soldiers lost their lives in the war; probably 10 million people in all were slaughtered, but of this number only 52,000 were Americans. These figures help explain why British and French leaders were so driven by hatred for Germany at the Paris peace conference in 1919 and why they scorned Wilson's pleas for moderation. Such feelings, combined with the president's great reluctance to place American troops under European commanders and his refusal to participate fully in several wartime planning conferences, did not augur well for the peace conference. But then the problems Wilson was enduring at home were also ominous for his postwar plans.

## 1919: RED SCARE

In 1919, as peace came to Europe, industrial warfare flared in the United States. That year more than 4 million workers took part in 3,600 strikes. Most of the walkouts had similar causes. Workers who had won union recognition and improved their working conditions during the war now attempted to solidify or extend those gains. It seemed essential to do so because wages were lagging behind rising prices, and many workers feared that they would lose their jobs as factories converted back to civilian production. Employers, however, wanted to withdraw many of the concessions made during the war; consequently, they often refused even to negotiate. These conflicts took place in the wake of the widespread anxiety aroused by the Russian Revolution. Although only a few strikes were led by radicals and none had radical objectives, employers, hoping to capture public opinion, claimed that labor turmoil posed a revolutionary threat.

Two of these disturbances in particular—the Seattle general strike and the Boston police strike—seemed to endanger law and order. In January 1919, when Seattle shipyard workers struck for higher wages, unions throughout the city voted to walk out in support. Many Americans viewed the general strike, in the words of one presidential adviser, as "the first appearance of the Soviet in this country." The government dispatched the U.S. Marines; the American Federation of Labor (AFL) leadership insisted that Seattle locals return to work; and Seattle's mayor, Ole Hanson, beefed up the police and issued an ultimatum. Under fierce pressure from all sides, the strikers capitulated. Then, in September, policemen in Boston demanded the right to join a union, a right denied them by the police commissioner. A strike followed during which some theft and looting occurred. The reaction was intense. The president branded the strike "a crime against civilization," and Governor Calvin Coolidge of Massachusetts proclaimed that there was "no right to strikes against the public safety by anybody, anywhere, anytime." The city dismissed everyone involved in the strike and recruited an entirely new police force.

In September 1919 the United States also faced the most massive industrial dispute in its history when 350,000 steelworkers left the mills. The men, many of whom still worked twelve hours a day, seven days a week, wanted an AFL union recognized as bargaining agent. The mill owners, for their part, welcomed a showdown over the principle of the open shop. Judge Elbert Gary, the president of United States Steel, accurately reflected the opinion of management when he claimed that most workers were satisfied with their conditions and wanted nothing to do with the union. As in Boston and Seattle, charges of radicalism were hurled at the union leaders. In this case the union gained nothing at all. By January 1920, its resources exhausted by a long and costly struggle, the AFL called off the strike.

In the spring of 1919, a series of bombings and attempted bombings badly frightened the American people. In April a bomb was sent to the mayor of Seattle. Another, mailed to a Georgia politician, exploded, and the maid who opened the package lost both her hands. When the post office intercepted thirty-four identical parcels addressed to J.P. Morgan, John D. Rockefeller, and other prominent business and civic leaders, and all were found to contain bombs, headlines blared: "REDS PLANNED MAY DAY MURDERS." In June bombs went off at about the same time in eight cities, adding to the fear that these acts were the work not of an individual but of a conspiracy. One of the bombs shattered windows in the home of Attorney General A. Mitchell Palmer.

As Americans felt increasingly threatened by signs of violent revolution, they hunted for preventive measures. No fewer than twenty-eight states passed peacetime sedition acts of some sort, under which 1,400 people were arrested and 300 convicted. Legislatures sometimes refused to admit those who held unorthodox views. In November 1919 the House of Representatives refused to seat Milwaukee socialist Victor Berger. When he won reelection, the House again balked at accepting him. In January 1920 the New York State legislature expelled five socialists, although most of them had held office during the war. States tried to uproot subversive influences by investigating public school teachers and requiring them to sign loyalty oaths. Congress further tightened immigration laws in 1920 by providing for the deportation of aliens who merely possessed revolutionary literature.

The Red Scare reached its crescendo with the Palmer raids. Shaken by the bombing attempt on his home, Attorney General Palmer, with the aid of other officials, worked out policies that effectively deprived radical aliens of due process. The Department of Justice launched surprise raids on the headquarters of radical organizations, seized correspondence and membership lists, detained suspects under astronomical bail, and cross-examined witnesses before they could obtain legal advice. Permitting a radical alien to see an attorney before interrogation, J. Edgar Hoover of the Justice Department explained, "defeats the ends of justice." In the first week of January 1920, federal agents, employing these tactics, arrested 3,000 alleged communists in thirty-three cities. Many were imprisoned, although no charges were brought against them; 550 were later deported. Palmer's action violated every civil libertarian principle, but instantly made him a national hero.

The wartime suppression of civil liberties differed in several respects from the postwar Red Scare. In the former, Americans feared subversion, but in the latter, revolution. The target in 1917 was frequently the German-American; the target in 1919 was often organized labor. But in important ways the two episodes resembled each other. Both occurred because society felt threatened from within, both involved legal and extralegal forms of repression, and both exploited anti-immigrant and antiradical sentiments. Each had a crippling effect on the American radical movement, which by 1920 was weak, fragmented, and in disarray. The Palmer raids, no less than wartime intolerance, angered many Progressives, who condemned Wilson for permitting, if not actually encouraging, these excesses. By mid-1920 the Red Scare had run its course. With communism clearly confined to Russia, with labor turmoil and bomb scares at an end, fears began to evaporate. The Wilson administration had won praise for its antiradical stance early in 1920, but had a more difficult time defending its record by the end of the year.

## 1919: BLACK SCARE

The postwar years were marked not only by labor turmoil but also by intense racial discord. In 1919 lynch mobs murdered seventy-eight African-Americans, at least ten of whom were veterans. From April to October race riots erupted in twenty-five cities, including Washington, DC; Omaha, Nebraska; and Longview, Texas. These riots claimed the lives of 120 people. The worst riot, during what came to be known as the "Red Summer," took place in Chicago; it left 38 dead and 537 injured. In truth, "race riot" was a less accurate term than "race war." Marauding bands of whites and blacks, armed with guns and clubs, roamed the streets and hunted each other down. Racial turbulence, like the Red Scare, had its roots in postwar social and economic dislocations. The war had dramatically altered the position of black Americans and raised their expectations. When those expectations clashed with the ingrained prejudices of whites, the stage was set for the Red Summer.

World War I spurred a mass exodus of blacks from southern farms to northern cities. In 1915 and 1916, floods and boll weevils ravaged crops in the cotton belt and forced many tenant farmers off the land. At about the same time, the war opened magnificent opportunities in the North. The demand for industrial labor seemed insatiable as factories were swamped

# BASEBALL
## SPORT AND BUSINESS

Babe Ruth and New York Giants manager John McGraw, 1923.
*(Library of Congress)*

Baseball has long been America's national pastime. It combines raw individual effort with precise team play, compiles masses of figures that enchant statistic-loving Americans, has a long tradition that allows fans to link past heroes to the present, and is played during the school-free, halcyon days of summer. Its complexity even makes it a favorite of intellectuals ("Base-ball is a religion," a distinguished philosopher proclaimed in 1919.).

The game's roots go back to ancient Egypt. Modern American teams appeared in the 1840s, organized—as has been every popular American sport except basketball—by wealthy gentlemen in the Northeast. Baseball was nationally popular by the Civil War. The first professional team, the Cincinnati Red Stockings, was formed in 1869. The National League appeared in 1876, the American League in 1901. World Series competition between the two leagues began two years later. Baseball grew quickly at the twentieth century's turn because of rapid urbanization, new street railways, and, particularly, increased leisure time created by the mechanization of farming and industry.

Equally important, the game was developed by men who viewed it as business, not sport. They organized it along the lines of such corporations as United States Steel. A division of labor existed between management and players, with owners monopolizing the players through a "reserve clause" that made players property of a single club. Owners controlled their market by giving each team absolute rights over its own urban area. Supreme Court rulings meanwhile exempted baseball from antitrust laws (a benefit not even United States Steel received from the courts). Attendance rose dramatically. The value of some clubs multiplied ten times between 1900 and 1918. Then, in 1919, members of the Chicago White Sox (soon tabbed the "Black Sox") were accused of accepting bribes to lose the World Series.

The sport was severely shaken. But four people managed to resurrect baseball so that

Brooklyn Dodgers president Branch Rickey talking to Jackie Robinson. *(National Baseball Hall of Fame Library, Cooperstown, New York)*

it became the rage of sport-minded Americans. Kenesaw Mountain Landis, a tough U.S. district court judge, was brought in as the first commissioner of professional baseball by the frightened owners to clean up the game. He did so brutally, even trying to ban players and owners from attending racetracks (where, Landis believed, lurked shadowy figures who "would sell out the Virgin Mary and their mothers"). He ruled baseball until his death in 1944. The second savior was George Herman ("Babe") Ruth of the Boston Red Sox and New York Yankees. His twenty-nine home runs in 1919 broke an 1884 record and revolutionized baseball by making it a game of exciting power. A son of a Baltimore barkeeper and a hard drinker at age eight, Ruth glamorously flouted Prohibition in the 1920s. He ordered the clubhouse boy to discard all letters except "those with checks or from broads." Landis was the puritanical Calvin Coolidge of baseball while Ruth was Babylonian America having an often illegal and immoral—but wonderful—time.

The third figure was Branch Rickey, a religious, Ohio-born, sharp-eyed lawyer who, as a general manager for several teams, developed the farm system whereby major league clubs developed their own players in minor leagues. This arrangement resembled Standard Oil's system of controlling its profitable product from the oil well to the filling station. The devout Rickey would not play ball on Sunday, but liked the player who "will break both your legs if you happen to be standing in his path to second base." His corporate techniques won championships at St. Louis, Brooklyn, and Pittsburgh. In 1947 he forced reluctant owners to allow him to hire Jackie Robinson, the first African-American to play in the Majors (for the Brooklyn Dodgers). Robinson became baseball's fourth savior.

He was followed by such other black superstars as Willie Mays, Hank Aaron (who broke Ruth's all-time home run record), and Bob Gibson (who struck out more hitters than any other National League pitcher). In 1958 the fabled Brooklyn Dodgers deserted Flatbush and became the Los Angeles Dodgers, making big league baseball a continental sport for the first time. And in the mid-1970s, the courts finally broke the owners' monopoly over their employees. Players with a specific number of years of experience, the courts decided, could test their worth in the open market. Wealthy clubs, such as the New York Yankees, were accused of "buying championships" when they won pennants after paying millions to several such stars. These huge sums were made possible by steadily increasing attendance and lucrative television contracts. The sport prospered, but it had been a close call, for in the 1920s baseball had nearly struck out before Landis, Ruth, Rickey, and Robinson stepped in to save it.

## Web Links

**www.pbs.org/kenburns/baseball**
The public broadcasting system program, with a list of additional websites.

**http://blackbaseball.com/**
A site that includes a video on the creation of the Negro Leagues.

National Guardsmen are called out to quell race riots in Chicago, July 1919. *(Jun Fujita/Getty Images)*

with military orders, workers left their jobs for the army, and the flow of immigration from Europe came to a virtual halt. Black newspapers, particularly the Chicago *Defender*, encouraged migration by playing up the opportunities available to blacks in the North. Labor agents swept through the South attempting to recruit black workers. Some companies even issued free railroad passes to anyone who promised to work for them. From 1916 to 1918, hundreds of thousands of African-Americans moved north. The black population of Chicago doubled in just four years.

For most, migration had a racial as well as an economic dimension. The letters written by migrants, and their behavior as well, reveal their sense of embarking on a pilgrimage out of bondage and into a promised land. "I am in the darkness of the south," said an Alabama black in explaining his request for train fare to Chicago; "please help me to get out of this low down country [where] i am counted no more thin a dog." A group of blacks from Hattiesburg, Mississippi, on crossing the Ohio River, knelt, prayed, kissed the ground, and sang hymns of deliverance. The North, with its absence of legal segregation, surely afforded some African-Americans an exhilarating sense of freedom. A black carpenter who had moved to Chicago wrote to his brother in Mississippi, "I should have been here 20 years ago. I just begun to feel like a man."

Most blacks genuinely believed that the war would usher in an era of social justice. The National Association for the Advancement of Colored People urged blacks to support the war by enlisting and buying bonds, for then whites could no longer ignore their appeals for equality. A similar conviction led W.E.B. DuBois to advise blacks to "close our ranks shoulder to shoulder with our own white fellow citizens and the allied nations that are fighting for democracy." Several concessions made by the Wilson administration bolstered the prevailing optimism. Although the army remained rigidly segregated, the War Department established an officers' training camp for blacks, created a black combat division, and accepted blacks into medical units. The Railroad Administration, while preserving separate facilities for passengers, paid the same wages to white and black workers and agreed to bargain with a black Pullman union. All this, in the context of 1918, represented progress.

The end of the war, however, disappointed the hopes of DuBois and many others. With the return of millions of veterans, competition for jobs and housing grew fierce. In 1919 African-Americans discovered that many of their wartime gains were vanishing. They were again the last hired and the first fired. They still paid the highest rents for the most squalid dwellings. The Wilson administration no longer showed the slightest interest in them. Disillusionment was profound. For the first time, a number of black spokesmen openly advocated the use of violence for purposes of self-defense. This heightened race consciousness coincided with heightened fears among whites that blacks would drive down property values or, more generally, forget their "proper place."

The race riots occurred against this background of blacks and whites being thrown together in cities, of competition for places to live and work, of increased black militancy and corresponding white anxiety. Though no two riots followed exactly the same pattern, there were some similarities. The riots, which usually broke out during a heat wave when tempers were on edge, were often triggered by rumors of an interracial assault. Once the rioting began, the police seldom acted impartially; rather, they treated blacks more brutally than whites. Both sides committed acts of violence. Usually whites were the aggressors, and blacks defended themselves by trading rifle fire with their foes and making sorties into white neighborhoods. A few riots lasted a long time. It took thirteen days to restore order to Chicago. Invariably the riots left a legacy of bitterness and led not to mutual understanding but to a hardening of racial animosities.

## THE ROAD TO PARIS

The class and racial antagonisms in the United States mirrored those of the world community. If Americans had difficulty handling these problems at home, there was little reason to think that they could make the entire world, or even Europe, safe for Progressive democracy. Yet Wilson set out to try.

He immediately ran into a string of disasters. Throughout the war the president had refused to discuss peace terms with the Allies. He feared that such talks could lead to splits that would retard the war effort. He also believed that as the war continued, American economic and military power would give him an increasingly stronger hand. But when he did approach the Allies to discuss the Fourteen Points in late 1918, Wilson discovered that the British refused to negotiate freedom of the seas (a principle that would protect neutrals against the powerful British fleet). The French insisted on destroying German power regardless of Wilsonian

"The Big Four" at the Paris Peace Conference in 1919: David Lloyd George, Vittorio Orlando, Georges Clemenceau, Woodrow Wilson. *(Library of Congress)*

principles. The president's position was weak, for he had refused to recognize neutral rights on the high seas in 1917 and 1918 and had singled out Germany as primarily responsible for starting the war. After all, such policies had been necessary to sustain the American commitment at home.

On the way to Paris Wilson told his advisers that "the United States was the only nation which was absolutely disinterested" in peace making. Allied leaders knew better, and they comprehended how history had shaped the American position as well as their own. Harold Nicolson, a member of the British delegation to Paris and later a distinguished historian, observed that Americans, like Europeans, had used brutal force to conquer territory in the nineteenth century. Then he asked, "Can we wonder that [Europeans] preferred the precisions of their old system to the vague idealism of a new system which America might refuse to apply even to her own continent?" As Europeans such as Nicolson understood, Wilsonian principles were designed to protect American interests.

The president also informed his advisers that, while he embodied the hopes of all progressive peoples, "the leaders of the allies did not really represent their peoples." This was a colossally mistaken belief. David Lloyd George and Georges Clemenceau, the prime ministers of Great Britain and France, respectively, received thumping votes of support at home before the peace conference convened, and both leaders ran on platforms pledging to squeeze every possible pfennig (penny) and acre out of Germany. Wilson, however, in one of the great American political fumbles, had proclaimed in late October 1918 that patriotism required the election of a Democratic Congress. In a congressional election year the Republicans would probably have gained some seats, but they won a major victory by blasting Wilson for questioning their wholehearted support of the war. Republicans even captured the Senate (49 to 47), the body that would have to ratify Wilson's work at Paris.

Nor did the president ease the situation by naming a peace commission that contained not a single important Republican or senator. This bland group was designed to raise few problems for the plans of the delegation's leader, Wilson himself. The president decided that no other person could be entrusted with the mission. He gave his political opponents and those who disliked the Fourteen Points a highly visible figure to attack.

## AT PARIS

In the wake of the war's devastation, communist uprisings took place in Germany. A communist government actually controlled Hungary for several months. An American warning that food supplies would be shut off if trouble occurred in part averted threatened left-wing riots in Austria. "We are sitting upon an open powder magazine," Colonel House worried, "and some day a spark may ignite it." By early 1919 Wilson's fear of bolshevism overshadowed his mistrust of the Europeans. He increasingly found himself on their side in a common effort to contain Leninism. He did reject their suggestions that a larger military force be sent to topple the Bolsheviks, but agreed that Lenin should not be invited to Paris. Wilson had decided to use pressure, not negotiation, in handling Lenin.

The president continued to have faith that Leninism could be conquered through a "slow process of reform." Since it was his League of Nations that would carry out the reform, Wilson, over the vigorous objections of the French and British (who wanted first to settle the precise terms for strangling Germany), forced the peace conference to begin in January 1919 with discussions on the League. Within a month the organization was created. The League of Nations consisted of an Assembly containing nearly forty nations (but not revolutionary Mexico, Russia, or Germany); a Council comprising nine nations, with the five permanent seats held by the United States, Great Britain, Japan, France, and Italy; and a Secretariat. Except for procedural matters, most decisions required unanimous consent in the Council.

Article XIV of the Covenant of the League of Nations established the Permanent Court of International Justice, which could decide international cases taken to the Court by the parties involved. Article XVI pledged all members to penalize aggressors by cutting off trade and economic aid. It was Article X, however, that Wilson termed "the heart of the covenant":

> The members of the League undertake to respect and preserve as against external aggression the territorial integrity and existing political independence of all members of the League. In case of any such aggression or in case of any threat or danger of such aggression the Council shall advise upon the means by which this obligation shall be fulfilled.

This wording deserves close study, for in the end Article X contributed to Wilson's doom.

Returning to the United State for a short time in February 1919, Wilson encountered strong opposition to the covenant from Senate Republicans led by Henry Cabot Lodge of Massachusetts. The opponents made public a petition signed by thirty-nine senators condemning the League, six more than the one-third necessary to defeat the pact. This opposition was partly personal. Some Republicans, Lodge and Theodore Roosevelt in particular, hated Wilson, a feeling not lessened by the president's partisan attack on Republicans and his often condescending manner. But his opponents primarily attacked several aspects of the treaty itself. Article X, they feared, committed Americans to uphold the status quo around the world, pledged the United States to preserve British and French imperial interests, and weakened Congress's power to declare war by providing a nearly automatic American commitment to intervene. League opponents also attacked the lack of a provision protecting America's use of the Monroe Doctrine in the Western Hemisphere and the failure to exclude domestic questions (such as tariffs) from League authority.

The president was furious with the Senate. "I am going to resume my study of the dictionary to find adequate terms in which to describe the fatuity of these gentlemen with the poor little minds that never get anywhere," he remarked privately. "I cannot express my contempt for their intelligence." Wilson then made another critical mistake. Returning to Paris, he demanded changes in the covenant—although not in Article X—that would meet some of the Senate's objections. Time that was to have been devoted to carefully drawing up the peace treaty with the Germans was, at the president's insistence, spent on rewriting the covenant. Lloyd George, Clemenceau, and Vittorio Orlando, the Italian leader, knew that they had Wilson at a disadvantage and consequently gave in to some of his requests only after he gave them much of what they wanted in the peace treaty. The president had to surrender parts of his Fourteen Points, particularly those concerning self-determination and territorial settlements.

As one American official later commented, "One came to Paris when hope was riding high, and each day you could see these hopes just—well, you soon detected that it was a great enormous balloon and gradually all the air was coming out of it. . . . Then there was Russia, a vast black cloud that overhung the whole thing." As the conference wore on and revolution threatened Germany, Hungary, and Austria, the key problem was, indeed, how the Soviet Union could be isolated and central Europe, particularly a weakened Germany, protected from the virus of communism. Wilson hoped to rebuild Germany so that it would be strong enough to provide its own immunity. Clemenceau, however, and to a lesser extent Lloyd George, determined that Germany must be stripped so that it could never again launch war. Territory taken from Germany was given to France, Poland, and the new independent state of Czechoslovakia. Millions of Germans were thereby wrenched from their native government and placed within the boundaries of other, weaker nations.

Equally important, Germany was saddled with $33 billion of war reparations that had to be paid out of a decimated economy. The French had actually asked for $200 billion, but Wilson fought Clemenceau and scaled down the French demands. In return, however, the president and Lloyd George signed a security treaty promising France aid if it were attacked by Germany. The plan thus became clear: in order to assist a weakened Germany to withstand the onslaughts of communism sweeping in from the east, the peace conference essentially threw out the principle of self-determination, particularly for Germans, in order to build the newly independent states of Poland, Hungary, and Czechoslovakia, which were to act as buffers, or a cordon sanitaire, between Russia and Germany. In reality, of course, these states were too weak to stand between two potential giants, so France gave territorial guarantees to the eastern Europeans by pledging to assist if they were attacked by a third party.

Self-determination was also sacrificed in the Pacific, where the Chinese province of Shantung, formerly controlled by Germany, was claimed by Japan. Wilson initially fought this transfer, but surrendered when the Japanese threatened to leave the League of Nations unless they received Shantung. The president did prevent Italy from claiming non-Italian territory along the Adriatic Sea, even though Orlando dramatically walked out of the conference in protest. Finally, Wilson accepted a compromise on the question of Germany's former colonies in Africa and the Pacific that, in actuality, gave France, England, and Japan the complete control they demanded in these areas. Germany was never consulted on these terms, but was simply given the hurriedly written treaty in May to sign—or else. The "or else" probably would have been an economic blockade designed to starve the Germans until they did sign. Berlin officials finally accepted the treaty only after bitterly protesting its terms. One war had finally ended.

## REJECTION

As Wilson returned to do battle with the Senate, he found three groups preparing to fight the Covenant of the League of Nations and the peace treaty. The first group, centering on Lodge and other conservative Republicans, determined to defeat anything Wilson recommended, but focused its objection on the automatic commitment implied in Article X. A second group comprised such Progressives as Herbert Hoover and Charles Evans Hughes. This group did not personally dislike Wilson (Hoover, indeed, had been one of the president's important advisers at Paris), but attacked Articles X and XVI and was afraid the covenant would endanger Congress's constitutional control over domestic affairs. A third group, led by Progressive Republicans William Borah of Idaho and Hiram Johnson of California, formed the "Irreconcilables," for they refused to agree to American participation in any international organization resembling the League of Nations. Moreover, they blasted Wilson's refusal to deal with Russia as, in Johnson's words, "an exhibition of the crassest stupidity." One common thread united the three groups: all wanted to maintain maximum freedom of action for the United States in the world, particularly so Americans could freely exploit their new economic power without having to worry about political restraints.

Wilson's opponents enjoyed a strong position. With the Republicans in control of the Senate, Lodge became chair of the Foreign Relations Committee, which would first have to act on the covenant and the treaty. As it became clear that Lodge was mustering opposition, the president attempted to pressure the Senate by embarking on an exhausting speaking tour. After thirty-six formal speeches in three weeks, the sixty-three-year-old Wilson suffered the beginnings of a paralytic stroke on September 26. Desperately ill, he nevertheless angrily stuck to his refusal to compromise with the Senate. When the Senate added reservations that modified Article X and condemned Japan's hold on Shantung, Wilson ordered Democratic senators not to vote for the amended covenant. In November 1919 the Senate rejected the League of Nations charter, with reservations, by a vote of 39 to 55. Four months later the charter again fell short of the necessary two-thirds needed for ratification, 49 to 35. Twenty-three Democrats, obeying Wilson's orders, ironically joined the Irreconcilables in defeating American entry into the League.

The president made one final effort during the 1920 presidential campaign. At first Wilson apparently decided to try for an unprecedented third term, but his illness and realistic Democratic political advisers ended that dream. He then declared the election a "solemn ref-

Senator Henry Cabot Lodge, chair of the Senate Foreign Relations Committee. *(Library of Congress)*

erendum" on the League of Nations. The president urged the Democratic ticket of Governor James Cox of Ohio and young Franklin D. Roosevelt of New York to support the covenant strongly. The Democratic ticket equivocated, however, while the Republicans, led by Senator Warren G. Harding of Ohio and Governor Calvin Coolidge of Massachusetts, talked on both sides of the League issue. Harding won overwhelmingly, obtaining 60.3 percent of the popular vote and carrying thirty-seven of the forty-eight states. Foreign policy issues, however, were peripheral. Once elected, Harding clearly stated that he would not push for American association with the League.

Wilson must bear primary responsibility for the American failure to join the League of Nations. His refusal to appoint an important Republican or senator to the delegation, his procedures at Paris, and his unwillingness to compromise with the Senate doomed the covenant. But in the end, American participation might have made little difference anyway. The fundamental problem was not the League of Nations but the ill-constructed peace treaty, which no organization of mere mortals could have saved. The treaty's treatment of Germany territorially and financially sowed the seeds for the terrible economic depression and the rise of Nazism in the 1930s. The exclusion of Russia from the peace conference and the League, and Wilson's announcement in March 1920 that the United States would not even recognize the existence of the Soviet government, piled unreality upon unreality. The failure to handle the problems posed by Germany and Russia set off a right-wing reaction not only in the United States, but also in Italy, France, Germany, and eastern and southern Europe, where the stage rapidly filled with fascists and National Socialists.

"What gave rise to the Russian Revolution?" Wilson finally queried in 1923, one year before his death. "The answer can only be that it was the product of a whole social system. It was not in fact a sudden thing." The same explanation can also be applied to the appearance of right-wing forces in the 1920s and 1930s. For the Paris conference in the end decided not on peace but on vengeance; not on economic justice—for there was little discussion of such issues at Paris—but on a political settlement that would allow economic exploitation; not on an inclusion of all people but on an exclusion of many, particularly revolutionary regimes.

In Paris, William Bullitt best summarized the result after he bitterly resigned from the American delegation. He declared that the peace treaty could result only in "a new century of wars." As he left his hotel, reporters asked Bullitt where he would go. "I am going to lie in the sands of the French Riviera," he replied, "and watch the world go to hell." He went. And it did.

# Chapter Five

# 1920–1929
## The New Era

President and Mrs. Coolidge, with their two sons and their pet dog in 1924. *(Library of Congress)*

Progressivism had appealed to many Americans because it promised stability to a nation experiencing rapid change. By 1920, however, the Wilsonian years had linked reform not with orderly change but with war and revolution. Consequently, Americans in the 1920s turned toward leaders who invoked traditional values and played on the widespread nostalgia for a simpler, happier past. But progressivism did not die. If anything, the decade was characterized by a quickening of those forces that were transforming American life—urban and corporate growth, racial and ethnic heterogeneity, concern for social morality, active government, and international involvement. The sharpest conflicts arose not over economic policy or foreign affairs, where something close to a consensus emerged, but over religion, ethnicity, and morality. Then, in 1929, Americans suddenly entered a chamber of economic horrors that transformed them, their world, and their progressivism.

## REPUBLICAN POLITICS: HARDING AND COOLIDGE

Benefiting from widespread disillusionment with Wilsonianism, Republican Warren G. Harding won a landslide victory in the 1920 election. A senator from Ohio since 1914 (and the first man ever to move directly from the Senate to the White House), Harding was jovial and expansive, a backslapper who joined as many fraternal lodges as possible. He loved to meet people, had a remarkable memory for faces, and played tennis or golf whenever he could. Harding's chief virtue was that he usually recognized his own limitations; his chief defect was that he believed in rewarding old friends with federal jobs. Many of them abused his trust by swindling the government, and when Harding died in August 1923, scandals were erupting on every side. The director of the Veterans Bureau was convicted of stealing hundreds of millions of dollars, the attorney general resigned when charged with authorizing the sale of alcohol from government warehouses to bootleggers, and the head of the Alien Property Custodian's Office was found guilty of accepting bribes. The most famous scandal centered on allegations that Harding's secretary of the interior, Albert Fall, had leased government oil reserves in Teapot Dome, Wyoming, to private owners in order to line his own pocket. Fall resigned in disgrace and later served a one-year prison sentence.

These revelations, however, did not harm the Republican Party, partly because Harding had not been personally involved in the scandals and partly because his successor, Calvin Coolidge, had a reputation for honesty and frugality. A former governor of Massachusetts, Coolidge was a cold, austere individual whose childhood, according to an admiring biographer, was "simple, wholesome and unfurtive." Miles apart in temperament, Harding and Coolidge nevertheless shared similar social and economic views. Both believed that government should foster business enterprise. This meant a hands-off policy in areas where businessmen wanted freedom of action and intervention in areas where they wanted help. "This is a business country," Coolidge remarked, "and it wants a business government." On the other hand, both presidents regarded intervention on behalf of other interest groups as socially undesirable, financially irresponsible, and morally wrong. The Supreme Court also sanctioned this outlook, which governed Republican policies toward business, labor, agriculture, and public power.

Big business benefited handsomely from Republican rule. In 1922 Congress enacted the Fordney-McCumber Tariff, which raised import duties to their highest level ever. Harding and Coolidge filled federal regulatory agencies with men who considered it their task to assist the business community. One of them was William E. Humphrey. Appointed to the Federal

Trade Commission in 1925, he decided not to prosecute companies that had violated the law so long as they promised to behave in the future. Republicans placed tax policy in the hands of Andrew Mellon, who served as secretary of the Treasury from 1921 to 1932. Mellon, who resigned from the boards of directors of fifty-one corporations on assuming office, feared that if high taxes deprived the businessman of a fair share of his earnings, then "he will no longer exert himself and the country will be deprived of the energy on which its continued greatness depends." Mellon fought long, hard, and successfully to reduce taxes on inheritances, corporate profits, and the well-to-do. By 1926 Congress had cut the tax rate on an income of $1 million from 66 percent to 20 percent.

While business received all kinds of support, organized labor went into eclipse. Union membership fell from 5 million in 1920 to 3.4 million in 1930 for several reasons: unions had no foothold in industries undergoing the most rapid expansion, such as automobiles, rubber, and chemicals; the American Federation of Labor clung to an increasingly obsolete craft structure; employers conducted a vigorous open-shop drive, which included the use of spies and blacklists to block organizers; and several large companies introduced welfare measures—pension, insurance, and stock-sharing plans—that stifled union growth. When walkouts occurred, however, the White House occasionally intervened on the side of management. This happened during the railroad strike of 1922, when Attorney General Harry Daugherty persuaded Harding that the nation faced imminent peril. In Daugherty's view, the workers' support for government control of the railroads "was a conspiracy worthy of Lenin." Daugherty obtained a sweeping court injunction that barred virtually all union activities and proved instrumental in breaking the strike.

Harding and Coolidge rejected any government role in supporting farm prices or in developing power facilities. At the time agricultural interests supported the McNary-Haugen plan, which authorized the government to purchase farm products at prices above those offered in the world market. The government would export the goods at the world market price, therefore taking a loss. Farmers would reimburse the government from the profits they realized on sales to American consumers at inflated domestic prices. Congress defeated this proposal in 1924 and 1926 but passed it in 1927 and 1928, only to have Coolidge veto it as "vicious" and "preposterous" special-interest legislation. Republicans also did their best to extract the government from its involvement in the construction of power facilities in the Tennessee Valley. During World War I the government had built power plants at Muscle Shoals. Harding and Coolidge wished to sell these facilities to private entrepreneurs, but Congress blocked their plans.

During the 1920s the Supreme Court mirrored the social philosophy that reigned in the White House. This was hardly surprising since Harding appointed four judges to the bench, including William Howard Taft, who served as chief justice from 1922 to 1930. In a series of decisions concerning organized labor, the Court ruled that unions engaging in certain types of strikes (such as secondary boycotts) were liable to antitrust prosecution, that strict limits could be placed on picketing outside factory gates, and that court injunctions could be used to enforce contracts in labor disputes. The Supreme Court also struck down key welfare legislation. In *Bailey v. Drexel Furniture Co.* (1922), the justices ruled against a child-labor act passed in 1919 that imposed a 10 percent tax on the profits of firms employing child labor. A majority found that the tax was levied to regulate business practices rather than to produce revenue and therefore was inappropriate. The Court decided in *Adkins v. Children's*

As secretary of commerce, Herbert Hoover had this small radio receiver installed in his home so he could understand complaints received by the department, c. 1925. *(Library of Congress)*

*Hospital* (1923) that states could not establish minimum wages for women workers. Since women could now vote, they no longer merited special protection. Chief Justice Taft, although generally content with the Court's performance, nevertheless feared for the future. "The only hope we have of keeping a consistent declaration of constitutional law," he noted, "is for us to live as long as we can."

## A NEW ORDER: REPUBLICAN ALTERNATIVES TO WILSON'S LEAGUE OF NATIONS

In foreign policy as at home, Harding and Coolidge knew that they could not retreat into isolationism or nostalgia for a pre-1914 world. "There never again will be precisely the old order," Harding declared in 1922. "Indeed, I know of no one who thinks it to be desirable. For out of the old order came the war itself." A new order, constructed and dominated by U.S. economic power, would avert future world wars and revolutions. That power was immense. In 1914 Americans owed the world about $3.5 billion; after they financed the Allies in war, the world suddenly owed the United States $13 billion. Fueled by the new radio, airplane, and especially automobile industries, the booming domestic economy doubled its industrial production between 1921 and 1929. Never had a nation become so rich so fast. That success seemed to confirm superiority in other areas. As the *Ladies' Home Journal* trumpeted, "There is only one first-class civilization in the world today. It is right here in the United States."

The new world order was to rest on certain principles. First, military force was to be reduced everywhere. Money spent on rifles would be better invested in automobiles so standards of living could rise. Second, money and trade would be the dynamics of the new order. Americans naturally wanted to set ground rules that played to their own greatest strength in international affairs. Third, economic activities were to be undertaken primarily by private individuals, not governments. If government directed investment and trade, individual rights could disappear and fascism or socialism result. "Constantly I insisted [in the 1920s] that spiritual and intellectual freedom could not continue to exist without economic freedom," Herbert Hoover recalled. "If one died, all would die."

Government's primary responsibility was to ensure that private investment and trade could flow freely into any market. Unfair monopolies were therefore to be broken up, state-controlled enterprises (as in Russia) undermined. Above all, freedom of enterprise was not to be shackled by such political alliances as provided for in Article X of the Covenant of the League of Nations. In 1928, for example, the French again pressed Washington for a political alliance against a revived Germany. Secretary of State Frank Kellogg quickly transformed the request into a meaningless fifteen-nation agreement in which each signatory renounced war, except, of course, for self-defense. The Kellogg-Briand Pact was later laughed at as nothing more than an "international kiss," but, most important for Americans, it retained their complete freedom of action. The most powerful decision makers in foreign affairs were Secretary of State Charles Evans Hughes and Secretary of Commerce Herbert Hoover. Both had long been identified with Progressive programs. Hoover emphasized that the key to happiness and prosperity was "American individualism," which he defined as "an equality of opportunity." To ensure such opportunity, Hoover, like Wilson, stressed the need for an expanding overseas economy. Hoover also believed that, to exploit global opportunities, American entrepreneurs should combine in global associations so they could both compete with foreign cartels and end cutthroat competition at home. One leading American banker caught this policy exactly: businessmen must stop "scrambling amongst each other for the plums which fall," and learn instead "by cooperative effort to plant more plum trees that we might share the larger yield." Since Hoover defined the national interest as the interest of business, his Commerce Department blazed the way. Particularly active was its Bureau of Foreign and Domestic Commerce, which during the 1920s quadrupled its budget as it established fifty offices around the world to help businessmen plant new "plum trees" in foreign markets. If the Republicans failed, it was because their assumptions were wrong, not because they attempted to retreat into a supposed isolationism.

## THE WASHINGTON NAVAL CONFERENCE

The first bold stroke of Republican diplomacy appeared when President Harding asked nine major nations to attend the Washington Naval Conference in November 1921. In a brilliantly conceived scheme, Hughes planned to reduce expenditures on warships drastically, dissolve political alliances dangerous to the United States (particularly the Anglo-Japanese alliance, in existence since 1902), and work out an international agreement to maintain the open door to the fabled China market. The last point was crucial, for since 1914 the Japanese, bolstered by their alliance with Great Britain, had been trying to close the door.

In February 1922 the conference produced three interrelated documents. In the Five-Power Treaty, the United States, Great Britain, Japan, France, and Italy received respective ratios of 5.00 to 5.00 to 3.00 to 1.75 to 1.75 for the size of their battleship fleets. In reality, the ratios gave Japan naval superiority in East Asia. American naval officers strongly protested the arrangement, but Hughes overruled the navy with the argument that the ratios also gave the United States dominance in the Western Hemisphere, and Great Britain and France control in European waters. Such a realistic division of world power satisfied the secretary of state.

More important, in return for naval superiority in East Asia, Hughes extracted from Japan an agreement to a Nine-Power Treaty pledging the maintenance of the open door in China. Clearly the United States was trusting that the Japanese would use their superior power to maintain an open marketplace in China for all nations. Hughes's successes were finally capped by a Four-Power Treaty that destroyed the Anglo-Japanese alliance. It was replaced by an agreement among the United States, Japan, Great Britain, and France in which each pledged to respect the others' possessions in the Pacific and to consult with the other powers in the event of aggression in that area.

These three agreements provided the framework for American diplomacy between 1921 and 1941. They marked a triumph for Hughes, for although Japan enjoyed a strong military position, it had now pledged itself to the open door. Moreover, after American pressure was applied, Japan also agreed to withdraw its troops from Siberia and to surrender Shantung to China.

China attended the conference, complained bitterly about being treated like a bone fought over by dogs, and then was ignored. To Western eyes China was doubly troublesome, for it was not only weak, but also unstable. In May 1919 the revolution led by Sun Yat-sen's Kuomintang party had accelerated. The major powers refused to recognize the revolutionaries. Americans tried to go on with business as usual, but in 1924 the revolution veered leftward as the Kuomintang cooperated with Soviet Russian agents. Effective economic boycotts and bloody personal attacks were launched against foreign missionaries and businessmen. One Chinese leader warned, "The time has come to speak to foreign imperialism in the language it understands." But with Sun's death in 1925, his mantle fell on Chiang Kai-shek. Chiang completed the Kuomintang triumph in 1927, broke with the Soviets, and greatly moderated the revolutionary program. In 1928 he worked out agreements with the United States and Western Europe that restored China's control over its own tariffs. Beyond this, however, Washington would not go. American Marines remained stationed in three Chinese cities to protect property, and six new U.S. gunboats moved to the Yangtze. A stable, wealthy, cooperative Japan, tied to American interests through the strong bonds of money, was a much-preferred partner to a revolutionary, erratic, and poverty-ridden China.

## THE NEW ORDER RECONSTRUCTS THE OLD

The Washington Naval Conference also aided American policy in Europe, that most crucial of all diplomatic priorities. Before World War I Europeans had taken half of all American exports. Some European nations had recovered from the war quickly. Italy was a model after 1922, when Benito Mussolini assumed power. Despite his fascism, many Americans admired the dictator for embodying their own supposed traits of efficiency, stability, and masculinity; in the words of former Progressive journalist Ida Tarbell, Mussolini was the "despot with a dimple." Germany, France, and Great Britain, however, recovered more slowly, and U.S. officials became concerned. "The prosperity of the United States largely depends upon the economic settlements which may be made in Europe," Hughes observed in 1921, "and the key to the future is with those who make those settlements."

Again American economic leverage allowed Hughes to shape such settlements. His levers were the flush New York money market and the $11 billion loaned to Europe during and immediately after the war. The Republicans insisted that this money be repaid on American terms, not because their Puritan conscience required it, but because these war debts and the European need for capital provided the United States with great power. Washington's attention centered on Germany, for European (and therefore American) prosperity was impossible without a healthy Germany. That nation had been the industrial hub of the continent before 1914 and promised to be so again if properly reconstructed. Moreover, only a stable Germany could protect Europe against the spread of bolshevism.

Disagreeing strongly with this moderate American approach, France pressed the Germans for high reparations payments until, in 1923, they defaulted. When the French army retaliated by trying to separate the Rhineland from Germany, the German economy went completely out of control. All of Europe was threatened with catastrophe. Hughes coolly stepped into the chaos. He convinced J.P. Morgan and British bankers to lend $200 million to Germany and demanded that Germany be given easier reparation terms. Despite some French objections, the deal was completed at a 1924 conference headed by Chicago banker Charles G. Dawes. The Dawes Plan became the key to rebuilding Europe.

But the results were rather different from what Hughes and Dawes anticipated. When Morgan sold $100 million of securities for the German loan in the United States, the offer was oversubscribed in hours. Americans, rushing to invest in a stabilized Germany, snapped up some 180 bond and stock issues amounting to nearly $2 billion. When some American investors discovered a German hamlet needing $125,000 for a small municipal project, they talked the village leaders into taking a $3 million loan instead. Dollars were not only flowing into increasingly questionable projects, but merely moving in a circular fashion: the United States sent money to Germany, which used it to pay reparations to Great Britain and France, which in turn sent it back to New York for payment of war debts and interest on loans. One broken link and the Western economies could collapse like a row of dominoes.

Between 1925 and 1929, however, those economies looked more like a game of Monopoly. During those four years Americans lent more than $5 billion abroad. By 1928 such giant corporations as Standard Oil of New Jersey, DuPont, Ford, General Motors, and Singer Sewing Machine had invested $3 billion in their own overseas subsidiaries. Americans put another $8 billion into overseas portfolio investments, that is, stocks and bonds of foreign-owned companies. In the Middle East, American capitalists bitterly struggled with the British and French for control over the world's greatest oil reserves. The competition ended in 1928 with the "Red Line" agreement, in which the giant oil companies divided a large Middle Eastern area, marked on a map with a red pencil, among themselves. Even Russia welcomed capital for development projects. Washington, despite its refusal to recognize the Bolsheviks, determined to encourage American businessmen to rush into what Hoover called "an economic vacuum" in order to beat out European entrepreneurs. Hoping that the Soviets could be transformed into capitalists, such American corporations as Ford, Westinghouse, and W. Averell Harriman's mining ventures invested millions of dollars in Lenin's country. In this area, however, Germany had become a foe, not a friend. Not only did it dominate foreign investments in Russia, but in 1922 the two outcasts publicly agreed to cooperate economically. Secretly they helped to rebuild each other's military machine.

Despite the successes in rebuilding Germany, the Middle East, and Russia, Hoover watched the outflow of capital with growing concern. He knew that much of it was going into doubtful enterprises and that other American money, such as that of U.S. bankers helping Japan develop Manchuria, injured American export interests. American bankers were following selfish policies that badly hurt other American businessmen. Manufacturers, for example, hated the bankers not only for helping Japanese industry take over former American markets in Manchuria, but also for investing money in bond issues abroad rather than in industrial export enterprises at home. Virtually uncontrolled, the bankers blithely went on, investing in dubious projects until, like lemmings, they nearly self-destructed in 1929.

## THE NEW ORDER IN LATIN AMERICA

American capital was also the key to relations with Latin America. In this region, however, Washington officials were not reluctant to use military force to maintain stability. Latin America had so long been counted a U.S. preserve that when new recruits entered the State Department's Foreign Service School in the mid-1920s, they were told not to expect too much from South Americans: their "Latin temperament" and "racial quality" were weaknesses, although Latin Americans could become "very easy people to deal with if properly managed." A 1924 survey revealed that of the twenty Latin American nations, only six were free of some kind of U.S. "management." The rest were either under the control of the U.S. Marine Corps or had their finances controlled by New York bankers. With stability supposedly assured, investments in Latin America more than doubled to $5.4 billion between 1924 and 1929, at a rate more than twice as great as that in any other part of the world. Much of this investment went into oil exploration and development. The southern part of the hemisphere was to provide raw materials for the industrial progress of the northern part.

U.S. officials tried to make Latin America the showcase of American foreign policy. They believed that through cooperation between government and business, the area could produce prosperity and democracy for its peoples and profits for its developers. Hoover's Commerce Department helped investors by coming up with new approaches for building the infrastructure (highways, communications, and utilities) needed to attract private capital. "The number of rebellions per capita is highest in those republics where the per capita mileage of highways is lowest," a Commerce Department official announced in 1929. "Romance may have been driven out by the concrete mixer, but the mixer has paved the way for law and order and for

Nicaraguan revolutionary General Sandino *(center)* and staff en route to Mexico, 1929. *(Time Life/ Getty Images)*

better understanding, as well as better business among the far-flung provinces of these sparsely populated commonwealths."

Hoover also tried to help by announcing new political policies. After becoming president in 1929, he repudiated the Roosevelt Corollary of 1904–1905 and began pulling U.S. Marines out of Caribbean nations. Problems did exist, however, particularly with revolutionary Mexico. The United States had finally recognized the Mexican government in 1923 but continued to object to the Mexican constitution's Article 27, which provided for national ownership of such subsurface minerals as oil. In 1927 a temporary compromise was finally reached on the oil controversy.

A case study of Republican policy took place in Nicaragua. U.S. Marines had occupied that Central American nation since 1912. Of special importance, Nicaragua was a possible site for an interoceanic canal that could rival the U.S. waterway in Panama. North Americans wanted no such competitor. Once the Marines landed, however, they could not leave: when Nicaraguan leaders cooperated with the United States, they became unpopular with their own people and needed protection. In 1925 President Coolidge nevertheless decided to pull the forces out. Rebellion immediately erupted. Coolidge thereupon sent back the Marines, but now the situation had changed. A guerrilla leader, Augusto Sandino, fought the Marines successfully from 1927 to 1933. He found increasing support from Nicaraguan peasants who had not benefited from the U.S. occupation. The costly war and growing protests in the United States finally led Hoover to pull the troops out in 1933. But he left behind a new diplomatic invention: a U.S.-trained Nicaraguan national guard that could replace the Marines in keeping order. In 1934, the U.S.-picked leader of the National Guard, Anastasio Somoza, arrested Sandino (who had quit fighting after the U.S. troops left) and murdered him in cold blood. Somoza then made himself dictator. He and his sons ruled Nicaragua as their personal plantation until 1979, when they were overthrown by anti-American revolutionaries calling themselves "Sandinistas." Such was the forty-five-year legacy of the Republicans' new order in Nicaragua.

By 1928 hemispheric relationships were becoming badly skewed. The United States had lent $2.5 billion and had increased exports to Latin Americans, but when they tried to pay their debts they ran into American tariff walls that prevented many of their products from entering the United States. As in Europe, United States investors swamped South America with dollars; in 1928 Peru received twice as much in loans as it could legitimately use. Anti-Yankeeism flourished in such conditions. At the 1928 Inter-American Conference, the Latin Americans proposed that no state had the right to intervene in the internal affairs of another. When the United States objected, it was joined by only four countries, three of which were under American control. A year later economic depression struck. Seven revolutions erupted in Latin America between 1929 and 1931. Given its own assumption that a foreign policy's success was measured by the stability it produced, the Latin American policies of the United States lay in shambles.

## THE POLITICS OF CULTURAL CONFLICT

Social reformers found that the most pressing domestic issues of the decade were precisely those on which they were most bitterly divided, such as immigration restriction and Prohibition. Cultural issues—those relating to ethnicity, morality, and religion—dominated political discourse because prosperity led to a decline in the relative importance of economic concerns and because the spread of cosmopolitan mores and values troubled many small-town Americans who associated big cities with vice, crime, and immorality. The most controversial of these issues, Prohibition assumed new importance simply because it had become the law of the land and could no longer be ignored. Where one stood on such an issue usually depended on where one's parents had been born, which church one attended (or did not attend), and whether one lived in a village or large city.

Proposals to curb immigration clearly exposed some of these cultural tensions. In 1921, after the arrival of 1.2 million immigrants in just one year, President Harding approved a measure drastically limiting further admission. But this was merely a prelude. In 1924 the National Origins Act sailed through Congress with a huge majority. The act provided for the annual entry until 1927 of only 164,000 European immigrants under a quota system determined by the composition of the U.S. population in 1890. Under this arrangement the combined quotas for Russia and Italy were less than that for Norway; the combined quotas for Poland and Greece were less than that for Sweden. Beginning in 1927 the United States would admit 150,000 European immigrants each year under quotas based on the national origins of the white population in 1920. The measure barred all Japanese, but set no limits on immigration from Canada, Mexico, or South America. The National Origins Act won broad support from Progressives, including senators Hiram Johnson of California and George Norris of Nebraska. But urban reformers, whose constituencies included the ethnic and religious groups under assault, expressed dismay at the bigotry of those who had "a fixed obsession on Anglo-Saxon superiority."

## BESSIE SMITH
## AND THE BLUES

Bessie Smith, 1936. *(Library of Congress, Carl Van Vechten Collection)*

Thomas A. Edison invented the phonograph in 1877. It did not come into general use, however, until the 1890s, when grooved records replaced cylinders and an inexpensive "gramophone" was developed. The popular demand for recordings soon proved overwhelming. In 1919 more than 2.25 million phonographs were manufactured; two years later, over 100 million records were produced. The first blues recording by a black singer—Mamie Smith's "Crazy Blues"—was released in 1920. It sold extremely well and encouraged record companies to sign other black artists. A large "race market" seemed to exist, particularly among African-Americans who had migrated to northern cities during World War I.

Of all the blues singers in the 1920s, none was more popular than Bessie Smith. Born in Tennessee in 1894, she began working with traveling road shows when she was a teenager. For a time she worked with another famous entertainer, Gertrude ("Ma") Rainey. In 1923 Bessie Smith made her first recording, "Down Hearted Blues." Columbia Records paid her $125 a side for the record, which sold 780,000 copies within six months. (Throughout her association with Columbia, which lasted until 1931, she never received royalties based on sales but instead was paid a flat recording fee.) In 1925 Smith organized a traveling tent show, "Harlem Frolics," which toured in a custom-made, seventy-eight-foot-long railroad car complete with seven staterooms, kitchen, and bath. Audiences acclaimed her performances and her records sold remarkably well.

The blues idiom had several characteristics. The music was intensely personal. Songs dealt with the singers' own experiences—broken love affairs, natural disasters, tragedy, sorrow. Bessie Smith's own life, while often marked by luxury and extravagance, had its full share of such misfortune. The blues appealed mainly to the lower classes, for middle-class blacks, and whites, were often offended by the emphasis on gambling, drugs, and sex, allusions to which were usually disguised. "Bought me a coffeegrinder, got the best one I could find," Smith sang, "So he could grind my coffee, 'cause he has a brand new grind." The blues, finally, was race music. Race records were advertised in separate catalogues and sold in stores in black communities. The first black-owned record company, Black Swan, advertised, "The Only Genuine Colored Record—Others Are Only Passing for Colored." Smith almost always sang before black audiences and was booked in black theaters. Only on rare occasions did she perform for whites.

With the stock market crash of 1929, Smith's career, and those of many other black performers, went into decline. Record sales nose-dived and theater attendance dropped. Increasingly, the radio replaced the phonograph as the chief source of home entertainment. The blues, rough and raw-edged, gave way to the softer sound of "swing." Bessie Smith continued to sing, but she never matched her earlier success. On September 26, 1937, she was fatally injured in an automobile accident outside Memphis, Tennessee. A legend quickly arose that she died after being refused admittance to a white hospital. Although unfounded, the legend provided the basis

American blues singer Ma Rainey, c. 1923. *(Frank Driggs Collection/Getty Images)*

for Edward Albee's play *The Death of Bessie Smith.* Her Philadelphia grave remained unmarked for over thirty years until in 1970 a plaque was placed on the site. Rock singer Janis Joplin donated half the cost, as a tribute to a woman who had exerted so important an influence.

## Web Links

**www.bluessearchengine.com/bluesartists/s/bessiesmith.html**
Biographical information, lyrics, and videos, including a clip from St. Louis Blues.

**www.redhotjazz.com/rainey.html**
A brief biography and many audio clips of Ma Rainey.

If immigration restriction illustrated the divisions among reformers, the experience of the Progressive Party in 1924 demonstrated their essential weakness. The party was formed by diverse groups uniting out of weakness rather than strength: former Bull Moose Progressives, leaderless since the death of Theodore Roosevelt; socialists, whose movement lay in ruins as a result of the war and the Red Scare; Midwestern farmers, resentful over a sharp decline in agricultural prices; and railroad workers, embittered by the Harding administration's role in breaking their 1922 strike. The Progressive platform called for public ownership of railroads, the dissolution of monopolies, direct election of the president, and a constitutional amendment barring child labor. The party also favored prohibiting the use of injunctions in labor disputes, promoting public works in time of depression, and imposing high taxes on business profits. To the Progressives and their sixty-nine-year-old presidential candidate, Robert M. La Follette of Wisconsin, "that government is deemed best which offers to the many the highest level of average happiness and well-being."

La Follette faced an uphill struggle in his race against Republican Calvin Coolidge and John W. Davis, the conservative lawyer nominated by the Democrats. His opponents, assailing La Follette for having opposed American entry into World War I, branded him a dangerous radical, the candidate of "the Reds, the Pinks, the Blues, and the Yellows." The Progressives, moreover, faced many of the same obstacles that traditionally hamper third parties: lack of funds, absence of grassroots organization, and inability to get on the ballot in every state. Although the American Federation of Labor formally endorsed La Follette's candidacy, labor gave the ticket less support than expected. Similarly, as agricultural prices improved in 1924, farmers' enthusiasm for La Follette waned. In November La Follette obtained 4.8 million votes—under 17 percent of the total—and captured only Wisconsin's thirteen electoral votes. Davis received 8.3 million votes, and Coolidge a whopping 15.7 million. Apparently the Republican slogan—"I like silence and success better than socialism and sovietism"—settled the fate of the reform-minded third party.

During the 1920s a new style of urban reform began to emerge, best symbolized, perhaps, by Democrat Alfred E. Smith and Republican Fiorello H. La Guardia. Both came from New York City. Smith, the son of Irish Catholic immigrants, had worked as a boy in the Fulton Fish Market, served an apprenticeship in Tammany Hall, and then became governor of New York. La Guardia, who represented East Harlem in Congress from 1922 to 1933, was an Italian-Jewish-American Episcopalian who spoke seven languages and whose wife was a German Lutheran. La Guardia, his biographer has commented, "was a balanced ticket all by himself." Smith and La Guardia supported a broad range of social welfare proposals, but were distinctive chiefly for their stand on cultural issues. Both championed the cause of immigrants. Both openly flouted Prohibition. Both served as spokesmen for urban cosmopolitanism in a bitter struggle with rural fundamentalism.

This struggle reached a climax when the Democrats selected Smith as their presidential candidate in 1928. Smith favored such reforms as government development of power facilities, but his contest with Republican Herbert Hoover centered not on economic issues but rather on issues of religion, immigration, Prohibition, and the city. One New England Protestant reformer expressed the sense of cultural cleavage when she wrote in her diary, "My American against Tammany's. Prairie, Plantation and Everlasting Hills against the Sidewalks of New York!" Given the prevailing prosperity, Hoover was probably unbeatable, but his margin of victory demonstrated the pervasiveness of cultural tensions. Smith received only 15 million

Governor Al Smith, giving a speech. *(Library of Congress)*

votes to Hoover's 21.4 million. For the first time since Reconstruction, the Republicans broke the Solid South, capturing Virginia, North Carolina, Texas, Florida, and Tennessee. The only consolation for the Democrats was that Smith did extremely well in the nation's largest cities.

## PROHIBITION AND CRIME

Many Americans greeted the advent of Prohibition in January 1920 with unwarranted optimism. Prohibitionists had long promised that, given a change, they would eradicate pauperism and improve the condition of the working class. They had also predicted a sudden reduction in crime since "90 percent of the adult criminals are whisky-made." Closing the saloons, many believed, would improve the nation's physical health and strengthen its moral fiber as well.

Yet not all Americans supported Prohibition, and the distinction often followed religious, ethnic, and geographic lines. Typically, prohibitionists were likely to be Baptists or Methodists rather than Catholics, Jews, Lutherans, or Episcopalians; old-stock Americans rather than first- or second-generation immigrants. They were more likely to live in small towns and in the South or Midwest than in New York, Boston, or Chicago. At the heart of the struggle between wets and drys were contrasting cultural styles.

The Eighteenth Amendment, ratified in January 1919 and ultimately approved by every state except Connecticut, Rhode Island, and New Jersey, contained several glaring loopholes. It did not forbid the consumption of intoxicating beverages—only their sale and manufacture. As a result, those who could afford to store up an adequate supply were not terribly inconvenienced. In deference to property rights, liquor dealers were permitted a full year's grace in which to wind up their business affairs. The amendment also failed to define the word "intoxicating" and to provide any means of enforcement. The Volstead Act (1920) attempted to remedy these deficiencies: it arbitrarily defined as "intoxicating" any beverage with one-half of 1 percent alcoholic content, and it provided rudimentary enforcement machinery.

Yet the task of enforcement proved truly Herculean, particularly in those communities where a majority saw no moral virtue in temperance. There seemed an endless number of ways to evade the law. People smuggled whiskey across the Canadian and Mexican borders, made denatured industrial alcohol palatable by adding chemical ingredients, prepared their own "moonshine" at home in one-gallon stills, falsified druggists' prescriptions, stole liquor reserved for legitimate medicinal and religious purposes in government warehouses, and pumped alcohol back into "near beer" to give it more of a kick. Those administering the law encountered many difficulties. The Prohibition Bureau, understaffed and underpaid, was the target of a series of attempted briberies. Some evidently succeeded, for one of every twelve agents was dismissed for corrupt behavior, and presumably others were never caught. The memoirs of a leading Prohibition agent testified to the laxity of enforcement. He related how long it took to buy a drink on arriving in different cities: Chicago—twenty-one minutes; Atlanta—seventeen minutes; and Pittsburgh—eleven minutes. In New Orleans it took thirty-five seconds: when the agent asked a cab driver where he could find a drink, the driver, offering him a bottle, replied, "Right here."

For all its inadequacies, the law almost certainly cut down on alcohol consumption. But the attempt to enforce a moral code to which many Americans did not adhere led to widespread hypocrisy and disrespect for the law. This problem received formal recognition when the Supreme Court ruled that the government could request income tax returns from bootleggers. The Court found no reason "why the fact that a business is unlawful should exempt it from paying the tax that if lawful it would have to pay."

Prohibition was associated not only with a cavalier attitude toward the law, but also with a more sinister phenomenon: the rise of organized crime. Criminal gangs had existed in the past, but in the 1920s they evidently became larger, wealthier, and more ostentatious. Gangland weddings—and funerals—became occasions for lavish displays of wealth and influence. The 1924 funeral of the Chicago gunman Dion O'Banion featured twenty-six truckloads of flowers, an eight-foot heart of American beauty roses, and 10,000 mourners, among whom were several prominent politicians. Gangs became increasingly efficient and mobile because of the availability of submachine guns and automobiles. And they grew somewhat more centralized, dividing territory in an effort to reduce internecine warfare. Although criminals made money through the control of prostitution, gambling, and racketeering, bootleg liquor provided a chief source of revenue.

By the end of the decade, opponents of Prohibition had begun to win over the public. Once the drys had promised that Prohibition would reduce crime; now the wets held Prohibition responsible for organized crime and pledged that, with repeal, "the immorality of the country, racketeering and bootlegging, will be a thing of the past." Formerly the drys had claimed that Prohibition would eliminate poverty; now the wets asserted that the liquor industry could provide needed jobs and revenue to a nation beginning to experience mass poverty in the Great Depression. Prohibition was repealed in 1933. Yet it failed less because it triggered a crime wave or weakened the economy than because it attempted the impossible: to ban allegedly immoral behavior in the absence of a genuine consensus that the proscribed behavior was, in any real sense, immoral.

## THE KU KLUX KLAN

In the years following the Civil War, white southerners had organized the Ku Klux Klan to terrorize blacks and prevent them from voting. This early organization faded with the end of Reconstruction, but in 1915 William J. Simmons, a preacher-turned-salesman, founded a new Klan. In the early 1920s millions of Americans joined the hooded order, although membership probably never exceeded 1.5 million at any time. Yet the new Klan was not simply a reincarnation of the old. The Klan of the 1920s, although strong in the South, was stronger still in Indiana, Illinois, and Ohio. Perhaps three of every five members did not live in the South or Southwest. The new Klan also was less heavily rural, enlisting members in Chicago, Detroit, Atlanta, Denver, and other cities. One of every three Klansmen lived in a city with a population of over 100,000. Finally, the Klan was no longer primarily a white supremacist group. Its chief targets in the 1920s were immigrants and Catholics.

The Klan began its rapid ascent in 1920, when two public relations experts, Edward Y. Clarke and Elizabeth Tyler, made an arrangement with Simmons that turned the Klan into a highly profitable business venture. To sell Klan memberships they recruited a legion of high-powered salesmen, known as Kleagles, and adopted shrewd sales techniques. More than 1,000 organizers set forth in search of recruits, and since each membership cost $10, of which the Kleagle kept $4, the incentive was rather high. Simmons and the other Klan leaders eventually grew wealthy by taking a rake-off on everything from membership fees to the sale of official robes and hoods. With so much at stake, power struggles inevitably occurred. In 1922 the Klan changed hands. Hiram Wesley Evans, a Dallas dentist, ousted Clarke and Tyler and agreed to buy out Simmons, who retained his title but no authority.

The Klan created a world of make-believe by carrying ritual, pageantry, and secrecy to the furthest extreme. Klansmen met in a Klavern, held Klonklaves, carried on Klonversations, and even sang Klodes. They aspired to such high offices as that of Grand Goblin, Grand Dragon, and Exalted Cyclops. They followed a Kalendar in which 1867 was the year 1 and in which awe-inspiring names were assigned to days (dark, deadly, dismal, doleful, desolate, dreadful, desperate), weeks (woeful, weeping, wailing, wonderful, weird), and months (bloody, gloomy, hideous, fearful, furious, alarming, terrible, horrible, mournful, sorrowful, frightful, appalling). Klan members spoke a secret language by forming strange, new words from the first letter of each word in a sentence. Thus "sanbog" meant "strangers are near, be on guard."

Clever organization and secret ritual did not alone account for the Klan's success. The Klan also preached an ideology that appealed to Americans who feared that alien groups were threatening a traditional way of life. Evans asserted that blacks could never "attain the Anglo-Saxon level" and regarded Jews as "alien and inassimilable." The Klan was hysterically anti-Catholic. Members believed in the existence of a papal conspiracy to subvert American liberties and blamed Catholics for the deaths of presidents Lincoln, McKinley, and Harding. Racism, anti-Semitism, and anti-Catholicism were all subsumed under a broader fear of the "mongrelization" of America through immigration. As Simmons put it, "The dangers were in the tremendous influx of foreign immigration, tutored in alien dogmas and alien creeds, slowly pushing the native-born white American population into the center of the country, there to be ultimately overwhelmed and smothered."

Klan activities were a strange mixture of benevolence and terrorism. In some cases the Klan functioned primarily as a fraternal organization. Members patronized each other's businesses, helped out in case of sickness or accident, and contributed to various churches and charities. But the Klan also set itself up as a watchdog of community morals. Klansmen spied on people, reported acts of marital infidelity, attacked "indecent" shows and publications, and promised "to drive the bootleggers forever out of this land and place whiskey-making on a parity with counterfeiting." To uncover every possible scandal, the Klan sometimes tapped telephone wires and intercepted mail at post offices. It punished transgressors by burning crosses outside their homes, ostracizing them, or brutally beating and torturing them. Some victims were immigrants or blacks; others were native white Protestants who failed to measure up to Klan standards.

The Klan acquired formidable political power. It helped elect senators in Oregon, Ohio, Tennessee, and several other states. In Texas it elected a senator, held a majority in the state legislature for a time, and controlled Dallas, Fort Worth, and Wichita Falls. The Indiana Klan, under David Stephenson, built a machine that dominated state politics and placed a functionary in the governor's mansion. The Klan's political goals, aside from power for its own sake, were to prohibit immigration, prevent U.S. entry into the World Court, enforce Prohibition, and weaken parochial schools. The Klan put up its own candidates, endorsed others it considered friendly, and above all sought to prevent the nomination of, or else defeat, candidates (such as Al Smith) who stood for everything it abhorred.

Despite Smith's defeat, the Klan by 1928 had passed its peak. Torn by internal conflicts between Evans and state leaders, placed on the defensive by politicians who considered it a disruptive force, and appeased by the enactment of the National Origins Act, the Klan after 1924 began losing members and influence. Stephenson was arrested for abducting a young woman, sexually molesting her, and refusing to let her visit a doctor after she poisoned herself. Convicted of murder and sentenced to life in the penitentiary, Stephenson opened his private files, which exposed Klan lawlessness. Supposedly created to enforce strict moral codes, the Klan could not survive this scandal or the ensuing revelations. By 1930 the organization was everywhere in shambles.

## FUNDAMENTALISM AND THE SCHOOLS

In the summer of 1925 the town of Dayton, Tennessee, witnessed an event that symbolized the decade's cultural conflicts. John Thomas Scopes was put on trial for having violated state law by teaching the theory of evolution in the public schools, but the nation's attention was focused on the lawyers for the two sides. Prosecutor William Jennings Bryan was the most prominent spokesman for the traditional values of rural, Protestant America. Defense attorney Clarence Darrow, by contrast, was a skeptic, a relativist, and an agnostic. There seemed no common ground between them. To fundamentalists, the theory of evolution was a scientific sham whose acceptance would erode the moral underpinnings of society. Evolutionists, on the other hand, placed fundamentalists on a par with those who had once refused to believe that the earth revolved about the sun.

Religious fundamentalists believed in the literal truth of the Bible. The story of Adam and Eve was, in their view, a matter of historical fact. Charles Darwin's theory of evolution, as expounded in his 1859 volume, *The Origin of Species*, contradicted the biblical account of Creation, and was therefore wrong. Fundamentalists sometimes assumed an overt posture of anti-intellectualism, as when Bryan declared it more important to know the hymn "Rock of Ages" than to know the age of rocks. Yet fundamentalists oversimplified Darwin: the theory of natural selection—that evolution occurred through a gradual accretion of useful variations that fit an organism to survive—had by no means been proved. Bryan noted sarcastically that Darwin, in two major books, resorted to the phrase "we may suppose" more than 800 times.

Fundamentalists were disturbed by what they considered a breakdown in moral values, by which they meant everything from "vile and suggestive" motion pictures and dance styles to "unchaperoned automobile riding at night." They attributed this breakdown, at least in part, to the popularity of the theory of evolution. By calling the Scriptures into question, Darwin had undermined Christian faith. By emphasizing man's animal nature, he excused immoral conduct. In addition, reformers understood that conservatives had used Darwin's theory to assert that government assistance to the needy violated the natural law of survival of the fittest. If Darwin was not responsible for the uses to which his theory had been put, the application nevertheless had pernicious results.

Fundamentalist opinion was strongest in the South and Southwest, but hardly dominated those regions. During the 1920s, bills designed to prohibit the teaching of evolution were introduced in twenty state legislatures. The measures always encountered stiff opposition and were usually defeated. Only five states—Oklahoma, Florida, Tennessee, Mississippi, and Arkansas—enacted such bills, and even there they were regarded less as weapons of repression than as symbolic expressions of legislative concern. The Butler bill in Tennessee, which led to the Scopes trial, barred the teaching of "any theory that denies the Story of the Divine Creation of Man as taught in the Bible, and [holds] instead that man has descended from a lower order of animals." The bill passed easily since educators feared that opposing a popular measure might jeopardize state university appropriations. No one took it very seriously. "Probably the law will never be applied," said the governor when signing it.

The law was applied when some acquaintances persuaded Scopes to test it and the American Civil Liberties Union agreed to provide legal counsel. No one had interfered with the way Scopes conducted his high school biology class, but he agreed to the trial as a matter of principle. The chief courtroom drama occurred when Bryan took the witness stand and engaged Darrow in a verbal duel over the literal interpretation of the Bible, the exchange revealing Bryan's limited knowledge of science. The outcome, however, was a foregone conclusion, for Scopes had admitted breaking the law and the judge ruled that evidence supporting the theory of evolution was inadmissible. The jury took nine minutes to find Scopes guilty, and he was fined $100. William Jennings Bryan died five days after the trial ended. Forty-two years later, Tennessee repealed the law.

Marcus Garvey, 1924. *(Library of Congress)*

The furor surrounding the evolution controversy concealed the more subtle pressures exerted on teachers nearly everywhere in the United States. Most Americans believed that the public schools should instill certain values in the young, but usually the sensitive areas involved politics or economics rather than religion. In 1927 Nebraska ruled that its teachers emphasize "honesty, morality, courtesy, obedience to law, respect for the national flag, the constitution, . . . respect for parents and the home, the dignity and necessity of honest labor and other lessons of a steady-ing influence, which tend to promote and develop an upright and desirable citizenry." School boards commonly established curricula, selected textbooks, and hired teachers with the goal of excluding unpopular ideas. In this sense the antievolution crusade did not represent an entirely atypical effort to restrict what teachers might tell their students even as it expressed the cultural tensions that characterized the 1920s.

## THE GARVEY MOVEMENT AND THE "NEW NEGRO"

As cities in America got larger, so too did their black ghettos. The northward migration of African-Americans, stimulated by the war, continued into the 1920s. During the decade New York City's black population climbed from 152,000 to 328,000; Chicago's grew from 109,000 to 233,000. People left the rural South to improve their lives and some undoubtedly succeeded, but large numbers did not. In New York's Harlem and Chicago's South Side, they crowded into grimy tenements for which they paid exorbitant rents. In 1927 an investigator said of Harlem, "the State would not allow cows to live in some of these apartments." Most blacks could find jobs only as menial or unskilled workers and even then took home less pay than their white counterparts. As always, poverty produced chronic ill health; in the mid-1920s the death rate in Harlem was 42 percent higher, and the infant mortality rate 70 percent higher, than elsewhere in the city.

These conditions made possible the spectacular success of Marcus Garvey and his nationalist doctrine. A Jamaican who came to the United States in 1917, Garvey dreamed of "uniting all the Negro peoples of the world into one great body to establish a country and Government absolutely their own." His Universal Negro Improvement Association claimed hundreds of thousands of followers in the early 1920s, most of them uprooted blacks who had left the rural South for the urban North. Garvey appealed to race pride by glorifying blackness. His newspaper, unlike other black journals, did not ordinarily accept advertisements for skin-lightening lotions or hair-straightening formulas. Whites, he claimed, had distorted the black past: "When Europe was inhabited by a race of cannibals, a race of savage naked men, heathens and pagans, Africa was peopled with a race of cultured black men, who were masters in art, science and literature."

The coin of black pride had a reverse side: distrust of whites. In Garvey's view, "potentially every white man is a Klansman." As competition for jobs and resources increased, he reasoned, whites would become ever less tolerant of black success. The goal of integration, therefore, was a delusion, for the white majority would never accord justice to the black minority. Instead, blacks should build their own nation in Africa. Garvey did not expect the emigration of all black Americans, but rather envisioned a dedicated cadre of trained people. When whites saw that blacks were capable of constructing an advanced civilization of their own, they would learn to respect blacks. A powerful African state would drape a protective mantle around blacks wherever they might live.

Garvey's approach to economics was wholly in keeping with the business ethos of the 1920s. He asserted that black workers' only ally was the white capitalist who needed their labor. Blacks should shun white trade unions and, indeed, work for just under union wages because employers would always prefer to hire a white unless there was some incentive to hire a black. In the end, though, blacks could become autonomous only by developing their own business and commercial establishments. Garvey sponsored several such undertakings, but by far the most important was the Black Star Line, a steamship company designed to link the non-Caucasian peoples of the world commercially and to transport repatriates to Africa. It thus united the twin themes of African redemption and black entrepreneurship.

But the Black Star Line was also the immediate cause of Garvey's downfall. The company sold thousands of shares at five dollars each to black investors, but it quickly went bankrupt. Lacking managerial experience, Garvey fell victim to unscrupulous dealers who sold him run-down ships at inflated prices. The vessels constantly broke down and failed to pass inspection. The fiasco led to charges in 1922 that Garvey had used the mails to defraud investors. The government was very happy to prosecute, for it had long regarded Garvey, in the words of a State Department official, as "an undesirable, and indeed a very dangerous, alien" who was organizing "all of the Negroes in the world against the white people." The trial began in May 1923; Garvey, who believed himself the victim of persecution, conducted his own defense. He was found guilty and sentenced to five years in prison. In February 1925, when the courts rejected his appeal, Garvey entered the penitentiary. Late in 1927 President Coolidge commuted his sentence and the government deported him as an undesirable alien.

Most other black leaders, who had always considered Garvey's ideology dangerous and his movement a threat, seemed relieved by the outcome. The National Association for the Advancement of Colored People opposed Garvey because he rejected integration and challenged its authority as spokesman for African-Americans. A. Phillip Randolph and other socialists placed their hopes in an alliance of black and white workers. They resented Garvey's enmity toward unions, emphasis on black enterprise, and insistence that race was more important than class. Yet while Garvey's movement failed, his emphasis on race pride had lasting import. In 1927 the *Amsterdam News* assessed Garvey's influence on blacks this way: "In a world where black is despised, he taught them black is beautiful. He taught them to admire and praise black things and black people."

In this respect, Garveyism had much in common with the "New Negro Renaissance," the name given to the work of black poets, novelists, scholars and artists, most of whom lived in Harlem, all of whom were self-conscious participants in a cultural awakening. The person who did most to publicize the movement was Alaine Locke. A Phi Beta Kappa graduate of Harvard, Locke, in 1907, had been the first black Rhodes scholar at Oxford. He went on to study in Berlin and Paris and then became a professor of philosophy at Howard University. In 1925 he published an anthology, *The New Negro*, with contributions by Langston Hughes, Claude McKay, Jean Toomer, Countee Cullen, and most of the other writers prominently associated with the Harlem renaissance. Locke believed that the race consciousness cultivated by the urban ghetto was largely responsible for the new literary and artistic awakening. "In Harlem," he wrote, "Negro life is seizing upon its first chances for group expression and self-determination."

Most of the writers identified with the New Negro Renaissance shared common concerns. They emphasized the African roots of black culture and conveyed a sense that American blacks were spiritual aliens, cut off from their native land. They emphasized the dignity of the common people and the importance of the folk tradition. Writers began to use the cadences and idioms associated with spirituals and jazz, and Langston Hughes published a book of poems titled *Weary Blues* (1925). There were also denunciations of racial injustice, lynching, and segregation. But for all their bitter indignation, these writers, according to historian John Hope Franklin, "were not revolting so much against the system as they were protesting against the inefficient operation of the system. In this approach they proved to be as characteristically American as any writers of the period."

## NEW WOMEN AND THE NEW MORALITY

For women, the decade after World War I was decidedly a new era, though in ways unanticipated by suffragists of the Progressive years. Politically, the decade began on a note of elation. The national committees of political parties welcomed women, women candidates ran for office, and politicians catered to the new "woman's vote." In 1921, Congress passed the Sheppard Towner Act, the first federally funded health care plan, which supported maternal and child care services in rural areas. But women's welcome in politics, like the Sheppard-Towner Act, was short-lived. Since women voters did not seem to vote as a bloc or unite behind women's issues, Congress made no further gestures. As progressivism lost momentum, so did the women's movement that had long been associated with it. A prolonged feud arose over an equal rights amendment (ERA), first proposed by the National Woman's Party in 1923. An ERA, its backers claimed, would "secure for women complete equality under the law and in all human relationships." But most women reformers feared that the amendment would harm working women by vitiating protective laws, and they loudly denounced it. The ERA, charged Florence Kelley, was "a slogan of the insane."

While arguments over the ERA raged, women's organizations failed to mobilize the enthusiasm that once had been generated by the suffrage campaign. Young women of the 1920s seemed to have lost interest in both feminist goals and social causes. "Feminism has become a term of opprobrium to the modern young woman," a 1927 article in *Harper's* claimed. As collective purpose waned, attention turned toward private lives and individuals goals. Some "new women" of the decade directed their attention toward jobs, careers, and self-support. A major achievement, one woman journalist claimed in 1926, was "invading every field that had been held the special province of men." Spectacular breakthroughs, such as former suffragist Amelia Earhart's aviation career, drew the most attention. Less spectacularly, large numbers of women entered the labor force in white-collar jobs, and educated women moved into professional work. In the 1920s, women professionals increased by 50 percent and the number of married women in the workforce rose 30 percent. The new woman of the 1920s wanted marriage and family, *Nation* editor Freda Kirchwey explained, but she also wanted "some way of satisfying her personal ambition."

In popular culture, the new woman of the 1920s sought personal independence, often of a sexual nature. Americans of the 1920s witnessed a transformation in private life, one that had been building up since the turn of the century. The much-heralded "new morality" (a label affixed by its defenders) was part of a long-term revolution, or evolution, in moral values and sexual behavior that rose into view after World War I and thereafter became a national preoccupation. Symptoms of moral change had been visible before the war, when dance crazes first burst into vogue and issues such as venereal disease were discussed in the press. But then sexual emancipation was the province of socialists, radicals, and urban sophisticates. Now it was a far more widespread phenomenon that seemed to take hold of the entire young generation, whose antics and attitudes dominated the press. The young and old were as far apart in point of view, an *Atlantic* editorial observed, "as if they belonged to different races."

Behavior, moreover, changed as dramatically as point of view. "The more sophisticated social life of today," reported Helen and Robert Lynd in their classic study of a Midwestern city, *Middletown* (1928), "has brought with it . . . the apparently increasing relaxation of some of the traditional prohibitions upon the approaches of boys and girls to each other's persons." Such relaxation, they observed, was greatly abetted by the automobile. The media played a role, too. Movies depicted attractive young women bickering over men, transforming their image with flapper wardrobes, and frolicking in novel locales, such as bathtubs. Newspapers featured pictures of beauty contests that catered to the decade's competitive and exhibitionist instincts. Popular magazines offered advice on "How to Keep the Thrill in Marriage," and best sellers like *Flaming Youth* (1923), the tale of an adventurous young home wrecker, promised "the truth, bold, naked, sensational." According to social scientists, middle-class morals were in transition. A pioneer study of the sex lives of 2,200 middle-aged, middle-class women, by social worker Katherine Bement Davis, revealed more sexual activity than readers or surveyor anticipated. Subsequent studies suggested that birth control, though illegal, was widely used, especially among the well off.

The new morality fomented conflict between liberals and traditionalists. In some quarters, any dent in Victorian repression meant a gain for women. "The Myth of the Pure Woman is almost at an end," declared enthusiast C.V. Calverton, once editor of *The Masses*, a prewar radical vanguard. "Women's demands for equal rights have extended to the sexual sphere as well as the social." Judge Ben Lindsey of Denver, who applauded the young generation, proposed a new type of "companionate marriage," which would provide a trial run of compatibility and could easily be terminated by divorce. (The divorce rate in 1930 was twice the pre–World War I rate.) But traditionalists feared social disintegration and suspected that the new morality was no morality at all. Progressive Era feminists sometimes agreed with them. Charlotte Perkins Gilman contended that "indulgence" was not necessarily an improvement over "repression" and voiced considerable disgust at the irresponsibility of young women. "It is sickening," she wrote in 1923, "to see so many of the newly freed abusing that freedom in mere imitation of masculine vice and weakness." Contraception, in particular, was an issue that separated prewar feminists from emancipated new women of the next generation. "Your reform is too narrow to appeal to me and too sordid," suffrage leader Carrie Chapman Catt wrote to birth control pioneer Margaret Sanger in 1920.

As with much else in the 1920s, the new morality was less radical a transformation than either proponents or critics believed. Some observers suggested that release from verbal inhibition gave an impression of greater change than actually occurred. Others pointed out that the new morality changed courtship customs, but did not challenge traditional goals. According to surveys, young women's newly liberated attitudes were wedded to old-fashioned aspirations. Few were willing to sacrifice marriage for career; most hoped, rather, to attain "a richer and fuller life" with "an all-round companion." The 1920s popularized the ideal of romantic, companionate marriage, although not the trial run proposed by Ben Lindsey. Women could find fulfillment in traditional domestic roles, now enlivened by a celebrated sexual dimension. Some feminists objected to the emphasis on domesticity. But *Middletown* readers were more likely to listen to columnist Dorothy Dix, who advised wives to join clubs, cultivate worthwhile connections, and strive for upward mobility. "Woman," said Dix, "makes the family status."

Significantly, the birth control campaign, the most radical of prewar reform movements, adapted swiftly to the conservative tone of the decade. Before the war, when Margaret Sanger began her campaign in the 1914 *Woman Rebel*, birth controllers intended to reach a working-class following, end the production of "slaves to capital," and foster proletarian revolution. Since spreading information about contraception violated federal and state laws, advocates of birth control were inviting trouble. When Sanger opened a Brooklyn clinic in 1916, she and her colleagues were arrested, tried, convicted, and jailed. During the 1920s the laws remained on the books, but the mood of the times—and of the birth control movement—had changed. After the war, Sanger's organization, the American Birth Control League, became a middle-

Margaret Sanger, American birth control activist. *(Library of Congress)*

class reform movement, courting the support of physicians, academics, and eugenicists. Birth control clinics, now run by physicians, multiplied. And the arguments in favor of contraception changed. Birth control would emancipate women, Sanger asserted, as she had before the war; but it would also produce "more children from the fit, less from the unfit." It would eliminate the diseased and degenerate, and rid society of "poverty, mental defects, feeble-mindedness, and other transmissible traits." Capitalizing on its scientific and eugenic thrust, rather than on its radical origins, the birth control movement was able to win the approval of the medical profession and the appreciation of a large segment of middle-class practitioners. A pivot of the new morality, it was able to adjust to conservative times as Progressive Era feminism could not.

Nicola Sacco and Bartolomeo Vanzetti, handcuffed together and under guard, in Massachusetts, 1927. *(AP Photo)*

## THE DISCONTENT OF THE INTELLECTUALS

Intellectuals in the Progressive Era had been outraged by economic injustice and political corruption. Intellectuals in the 1920s, however, while by no means apologists for Harding and Coolidge, were more often incensed by the materialism and conformity they found at all levels of society. Where one target had once been the crooked politician, now it was more likely to be the narrow-minded puritan who, unable to enjoy life, wanted to make sure that no one else did either. Formerly, intellectuals had drawn up manifestos for social betterment; in the 1920s they were more acutely conscious of the barriers to change, and some lost interest in politics altogether. Two books published in 1922 illustrate these themes: Sinclair Lewis's *Babbitt* and Walter Lippmann's *Public Opinion.*

Of the writers who satirized the values of the business culture, perhaps none did so more effectively than Sinclair Lewis. In George F. Babbitt, Lewis created a figure that personifies boosterism, complacency, and conformity. A small-town real estate agent, Babbitt is a thoroughgoing materialist whose "symbols of truth and beauty" are mechanical contraptions. He advises his son that "there's a whole lot of valuable time lost even at the U., studying poetry and French and subjects that never brought in anybody a cent." In a speech to his fellow realtors, Babbitt defines "the ideal of American manhood and culture" as "a God-fearing hustling, successful, two-fisted Regular Guy, who belongs to some church with pep and piety to it, who belongs to the Boosters or the Rotarians or the Kiwanis, to the Elks or Moose or Red Men or Knights of Columbus." Vaguely discontented with these values, Babbitt finally rebels against them. But finding "nonconformity" hardly more satisfying, he is disillusioned, and when he is subjected to terrific personal and financial pressure from the community, he gratefully reenters the fold. Lewis's target, therefore, was not Babbitt himself so much as the society that produced him and prevented him from becoming anything else.

Walter Lippmann, meanwhile, expressed profound disillusionment with traditional American political beliefs. Lippmann believed that people think in stereotypes—"for the most part we do not first see, and then define; we define first and then see"—and therefore act irrationally. Democratic theory, he held, had "never seriously faced the problem which arises because the pictures inside people's heads do not automatically correspond with the world outside." Since public affairs are too complex for most people to grasp even if they wanted to, and since most people lack the time and interest to try, it is not reasonable to suppose that voters would instinctively or intuitively make the right choices. Instead, Lippmann called for "an independent, expert organization for making the unseen facts intelligible to those who have to make the decisions." Social scientists, organized in a network of intelligence bureaus, might perform such a function. Social progress, Lippmann argued, depended not on the old Progressive faith in an enlightened citizenry, but rather on the scientific organization of intelligence.

Many intellectuals in the 1920s assumed a coolly detached stance toward public affairs. "It was characteristic of the Jazz Age," said F. Scott Fitzgerald, "that it had no interest in politics at all." But even those who held themselves most aloof were caught up in the Sacco-Vanzetti case. Anarchists Nicola Sacco and Bartolomeo Vanzetti were charged with robbery and murder in 1920, convicted the following year, and sentenced to die. Legal appeals dragged on for six years until, in August 1927, both men were electrocuted. The case stirred immense moral outrage because elementary rules of due process were ignored, the judge, Webster Thayer, was viciously biased, and the Commonwealth of Massachusetts seemed determined to carry out an unjust sentence rather than concede the possibility of error. For a generation of intellectuals, Sacco and Vanzetti came to symbolize all that America was not. In a nation of conformists, they were rebels; in a nation of materialists, they were "the good shoemaker and poor fish peddler." They were, many believed, martyrs crucified by an unfeeling society.

## THE END OF THE NEW ORDER: 1929

Unfeeling or not at home, Americans had a strongly held view about how they might save the world. "The work that religion, government, and war have failed in must be done by business," an *Atlantic Monthly* correspondent declared in 1928. "That eternal job of administering the planet must be turned over to the despised business man."

One of these businessmen, not all despised, was the newly elected president. A multimillionaire mining engineer, Herbert Hoover embodied the success stories of the 1920s. His efficiency, realism, and faith in technology were exemplified when he installed the first telephone on the president's desk. (Before that, the chief executive had to use a booth in an adjoining room.) For Hoover, the roots of the system needed no examination. As he told a crowded Stanford stadium in 1928, "We in America today are nearer to the final triumph over poverty than ever before in the history of any land. The poorhouse is vanishing from among us."

The economic triumph of American individualism, moreover, had eradicated the causes of world wars. "It seems to me," Hoover wrote to his secretary of state, Henry Stimson, in 1929, "that there is the most profound outlook for peace today that we have had at any time in the last half century." Most Democrats were forced to agree. When the influential periodical *Foreign Affairs* asked a Republican and a Democrat to discuss their differences on foreign policy in 1928, the Democrat, Franklin D. Roosevelt, could find little of substance wrong with Republican diplomacy.

Hoover and many others fully realized that international stability depended on the strength of the American economy. Since becoming the world's leading creditor during World War I, the United States had dominated the international economy as Great Britain had before 1914. That power increased during the 1920s, as the efficient American system exported ever-larger amounts of goods. When foreign customers tried to repay with their own products, however, they encountered walls erected by the 1922 Fordney-McCumber Tariff, which raised average rates on imports to 33 percent. In 1923, U.S. merchandise exports exceeded imports by $375 million; in 1928, by $1.1 billion. Profiting handsomely, Americans covered the difference by lending their dollars to foreigners for the purchase of U.S. goods and by investing directly in overseas stocks and bonds. The dollar made the world economy go around.

By 1929, however, the dollar had begun staying home. New overseas investment opportunities did not appear, and a glamorous alternative, the New York Stock Exchange, quickly seduced big and small spenders. In 1924 the *New York Times* industrial average of stocks was 106; by 1928, it was 331, and during the summer of 1929, it shot up another 110 points. This wild speculation was fueled by "buying on margin," in which an investor bought stocks for a small down payment while borrowing the remainder at interest rates as high as 10 to 20 percent. The government and the banking community watched happily, even encouraging the speculation since they believed the stock exchange rested on a sound American economy.

But that economy was being eaten away by a rash of illnesses. First, the mass of Americans was too poor to buy the glut of goods being produced. Productivity shot up nearly 50 percent between 1919 and 1929 until the gross national product (the sum of all goods and services produced in the country) reached $104 billion in 1929. But wages did not keep pace. By 1929, 5 percent of the people received one-third of all personal income. As the gap between rich and poor widened, the economy became increasingly unstable. The government refused to consider measures, such as higher income taxes, to make income more equal. Farmers, miners, and textile workers especially suffered. Between 1919 and 1929, farm debt more than doubled. Farmers were further hurt in 1928 and 1929 when their foreign markets, now lacking American dollars, were no longer able to buy large amounts of wheat and cotton. Throughout the decade the rate of bank failures was also high. In truth, stock prices rested not on a strong economy, but on bankers' loans and on holding companies that had gained control of smaller firms through complex stock manipulations and business hocus-pocus. In October 1929 the stock market suddenly stalled. Excited bankers demanded repayment of their loans, forcing borrowers to declare bankruptcy, disappear, or jump from high buildings. A run on stocks began. Within a month after "Black Thursday," October 24, stock prices plummeted 50 percent.

A second illness, the inability of the government to control the economy, became obvious next. Throughout 1927 and 1928, the Federal Reserve System had fueled stock speculation with a low-interest, easy-money policy. When the system tried finally to slow the wild lending, large private banks refused to cooperate. As the stock decline accelerated, 800 banks closed in

1930. The government did little to save the banking system. Unemployment, at 1.5 million in 1929, shot up to 4.2 million in 1930, further cutting purchasing power. The Federal Reserve System then set lending rates at historically low levels so money would be very cheap. But there were no takers, for there appeared to be nowhere to invest the money profitably. As American capitalism crumbled, the government passed the Hawley-Smoot Tariff in 1930. It raised average rates on imports to 40 percent in order to keep out cheap foreign goods.

But the tariff starkly revealed the third illness. The world economy could survive only with the aid of either dollars or American markets. Now both disappeared. Without dollars foreigners could neither buy American goods nor repay earlier loans. As their own economies began to collapse, they too sought protection behind tariff walls that kept out American goods. From 1929 to 1933, world trade dropped 40 percent in value, with the leading exporters—Great Britain, Germany, Japan, and the United States—especially hard-hit. A domino effect occurred: the American depression caused foreign economies to decline, and the disappearance of these traditional markets for American products in turn worsened conditions in the United States. Meanwhile, President Hoover announced that the economy was basically sound. A group of Harvard economists declared, "a serious depression . . . is outside the range of possibility."

Actually, the world tottered on the edge of catastrophe. The great British economist John Maynard Keynes held out little hope: "A general breakdown is inevitable," he privately commented. "America will revert to a Texas type of civilization, France and Germany will go to war." Keynes's conclusions were appropriate, for without a healthy international economy the treaty system, so painfully constructed in Washington in 1922 and in Europe between 1924 and 1929, could not survive. The problem was not that Americans had become isolationist during the 1920s. Indeed, the internationalization of the American economic system had been so successful that as the domestic economy slowly sank, it dragged the rest of the world down with it.

# CHAPTER SIX

# 1929–1936
## The Depression and the New Deal

An unemployed woman sells apples in New York City, 1929.
*(Archive Holding, Inc./Getty Images)*

The Great Depression had a cataclysmic effect on all areas of American life. Producing unprecedented suffering, the economic crisis posed a severe challenge to the prevailing view of the social responsibilities of government. Within a few years that view, which sharply limited the role of government, proved a dismal failure. Yet the fear that disillusioned Americans would turn to revolution on the left, or to dictatorship on the right, proved groundless. Most people favored more moderate change, and that is exactly what the New Deal provided. Franklin D. Roosevelt's first administration erected the foundations of a welfare state. New Deal policies concerning business, agriculture, conservation, labor, and welfare, while benefiting certain interest groups considerably more than others, nevertheless enabled the Democrats to fashion a new political coalition that dominated American politics for several decades.

## HERBERT HOOVER AND THE DEPRESSION

Perhaps no one had ever assumed the office of president with more prestige, or left it so utterly discredited, as Herbert Hoover. Entering the White House in 1929 as a renowned humanitarian who would lead the nation "to the previously impossible state in which poverty in this country can be put on a purely voluntary basis," Hoover exited four years later with his name a synonym for suffering and hard times. People who spent the night on park benches covered by newspapers said they were sleeping under "Hoover blankets." Those who hitched broken-down cars to mules or horses said they were riding in "Hoover wagons." Men who turned their trouser pockets inside out to show they were empty claimed to be waving "Hoover flags." Hoover had once symbolized the application of scientific intelligence to social problems. By 1932 many considered his refusal to face facts squarely a national scandal.

During the 1920s Hoover had expressed boundless confidence in the potential of American capitalism. In *American Individualism* (1922) he asserted that the American system, by promoting equality of opportunity, permitted the "free rise of ability, character, and intelligence." Yet individualism, he added, by no means required the government to pursue a laissez-faire policy. As secretary of commerce under Harding and Coolidge (a position for which he turned down a $500,000-a-year offer as a mining and metallurgical engineer), Hoover endorsed government intervention in the domestic economy. He favored increased spending for public works to create jobs in periods of distress. He supported a constitutional amendment prohibiting child labor. He also advocated the creation of trade associations. By promulgating voluntary codes of business ethics, approved by the government, these associations would allow businessmen to avoid wasteful competition and to pool technical knowledge without violating the antitrust laws. In 1927, when floods ravaged the Mississippi Valley, Hoover brilliantly mobilized state, local, and private resources to aid the victims. Hoover's supporters in 1928 dubbed him "the Master of Emergencies."

His post-1929 program had five parts. First, Hoover summoned business and labor leaders to the White House in an effort to persuade them to maintain wages, keep up production, and proceed with plant expansion. Second, the president stepped up expenditures for the construction of roads, bridges, and public buildings. Federal aid for highway construction jumped from $105 million to $260 million annually, and the number of workers on such projects increased from 110,000 to 280,000. Third, Hoover signed the Hawley-Smoot Act (1930), which substantially raised tariff rates in the hope of protecting American manufacturers and farmers. Fourth, in June 1931 Hoover declared a moratorium on war debts. Convinced that economic collapse abroad was prolonging the depression in the United States, Hoover sought to improve the ability of European nations to purchase American goods and thereby stimulate domestic output. Fifth, the president somewhat grudgingly accepted direct aid to big business. Early in 1932 Congress created the Reconstruction Finance Corporation (RFC) in order to assist businesses in financial trouble. In Hoover's last year in office, the RFC lent $1.78 billion to 7,400 banks, insurance companies, railroads, and other institutions.

Some of these initiatives helped, but none succeeded in reversing the downturn. The "conferences for continued industrial progress," as they were called, produced little more than empty promises. Most business owners simply could not afford to maintain wages or prices while the economy continued to slide downward. The public works program did some good, but even as the federal government was expanding its program, bankrupt states and municipalities were trimming theirs. Consequently, the total amount spent on such improvements and the total number of men employed declined. The Hawley-Smoot tariff was an unqualified disaster; European countries, selling less to the United States, retaliated by erecting high tariff walls of their own. The debt moratorium had little domestic impact. Eventually it led to what its critics had feared—a decision by France, Great Britain, and most other nations to default on further payments. The RFC, whose activities were confined largely to bailing out large concerns, was said to dispense a "millionaire's dole."

By the end of 1932 Hoover's policy lay in ruins. Every statistic revealed a startling degree of deterioration. From 1929 to 1933, gross national product fell from $104 billion to $74 billion, and national income fell from $88 billion to $40 billion. Almost every day there were more bank failures: 1,350 closed their doors in 1930, followed by 2,293 and 1,453 in the next two years. Stock prices tumbled precipitously. General Motors had sold for a high of 91 in 1929; in January 1933 it sold for 13. In the same period Standard Oil declined from 83 to 30 and United States Steel declined from 261 to 27. Farmers watched in dismay as their income plummeted by 61 percent. A pound of cotton, which had sold for 16 cents in 1929, brought 6 cents in 1932; a bushel of corn, which had sold for 79 cents, brought 31 cents. Only the number of unemployed workers rose steadily. In 1929, 1.5 million workers—3 percent of the labor force—were jobless. By 1933, at least 13 million workers—25 percent of the total—were idle. An average of 75,000 workers lost their jobs every week for three years.

## THE BREAKDOWN OF RELIEF

Hoover's unwillingness to provide federal relief for the unemployed clearly revealed the inadequacy of his approach. The United States in the early 1930s had an unwieldy and anachronistic system of administering relief. Existing agencies were equipped to deal on a temporary basis with individual victims of accident or illness, but were not equipped to deal over a period of years with millions of jobless workers. Private charities had small staffs and limited funds; even municipalities often lacked the revenue to make sufficient money available. Only families that had become destitute, that had spent every dime of savings and sold every possession of value, could ordinarily qualify for assistance. Even then, those lucky enough to get on the relief rolls received barely enough for food. Rent, clothing, and medical care—all were considered luxuries.

Despite all this hardship, the president vigorously opposed direct federal relief in any form. To his mind it would open a Pandora's box, for it would cause a sizable increase in taxes, thereby discouraging private investment; lead to an unbalanced budget, thereby sabotaging confidence in the nation's credit; and require a gargantuan bureaucracy, thereby jeopardizing states' rights. Above all, the fearful "dole" would undermine its recipients' moral character, which Hoover took to mean "self-reliance," "sturdiness," and "independence." Yet as the situation worsened, the president was forced to take notice. The agencies he created to deal with the problem, however, illustrated perfectly Hoover's commitment to voluntary, cooperative action and his conviction that government could more properly dispense advice than funds.

In September 1930 Hoover set up the President's Emergency Committee for Employment under Colonel Arthur H. Woods. The committee at first subscribed to the view that relief was a local function, but by April 1931 even Woods recognized the need for federal involvement. When Hoover refused to concur, Woods resigned. In August Hoover created the President's Organization on Unemployment Relief, headed by Walter S. Gifford of American Telephone and Telegraph. Gifford arranged for a series of advertisements designed to stimulate charitable donations. But his group confined itself largely to a cheerleading function; as one member put it, "our job is not to raise funds ourselves." By November Gifford was assuring Hoover that "there is every indication that each state will take care of its own this winter." Two months later, testifying before a Senate committee, Gifford confessed that he did not know how many people were unemployed, how many were receiving relief, or how much money was available to the states to assist the needy.

By late 1932 the rickety relief system was collapsing in many places. Reports from cities across the country told of funds dried up and resources exhausted. Toledo: "There is only a commissary available for most families which is distributing the cheapest grades of food at a cost of six cents per person per day." Chicago: "Some families are being separated, husbands being sent to the men's shelter and wives to the women's shelter." Houston: "Applications are not taken from unemployed Mexican or colored families. They are being asked to shift for themselves." In Philadelphia, families on relief received $4.23 a week; in New York City, $2.39. Tragically, the special precautions taken to aid children revealed how bad things were. The American Friends Service Committee provided free lunches to children in the coal towns of Pennsylvania, West Virginia, and Kentucky. Funds were so limited that the Quakers could distribute meals only to children who were 10 percent underweight. In Oklahoma City, veterans collected discarded food from produce houses and scraps from butcher shops to feed the hungry. "All delicacies (such as figs that had spoiled and canned fruit that had gone a bit sour) were saved for the children."

## THE BONUS ARMY

The long years of hardship apparently left many Americans psychologically numb. No matter how bad conditions were throughout the country, many people regarded their inability to find work or support their families as a sign of personal inadequacy. Yet sporadic acts of protest, sometimes accompanied by violence and lawlessness, eventually occurred. The Midwest saw the invention of "penny auctions": when banks foreclosed farmers' mortgages and attempted to auction off their possessions, neighbors appeared, armed with rifles, and no one bid more than a penny. The two most important organized protests occurred in the summer of 1932—the Bonus Army and the Farm Holiday Association.

Soldiers in gas masks advance on Bonus Army demonstrators in Washington, DC, July 1932. The Bonus Marchers were unemployed World War I veterans urging the U.S. government to deliver their promised monetary bonus early. *(Jack Benton/Getty Images)*

The career of the Bonus Expeditionary Force demonstrated that even the most disillusioned Americans continued to seek improvement within the system rather than outside it. The bonus issue had originated in 1924 when Congress, over Coolidge's veto, promised a bonus of several hundred dollars (depending on length of military service) to World War I veterans, but deferred payment until 1945. By 1932, however, many unemployed veterans wanted to be paid immediately, since they considered the money rightfully theirs and desperately needed it. When Congress took up a bill providing immediate payment, veterans converged on Washington to lobby for passage. The veterans aroused considerable sympathy, but the Hoover administration believed the case against them to be overwhelming: payment of the bonus would wreck hopes for a balanced budget, give preferential treatment to veterans over other needy citizens, and entitle those veterans who were well-off to payment at a time of declining tax revenues.

In June 1932 some 22,000 veterans, led by Walter W. Waters of Oregon, streamed into Washington. They set up camp across the Anacostia River by building shanties furnished from garbage dumps. Their wives and children joined many veterans. The chief of police of Washington, Pelham D. Glassford, himself a former army officer, provided some funds and provisions. Although the House passed the bonus bill, the Senate rejected the measure on June 17 by a large margin. Congress adjourned in July after allocating $100,000 to provide loans for marchers who needed carfare to return home. Only 5,160 men took advantage of the offer. The rest, presumably having no home or jobs to return to, remained.

The presence of the Bonus Army embarrassed and frightened the Hoover administration. Hoover refused to meet with a delegation of veterans, assuming that an interview would only dignify their cause, raise false hopes, and bring even more demonstrators to Washington. In addition, the president came to accept the view that communist agitators had infiltrated the ranks of the Bonus Army. Ultimately the government increased its pressure on the veterans, demanding that they leave an abandoned Treasury Department building in downtown Washington in which some were living. The evacuation led to a scuffle with the police in which two veterans were killed, providing a pretext for dispersing the Bonus Army itself. On July 28, 1932, General Douglas MacArthur led cavalry and infantry troops, as well as a mounted machine-gun squadron, down Pennsylvania Avenue. With bayonets and tear gas, the soldiers drove the veterans out of the business district and across the bridge to Anacostia and there set fire to the encampment.

The decision to drive the veterans out of downtown Washington was made by Hoover, Secretary of War Patrick J. Hurley, and the District commissioners, but the decision to pursue them to Anacostia and break up their encampment was MacArthur's alone. Convinced that the Bonus Army was "a bad-looking mob animated by the essence of revolution," MacArthur ignored explicit instructions not to follow the veterans across the Anacostia River. But if Hoover had not ordered this pursuit, he accepted MacArthur's estimate of the revolutionary threat, believed that public opinion would support MacArthur's action, and therefore accepted responsibility for it. To have done otherwise would have required the president to repudiate his chief of staff and side with forces he considered subversive. The president thus not only misunderstood what the Bonus Army represented, but also misjudged public reaction to the government's panicky response.

## AGRARIAN PROTEST

Even as the government was driving out the Bonus Army, struggling corn and dairy farmers in Iowa and surrounding states were organizing the Farm Holiday Association. Like the veterans who went to Washington, the farmers wanted Congress to enact special-interest legislation. This took the form of the cost-of-production plan, under which the government would support food prices at a level that would guarantee farmers their operating cost, a 5 percent return on their investment, and a living wage for their operators. The plan would have raised the price of a bushel of oats from 11 to 45 cents, the price of a bushel of corn from 10 to 92 cents. The farmers, however, attempted to generate pressure on Congress not by camping on the Capitol doorstep but by withholding their products from market, hoping thereby to force prices upward.

The Farm Holiday Association began implementing its direct-action plan in August 1932. Despite wide support, the plan proved unworkable. Blockading a few markets could not significantly affect overall supply or price levels. Even if prices rose temporarily, they would drop as soon as farmers resumed normal operations. Nor did all farmers wish to cooperate with the strike. As Farm Holiday Association supporters set up patrols and picket lines, they clashed with farmers seeking to transport their goods to market and with sheriff's deputies attempting

# JAMES CAGNEY
## AND THE GANGSTER FILM

American actor James Cagney *(left)* plays gangster Tom Powers in the 1931 film
*Public Enemy*, directed by William A. Wellman for Warner Brothers. *(Hulton Archive/
Getty Images)*

In the early 1930s many Americans were troubled by the existence of organized crime, and
troubled even more by what they considered its source: the widespread disrespect for the
law bred by Prohibition and the closing of traditional paths to success because of the Great
Depression. The release of *Little Caesar* in 1931 marked the appearance of a new film
genre, the gangster film, which reflected these concerns. The picture's box-office success
led to the production of fifty other such films within a year.

The most revealing of these was *Public Enemy*, in which James Cagney played the gangster
Tommy Powers. Even as a youngster Tommy is tripping little girls on roller skates. As a teenager
he falls in with the wrong crowd and becomes a thief and bootlegger (although in Cagney's por-
trayal a rather jaunty, lovable one). As the archetypal gangster, Tommy Powers scorns traditional
values, most of which are embodied in his brother Mike. Tommy Powers cuts through social
convention with a scalpel. He sneers at education. When an accomplice asks him to involve
Mike in a gangland operation, Tommy replies, "He's too busy going to school. He's learning
to be poor." Similarly, Tommy exposes the hypocrisy of war. When Mike returns from military
service a hero and accuses his brother of murdering rival bootleggers, Tommy snaps, "You didn't
get those medals holding hands with Germans." Tommy refuses to be domesticated. When his
mistress, played by Mae Clarke, gently scolds him and says she wishes he would not drink so
early in the morning, Tommy mimics her savagely: "I wish, I wish, I wish you was a wishing
well. Then maybe you'd dry up!" Mashing a grapefruit in her face, he walks out.

In deference to the Hollywood production code, *Public Enemy* opens by stating that it does not intend to glorify the criminal but rather to "depict an environment." There is also a mandatory unhappy ending, in which a rival gang abducts Tommy Powers from a hospital and deposits his corpse on his mother's doorstep. But despite these concessions to convention, the film's message was plain. Its hero, after all, is a man who thumbs his nose at conventional virtues and follows the one career he finds open to his talents. The film was reassuring in another sense. For while Tommy Powers disregards the laws everyone else supposedly observes, his world had laws of its own. The underworld operated according to a clearly defined code, and gangsters dispensed an informal brand of justice by annihilating one another. Moreover, the world of the criminal was encapsulated. The gangster did not injure law-abiding citizens because he moved in a world separate and distinct from theirs.

FBI head J. Edgar Hoover aiming a Thompson submachine gun, 1925. *(Time & Life Pictures/ Getty Images)*

The image of the police officer in the gangster film was that of a dumb flatfoot, either incompetent or corrupt, or both. Yet with the advent of the welfare state under Franklin D. Roosevelt, crime films changed to reflect the new national mood. As the federal government extended its influence, the image of federal law enforcement was refurbished. Partly because of a massive public relations campaign by Federal Bureau of Investigation (FBI) director J. Edgar Hoover, Americans came to regard federal agents as fearless, intrepid, and incorruptible. The circle was not complete, however, until the release of *G-Men* in 1935, starring none other than James Cagney. In the film Cagney joins the FBI to avenge the gangland slaying of a friend. "'Public Enemy' Becomes Soldier of the Law," read advertisements: "Uncle Sam always gets his man." Now Cagney did his shooting from behind a badge—and, even more significant, it was a federal badge.

## Web Links

**http://lafenty.hubpages.com/hub/Gangster-Movies-1930s-1940s**
Clips from many gangster films including *Public Enemy*.

**http://themave.com/Cagney/**
A website devoted to James Cagney with a biography and video clips.

to keep the road open. The resulting violence dismayed the movement's leaders, who called off the strike in September. By then attention was shifting to the presidential campaign and the opportunity to elect candidates who might relieve the distress. In November 1932 Herbert Hoover failed to carry a single rural county in his home state of Iowa.

## ROOSEVELT AND THE NEW DEAL

To face Hoover in that election the Democrats nominated Franklin Delano Roosevelt, often referred to as FDR. Born in Hyde Park, New York, in 1882, the only child of wealthy parents, Roosevelt entered Groton in 1896 and Harvard in 1900, then attended Columbia Law School. In 1910, having practiced law for a time, he entered politics and was elected to the New York State Senate. He strongly backed Woodrow Wilson, whom he later served as assistant secretary of the navy, and in 1920 he ran for vice president on the Democratic ticket with James M. Cox. In August 1921 Roosevelt, until then a vigorous and athletic man, was struck by poliomyelitis. Years of physical therapy helped somewhat, but his legs remained paralyzed. For the rest of his life he wore steel braces, could walk only with assistance, and had to be lifted into and out of automobiles. While Roosevelt adjusted to permanent paralysis, his wife Eleanor threw her energies into Democratic politics in New York State to keep the Roosevelt name in the public eye. In 1928 he had recuperated sufficiently to run for governor. Although Democratic presidential candidate Al Smith lost New York State, Roosevelt won the governorship by a narrow margin and easily gained reelection two years later. In 1932, recognizing that Hoover's policies had alienated millions and that the name Roosevelt was "still almost as much a Republican name as a Democratic one," he purposely conducted a vague presidential campaign, promising to end hard times without ever explaining how.

Roosevelt entered the White House in March 1933 with several advantages. With 22.8 million votes to Hoover's 15.8 million, Roosevelt could claim an undisputed popular mandate. He also had comfortable majorities with which to work in Congress. Democrats outnumbered Republicans 59 to 36 in the Senate, 313 to 117 in the House. For economic advice Roosevelt could turn to members of his "brain trust," which included Columbia University professors Adolf A. Berle, Rexford G. Tugwell, and Raymond Moley. For political advice the president could rely on Louis Howe—an old friend and supporter—and James A. Farley, whom he made postmaster general. Roosevelt's cabinet contained talented administrators, among them Secretary of the Interior Harold L. Ickes, Secretary of Agriculture Henry A. Wallace, and Secretary of Labor Frances C. Perkins. Above all, Roosevelt took office in the midst of a severe national crisis, one he likened to a war. He could depend, therefore, on an extraordinary amount of cooperation from Congress and the public.

As he entered office, Roosevelt affirmed that the government owed each person the "right to make a comfortable living." This as well as anything else marked the distance between his approach and Hoover's. For New Dealers, the depression had exposed the bankruptcy of the existing order, characterized by what Tugwell termed its "violent contrasts of well-being, its irrational allotments of individual liberty, its unconsidered exploitation of human and natural resources." The New Deal, Berle noted, brought "a tremendous expansion of the area in which . . . government is prepared to accept responsibility." Roosevelt indeed saw no practical alternative. To rehabilitate the private enterprise system, government must rescue its victims. Roosevelt feared that a revolution "could hardly be avoided if another president should fail as Hoover has failed."

Pragmatic in outlook, Roosevelt's followers said they wanted "hard facts," declared it "unwise to lay down too specifically the structure of new things," and even announced that "'truth' is irrelevant as a test of an economic philosophy." They believed in trying something to see if it worked, discarding it if it did not, and then trying something else. This willingness to improvise, surely a source of strength, nevertheless raised certain problems. For one thing, it was not always clear how long a period was needed to judge whether a program was working or what criteria would be used in making that judgment. For another, new programs attracted support from political interests and developed bureaucratic structures that resisted change. Policies, once instituted, proved less adaptable in practice than they seemed in theory.

## THE BLUE EAGLE

The keystone of the early New Deal was the National Recovery Administration (NRA), created in June 1933. The NRA, rejecting the model of competition, favored business cooperation in partnership with government. Business executives were permitted to draft codes, subject to presidential approval, that regulated prices and wages and forbade a broad range of competitive practices. Those participating in such agreements were exempted from the antitrust laws. In addition, the NRA supposedly guaranteed labor the right to organize, and it inaugurated a public works program to pump money into the economy. This latter function was performed through the Public Works Administration, which Roosevelt placed under Harold Ickes. To head the NRA, however, Roosevelt chose General Hugh Johnson, who had played an instrumental role in the world war mobilization.

Although Congress clothed the NRA with licensing powers, Johnson, fearing that they might not withstand the scrutiny of the courts, attempted to gain voluntary compliance from business. He marshaled public opinion through parades and publicity, and all who took part displayed the NRA symbol—a blue eagle with the slogan "We Do Our Part." Just as soldiers used certain insignia to distinguish friend from foe, Roosevelt said, so those fighting the depression "must know each other at a glance." "May God have mercy on the man or group of men who attempt to trifle with that bird," proclaimed Johnson. The codes, he explained, resembled the Marquis of Queensberry rules in boxing. "They eliminate eye-gouging and knee-groining and ear-chewing in business. Above the belt any man can be just as rugged and just as individual as he pleases." By the fall of 1933 every major industry had pledged its cooperation.

But in economics, as in the ring, heavyweights enjoyed a distinct advantage. Many corporate leaders had always disliked what they regarded as excessive competition. They saw nothing wrong with fixing prices, so long as they did the fixing. The antitrust laws had presumably blocked such concerted action, but their suspension provided business leaders with a long-awaited opportunity. As things worked out, big business played the dominant role in drawing up the codes. The NRA, in consequence, generally kept production down and prices up. The codes restricted output by limiting factory hours and banning new plant construction. Similarly, the codes set minimum prices, prohibited sales below cost, and restricted combination sales, trade-in allowances, credit terms, and other competitive practices.

These policies caused a good deal of dissatisfaction. Consumers resented an arrangement that hurt their pocketbooks, and many owners of small businesses believed that the codes discriminated in favor of large concerns. Women's organizations, led by the League of Women Voters and the National Consumer's League, protested that one out of four NRA codes discriminated against women by setting lower minimum wages for women than for men. At the same time, labor was becoming increasingly dissatisfied because Section 7(a), which was intended to protect the right to organize, was proving insufficient. While it prohibited employers from interfering with their workers' right to join unions and choose bargaining officials, it did not create adequate enforcement machinery or require employers to bargain in good faith. In 1934 Roosevelt appointed a commission, under Clarence Darrow, that investigated the NRA and submitted a highly critical report. "NRA," said the disaffected, stood for "No Recovery Allowed" or "National Run-Around."

The experiment in industrial planning had mixed results. The NRA apparently brought about a measure of economic improvement and, perhaps as important, established the principle of federal responsibility for working conditions. Yet the agency did not live up to expectations, in part because different groups—consumers and workers, large and small businesses—expected different things of it. There was, in truth, little chance that the NRA could have satisfied all the competing demands made of it. Having relied so heavily on public support at the outset, the NRA found itself in difficulty when enthusiasm waned. In early 1935 the Senate agreed to extend the NRA for one, not two, years. That May, the Supreme Court brought the troubled flight of the blue eagle to an end.

It did so in the "sick chicken" case. The Schechter brothers, who owned a poultry market in Brooklyn, purchased chickens raised in surrounding states, slaughtered them, and sold them to retailers. In October 1934 the firm was found guilty of violating NRA wage and hour provisions and of selling unfit poultry. The case eventually reached the Supreme Court, which handed down a unanimous opinion. Chief Justice Charles Evans Hughes ruled that the depression did not confer upon the government powers it might not otherwise exercise, that an excessive delegation of legislative powers occurred in the code-drafting process, and that the Schechter brothers were involved in intrastate commerce and therefore outside the scope of federal regulation. Hughes admitted that the chickens had crossed state lines but reasoned that they had come to a "permanent rest"—that is, were killed and eaten—within New York. They therefore were no longer part of a flow of interstate commerce. Through an extremely narrow reading of the Constitution, therefore, the Court declared the NRA illegal.

## TRIPLE A

The New Deal attempted to aid agriculture by helping farmers pay off their mortgages, encouraging inflation to facilitate the payment of debts, acquiring foreign markets for farm products, and reducing acreage to limit supply. The last, known as the "domestic allotment plan," served as the foundation of the Agricultural Adjustment Administration (AAA or Triple A), which was established in May 1933. Under the plan—which affected wheat, cotton, hogs, tobacco, corn, rice, and milk—farmers signed acreage-reduction contracts. In return for curbing output, they received government subsidies. In some respects the AAA was a counterpart of the NRA, for each involved a planned limitation of production under government auspices.

At the outset, the AAA had to persuade farmers to destroy part of their existing crops. Making agreements to curb future output was relatively simple but did not affect the current harvest. The AAA therefore paid farmers $160 million to destroy one-fourth of their cotton. They plowed up 10 million acres, reducing the crop from 17 to 13 million bales. The administration also induced farmers to slaughter 6 million baby pigs and 200,000 sows. Although farmers received $30 million and relief agencies distributed the pork to needy families, the extermination led to howls of anguish. "To hear them talk," Secretary of Agriculture Wallace said disgustedly, "you would have thought that pigs were raised for pets!" Roosevelt apparently regarded the matter less seriously than did his critics. He inquired jokingly, "Wouldn't birth control be more effective in the long run?"

The AAA helped farmers who owned their own land, but it often hurt those who did not. Of the 2.86 million tenant farmers and sharecroppers, 1.6 million, many of them black, labored in southern cotton fields. The AAA policy of reducing farm acreage obviously reduced the need for farm laborers and consequently led to evictions and unemployment. Those tenants and croppers who remained received little, since payments were made only to landowners. They were supposed to apportion the money fairly among their tenants, but seldom did. The Roosevelt administration, believing that the AAA's success hinged on the cooperation of the owners of big farms, would do nothing to jeopardize that support. As AAA director Chester Davis noted in February 1936, the elevation of sharecroppers "cannot be forced by the Federal Government to proceed much faster than the rate that the Southern opinion and Southern leadership will heartily support. To try to force a faster pace would merely be to insure violent controversy, lack of local cooperation in administration, evasion and ineffectiveness for the plan."

Not everyone shared this outlook. A number of AAA officials, led by General Counsel Jerome Frank, wished to protect the sharecroppers' position by requiring that planters continue to employ the same workers. Frank's dispute with Davis eventually forced Wallace to choose between them. Early in 1935 he "purged" the AAA of Frank and those who wanted to make agricultural policy into a vehicle of reform. In July 1935, however, the administration partially appeased Frank's group by supporting the creation of the Resettlement Administration, which took the first, tentative steps toward helping landless farmers acquire their own land and tools. In some cases dissatisfied tenant farmers took independent action. In mid-1934, black and white sharecroppers in Arkansas organized the Southern Tenant Farmers Union. Too frequently, they complained, Roosevelt "talked like a cropper and acted like a planter." When they sang "We Shall Not Be Moved," they were protesting against a New Deal policy that was driving them from the land they worked but did not own.

Despite these difficulties, by 1936 the AAA had succeeded in raising gross farm income by 50 percent, boosting commodity prices by 66 percent, and reducing farm indebtedness by $1 billion. Then the agency met the same fate as the NRA. In January 1936, in *United States v. Butler*, the Supreme Court struck down the AAA by a vote of 6 to 3. Justice Owen Roberts, delivering the majority opinion, held that benefits paid to farmers for reducing acreage actually imposed a system of agricultural regulation under the guise of appropriations for the general welfare. In effect, Roberts said, Congress could not stipulate how its appropriations were to be used. In a stinging dissent, Justice Harlan Fiske Stone termed this "a tortured construction of the Constitution." He added, "the power to tax and spend includes the power to relieve a nationwide economic maladjustment by conditional gifts of money." This view New Dealers considered axiomatic for the continued functioning of the welfare state.

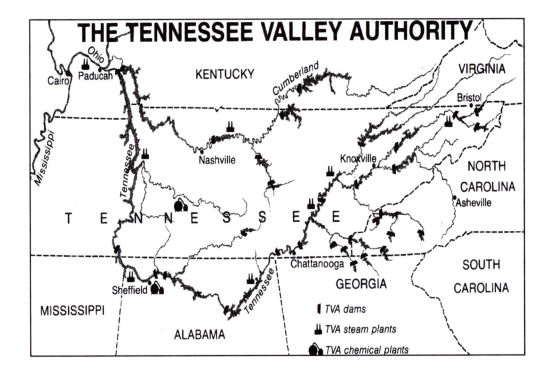

## CONSERVATION AND PUBLIC POWER:
## THE TENNESSEE VALLEY AUTHORITY

Few causes meant more to Roosevelt than conservation. The existing pool of unemployed young people provided an opportunity to unite the functions of forestry and relief, and this the president proceeded to do in the Civilian Conservation Corps (CCC). Within three months after its creation in April 1933, the CCC had enrolled 250,000 young men in their teens and twenties. The volunteers fought forest fires, built water-storage basins, and reseeded grazing lands. They constructed roads, bridges, and camping facilities. They protected trees against blister rust, bark beetle, and gypsy moths. In three years CCC volunteers planted 570 million trees in the national forests. They also showed farmers how to prevent soil erosion. To conserve wildlife, the agency built refuges, fish-rearing ponds, and animal shelters. In September 1935 the CCC reached a high point with 500,000 volunteers in more than 2,500 camps. The young men received $30 per month, of which $25 went directly to their families as part of a relief program.

New Dealers proposed a still more ambitious plan to transform social and economic conditions in the 40,000-square-mile Tennessee River Valley. There, Roosevelt said shortly before his inauguration, "we have an opportunity of setting an example of planning . . . tying in industry and agriculture and forestry and flood prevention, tying them all into a unified whole." In May 1933 Congress established the Tennessee Valley Authority (TVA), thereby fulfilling—indeed, exceeding—the hopes of such public-power advocates as Senator George

Norris of Nebraska. The TVA promised coordinated, multipurpose development. It not only provided electric power but also prevented soil erosion, helped control floods, allowed for navigation, and experimented with new fertilizers. It meant, Roosevelt said, "national planning for a complete river watershed."

During the 1930s the TVA erected more than twenty dams with a generating capacity of 1 million kilowatts. Consumption of electricity in the region more than doubled. The TVA also cleared a 650-mile channel from Paducah to Knoxville, which greatly stimulated traffic on the river. Inevitably, though, the agency provoked sharp opposition from private electric companies, which took a dim view of government competition. These companies also resented the concept of a federal "yardstick" against which their rates would be measured, arguing, with considerable justice, that TVA costs were not comparable with their own. Wendell Willkie of the Commonwealth and Southern Corporation, a leader of the opposition, branded the TVA "the most useless and unnecessary of all the alphabetical joyrides." Private utilities engaged the TVA in a long series of legal tussles. In February 1936 the agency won breathing room when the Supreme Court, in *Ashwander v. TVA*, upheld the government's right to sell the excess energy generated by Wilson Dam. The Court did not finally resolve the broader constitutional question in favor of the TVA until early 1939.

The TVA accomplished a great deal—as much as, if not more than, any other New Deal program—but it never brought about the "designed and planned social and economic order" for which some had hoped. Spokesmen for the agency advocated what David E. Lilienthal, one of its directors, termed "grass-roots democracy." Lilienthal believed that in assuming broad powers, the federal government must not lose touch with local mores and institutions. This required the "decentralized administration of centralized authority." The policy of encouraging local involvement, while helping to secure support, in effect made the TVA responsive to the largest and most influential interest groups. Its agricultural program, for example, was geared to wealthy farmers rather than to sharecroppers. Those who had the most extravagant expectations were most unhappy at what they viewed as the TVA's capitulation. No less than the NRA and AAA, the TVA often catered to the already powerful.

## SOLIDARITY FOREVER?

When Franklin Roosevelt took office, 3 million workers belonged to trade unions, compared with 5 million in 1920. Only one in ten nonfarm workers carried union cards, about the same percentage as in 1910. In the steel, rubber, and automobile industries, unions played virtually no role at all. Thrown on the defensive in the 1920s by the open-shop drive and adverse Supreme Court rulings, labor suffered further losses in the early depression years. Unions found it impossible to keep old members, much less attract new ones, in a shrinking job market. Many workers shied away from union activities for fear of antagonizing employers. After 1933, although the economy slowly revived, the policies adopted by employers and American Federation of Labor (AFL) officials continued to retard unionization.

The techniques employers used to block organizing drives included hiring spies and private policemen, stockpiling small arsenals for use in case of strikes, and recruiting professional strikebreakers. But in the years 1933 to 1935, employers relied chiefly on the company union, which had the advantage of appearing to comply with Section 7(a) of the legislation that created the NRA without actually doing so. These unions, set up and controlled by employers, lacked any semblance of autonomy. Management expected great things of them. A vice president in charge of industrial relations at United States Steel declared that the union he had just organized would lead to "sound and harmonious relationships between men and management," similar to those prevailing "between a man and his wife." Finley Peter Dunne's political cartoon character Mr. Dooley had once said that an employer's ideal union was one with "no strikes, no rules, no contracts, . . . hardly iny wages, an 'dam' few members." Except for the last point, company unions nicely fitted the definition. By 1935 nearly 600 of them existed, with well over 2 million members.

The AFL meanwhile was proving itself unequal to—indeed uninterested in—the task of organizing the unorganized, particularly unskilled workers in mass-production industries. With few exceptions, AFL unions followed craft rather than industrial lines. The AFL adhered to the principle of exclusive jurisdiction under which, for example, its metalworkers' affiliate had a claim on all metalworkers, no matter where they worked or what their preferences. The creation of industrial unions in steel plants or automobile factories could easily demolish these jurisdictional rights. To justify their position, AFL leaders insisted that unskilled workers lacked the leverage to bargain successfully, for if they went on strike, employers could easily replace them. The eventual collapse of such old AFL rivals as the American Railway Union and the Industrial Workers of the World supposedly provided ironclad proof that industrial unionism led up a blind alley.

The Roosevelt administration, unwilling to abandon the NRA concept of a business-government partnership, did little at first to spur union growth. "This is a time for mutual confidence and help," the president said in creating the NRA, but during 1934 capital and labor exhibited little of either. Not only were employers setting up company unions to avoid bargaining in good faith, but labor militancy rose sharply. In 1934, 1.5 million workers went on strike, and industrial violence reached its highest level since 1919. San Francisco longshoremen, Minneapolis truck drivers, Alabama cotton-mill workers—all struck for union recognition and improved conditions, and all clashed with the police or the National Guard. Simultaneously, pressure began to mount in Congress, where Senator Robert F. Wagner of New York drew up a measure to make collective bargaining guarantees meaningful. Roosevelt, claiming that the bill needed more study, succeeded in having it shelved.

With the various strands of his labor policy unraveling, the president finally accepted Wagner's position in the spring of 1935. At the last minute, when the Senate had passed the Wagner Act (1935) and the House was about to do so, Roosevelt endorsed it. The act upheld the right of workers to join unions and created the National Labor Relations Board to conduct shop elections. Most important, the measure substituted the principle of majority rule for that of proportional representation, thereby ensuring that the union winning a majority of votes would represent all the employees. The act prohibited employers from blacklisting workers, refusing to reinstate strikers, engaging in industrial espionage, or setting up company unions. The bill passed by huge margins, in part because many congressmen assumed—mistakenly as it turned out—that the Supreme Court would nullify it.

Enactment of this legislation was like a shot of adrenaline to advocates of industrial unionism. A sizable group within the AFL, led by John L. Lewis of the United Mine Workers, now demanded that the AFL accept industrial unions. Craft unions, Lewis asserted, may have served adequately in the past but were not suited to modern factories, in which technology

Labor leader John L. Lewis, head of the CIO, 1937. *(Library of Congress)*

had erased old craft distinctions. At the AFL convention in September 1935, Lewis presented a plan to allow the chartering of industrial unions. When the delegates rejected his motion by nearly a 2-to-1 margin, Lewis led a walkout. In November Lewis, Sidney Hillman of the Amalgamated Clothing Workers of America, David Dubinsky of the International Ladies Garment Workers Union, and leaders of fledgling unions in the automobile, rubber, and steel industries created what became the Congress of Industrial Organizations (CIO). The AFL demanded the dissolution of the congress and, when it refused, the AFL suspended and later expelled the unions composing the congress. Yet in the long run, the split proved a prelude to success, for it enabled labor to take advantage of the spectacular opportunities for organizing unskilled workers provided by the Wagner Act.

## RELIEF AND SECURITY

New Deal policies concerning relief, like those affecting labor, evolved in a halting fashion. This was no fault of Harry Hopkins, who, before Roosevelt brought him to Washington to direct relief efforts, had performed a similar function in New York State. Hopkins's approach diverged sharply from prevailing practice. He believed that all needy persons, the unemployed as well as the chronically unemployable, were entitled to receive relief. He favored raising

Applicants waiting for jobs in front of FERA offices, New Orleans, Louisiana, October 1935. *(Library of Congress)*

standards to furnish such necessities as clothing and medical care. He also believed that payments in cash rather than grocery slips preserved recipients' self-respect. Finally, Hopkins preferred work relief, which made individuals feel like productive members of society, to home relief, which was often degrading. Work relief should, where possible, utilize existing training and skills. Hopkins saw no reason to insist that, as the price of obtaining relief, a teacher or engineer should have to dig ditches.

Hopkins's views regarding eligibility, standards, and programs went far beyond those of the Roosevelt administration and Congress. The first New Deal relief venture—the Federal Emergency Relief Administration (FERA)—showed this clearly. The FERA supervised relief activities from April 1933 to April 1935, except for a six-month period during the winter of 1934. Administration of the program was left largely in state hands. The matching-grants provision had unfortunate consequences. States, hard-pressed to raise the money necessary to obtain such funds, had either to enact sales taxes, which imposed an unfair burden on the poor, or cut other expenditures, such as those for education. If providing outright grants for relief broke sharply with existing practice, echoes of Herbert Hoover's policy lingered on in the decision to leave supervision to the states and in the attempt to squeeze yet more money out of them.

In November 1933, with the unemployed facing a long, cold winter, the administration conceded the FERA's inadequacy and temporarily replaced it with the Civil Works Administration (CWA). The CWA differed from its predecessor in that the federal government administered it and met 90 percent of its cost. The agency also took on some workers who, although unemployed, had not qualified for relief. The CWA offered relatively high wages, paying unskilled workers forty to fifty cents an hour, up to a maximum of thirty hours a week. Within two months the new agency had put 4.2 million men to work repairing streets, laying sewer pipe, building roads, improving schools and playgrounds, and, as critics always pointed out, raking leaves. By the start of 1934, 300,000 women worked for the CWA in sewing, canning, and clerical jobs. Undoubtedly some projects were poorly conceived, but most accomplished useful purposes. Then, in April 1934, the administration, worried by the CWA's high cost and controversial nature, canceled the experiment and reverted to the FERA.

Not until April 1935, when it established the Works Progress Administration (WPA), did the New Deal fashion a workable relief program. The WPA employed only those certified as needing relief, but was federally run, paid good wages, and made room for white-collar and professional workers. At its height, the WPA employed 3 million people a year, and, although starting with an initial appropriation of $4.8 billion, it ultimately spent $10.7 billion over seven years. The WPA included writers' and artists' projects and the Federal Theater Project, which in 1936 employed 12,500 actors who performed before audiences of 350,000 every week. The WPA never helped all the needy, and it was continually fighting off attempts to slice its budget. Yet it embodied many of the principles in which Hopkins believed: decent standards, work relief, and utilization of existing skills.

Roosevelt created the WPA in April, endorsed the Wagner Act in May, and in August 1935 signed a third measure—the Social Security Act—that further institutionalized government responsibility for the disadvantaged. First, the act set up an old-age pension system administered by the federal government and funded by a 1 percent payroll tax. Beginning in 1942 (the date was advanced to 1940), retired workers over sixty-five would receive $10 to $85 a month, depending on the amount that they had contributed. Those who had already retired would receive pensions to which the government would contribute up to $15 a month. Second, the measure provided for a joint federal-state system of unemployment insurance based on employer contributions. Third, the act authorized federal aid for the care of the blind, training for the physically handicapped, and aid to dependent children. Certainly, the Social Security Act had many imperfections: farm workers and domestic servants were excluded from its retirement provisions; state standards for unemployment compensation varied tremendously; and the payroll tax reduced mass purchasing power at the wrong time. Yet the act placed another brick in the arch of the welfare state.

## THE NEW DEAL COALITION

Harry Hopkins was once quoted as saying, "We shall tax and tax, and spend and spend, and elect and elect." The remark may have been apocryphal, but it infuriated those who objected to New Deal relief and security policies. Many Republicans asserted, without justification, that Social Security would require federal prying into the private lives of citizens and would force millions of people to submit to fingerprinting or wear dog tags for identification purposes. Many of these same critics argued, with considerably better reason, that Democrats were attempting to extract partisan advantage from federal relief. Officials sometimes dispensed relief in ways calculated to bolster their political position and occasionally pressured WPA workers into voting a certain way. One Democratic leader privately requested the appointment of administrators who favored "using these Democratic projects to make votes for the Democratic Party."

In the 1936 presidential election, when Roosevelt defeated his opponent Alf M. Landon of Kansas, some Republicans blamed the magnitude of their loss on such unfair tactics. Certainly the dimensions of that defeat were stunning. Roosevelt received 27.5 million votes to Landon's 16.7 million and carried every state but Vermont and Maine. The voters sent only ninety Republicans to the House of Representatives and left only sixteen in the Senate, giving the Democrats the largest congressional majorities since the mid-nineteenth century. The vote revealed a sharp split along class lines, with Roosevelt in effect receiving most of his support from the lower classes and Landon receiving most of his from more prosperous groups. Politics had moved full circle from the 1920s, when cultural tensions had overshadowed economic issues. The Roosevelt coalition embraced southern whites and northern blacks, rural dwellers and urban immigrants, middle-class intellectuals and blue-collar workers. In 1936 a person's income and occupation (or lack of one) provided the surest clues to party preference.

The Democratic triumph reflected not illicit pressure exerted on relief recipients, but rather public approval of the programs Roosevelt had instituted. At the time those policies were criticized as inadequate, and in retrospect they may appear even less adequate. In almost every field—business, agriculture, conservation, labor, and relief—the New Deal moved cautiously and catered to more powerful groups at the expense of weaker ones. But this should not obscure the improvements in American life, or the changes in the role of government, that had occurred. In 1936 the clearest point of reference was 1932. The inadequacies of Roosevelt's policies, when compared with those of Hoover, did not seem so great after all.

# CHAPTER SEVEN

# 1933–1941
## Hard Times—Politics and Society

The wife of a migratory laborer with three children, near Childress, Texas, 1938. *(Library of Congress)*

Despite his efforts to combat the Great Depression and despite the vote of confidence he received in 1936, President Franklin Roosevelt by no means succeeded in restoring prosperity during his first or, for that matter, his second administration. Millions of Americans who remained poor and insecure concluded that New Deal policies were inadequate. Some turned to socialism or communism, but more supported the proposals of Dr. Francis E. Townsend, Huey Long, and Father Charles E. Coughlin, who promised instant abundance without a radical alteration of the social order. If some complained that the New Deal was proceeding too slowly, conservatives believed it was traveling at breakneck speed. Limited at first to sniping at New Deal policies, Roosevelt's conservative critics launched a massive offensive after 1937. Faced with mounting hostility in Congress and declining public support, New Dealers went on the defensive. By the end of the decade the Roosevelt administration was devoting most of its attention to national defense and foreign policy, not to domestic reform.

## THE OLD FOLKS' CRUSADE

In 1935 a California congressman rose in the House of Representatives to reflect on the passing of his mother. "She is the sweetest memory of my life," he said, "and the hands that used to feed me and cool my fevered brow now touch me only in my dreams. But if she were living today, . . . that little frail mother of mine . . . would say, 'Son, you be good to the old folks, and God will bless you.'" In the year 1935 being "good to the old folks" meant one thing: supporting the Townsend Old Age Revolving Pension Plan. Named for its creator, Dr. Francis E. Townsend, the plan gave birth to a movement whose widespread popularity pointed up the deficiencies of the New Deal and influenced the policies of the Roosevelt administration. Better than anything else, the appeal of the Townsend plan illustrated the devastating impact of the depression on the elderly.

For many elderly people the depression was in fact a nightmare. Many who wanted to continue working could not compete with younger workers. Unemployment among those over the age of sixty climbed to 40 percent. Many who had expected to retire on savings found themselves destitute when the banks failed. Others saw their incomes shrivel as the stock market fell and as private pension plans—often poorly conceived and badly financed—collapsed. Of the 7.5 million Americans over the age of sixty-five, fully half could not support themselves. Some were forced to seek assistance from their children who, given the difficult times that everyone faced, were already experiencing hardship. Others had to apply for public charity at the cost of sacrificing their self-respect. Only twenty-eight states provided old-age pensions. For the most part they were sadly inadequate, with monthly payments ranging from $7 to $30. In twenty states no pensions of any kind existed.

All these problems were greatly magnified in California, which, as a haven for retirees, had seen its aged population climb from 200,000 to 366,000 during the 1920s. Five times as many people over the age of sixty-five lived in California as in any other state except Washington. Large numbers of retired men and women, separated from their relatives by hundreds or thousands of miles, had no one to fall back on when the depression hit. California's old-age pension plan was defective by every standard. No elderly person with a legally responsible relative able to provide support could receive aid. To qualify for assistance, an elderly person had to go on the relief rolls, sign a pauper's oath, submit to a "needs" test, and accept a lien on any property so that the state could recover part of the cost of the pension upon the person's death. Then, and only then, were the aged eligible for a sum of $22 a month. The system could hardly have been better calculated to deprive the aged of their dignity.

These conditions help explain the overwhelming response to the Townsend plan. Townsend, who had worked as a ranch hand and traveling salesman before becoming a doctor, had gone to Long Beach after the world war. In 1933, at the age of sixty-six, he presented his "Cure for Depressions." Everyone in the country over the age of sixty would receive $200 a month, on two conditions: that they spend the full amount each month and retire if still employed. This would pump money into the economy, open jobs for younger people, and permit a dignified retirement. The plan would be financed by a national sales tax, later called a transactions tax. Asked why he chose the figure of $200, Townsend explained, "The main reason was so that nobody would come along and offer more." In collaboration with Robert Earl Clements, Townsend set up Old Age Revolving Pensions Ltd. in January 1934. Within two years 7,000 Townsend clubs with about 1.5 million members had sprung up across the country.

The Townsend plan offered a married couple over sixty years of age $4,800 a year, at a time when 87 percent of all American families had annual incomes below $2,500. Yet the plan won support from many who believed in the values of thrift, hard work, and individualism precisely because the plan did not seem at all radical. For example, it did not call for deficit spending. The government would collect in sales taxes what it disbursed, and those taxes would not be levied on the rich but on all consumers. The plan required no bureaucracy other than the Treasury Department to make out the checks and the post office to deliver them. The plan in no way compromised private property rights. Nor did it imply a dole. Rather, Townsend viewed the elderly as "Distributor Custodians," entrusted by society to spend $200 a month wisely. Critics, however, doubted the plan's feasibility, pointing out that it would cost $20 to $24 billion a year (or nearly half the total national income), that it would injure the poor through a regressive sales tax, and that it would require a far-flung bureaucracy to see that recipients spent their allotments.

The Townsend movement nevertheless crystallized popular sentiment for old-age pensions and helped move Congress and the administration to support the Social Security Act of 1935. Townsend condemned that measure because it excluded too many people from coverage and provided inadequate benefits. But, limited as it was, the act eroded Townsend's basis of support. His own plan lost on a voice vote in the House of Representatives. New Dealers responded to Townsend's challenge by attempting to discredit his movement. In the spring of 1936 a Senate committee began investigating the clubs in an effort to prove them a financial fraud. The investigators found that Clements had profited handsomely and that Townsend not only exercised absolute control over the clubs, but privately referred to the members as "old fossils." (When Townsend refused to testify, he was cited for contempt and sentenced to a year in jail; Roosevelt later commuted the sentence because of Townsend's age.) By the summer of 1936 Townsend's estrangement from the New Deal was complete. Certain that "we shall be able to lick the stuffing" out of both major political parties, Townsend prepared to join forces with other foes of the administration.

## "SHARE OUR WEALTH"

In 1933 Sinclair Lewis published a novel titled *It Can't Happen Here*, in which a senator named Buzz Windrip established a fascist regime in the United States. One character described

American politician Huey Pierce Long, c. 1932. *(Hulton Archive/Getty Images)*

Windrip as "a dictator seemingly so different from the fervent Hitler and the gesticulating Fascists . . . a dictator with something of the earthy American sense of humor of a Mark Twain." None doubted that this figure was patterned after Senator Huey Long of Louisiana or that Lewis was asserting that it could indeed happen here. In the highly charged political atmosphere of the 1930s, perhaps no one aroused more intense feelings of love and hatred than did the Louisianan. To his supporters, Long had "changed Louisiana from a hellhole to a paradise. He was emancipator. He brought light." To his critics, Long was an unprincipled demagogue. In the summer of 1932 Franklin Roosevelt privately termed him one of the most dangerous men in America.

Born in 1893, Long as a boy had done odd jobs—driving a bakery wagon, carrying water to construction crews, learning to set type—primarily, it seems, to avoid the drudgery of working on his father's farm. He spent his teens as a traveling salesman and gambler, then borrowed money to attend Tulane Law School, where he crammed a three-year program into eight months and arranged to take a special bar examination. At age twenty-four Long was elected to the Louisiana Public Service Commission and over the next several years gained a reputation for his attacks on the oil and railroad companies that dominated state politics. Although Long cultivated a comical public image, adopting the name "Kingfish" and dubbing his opponents "Turkeyhead" or "Old Trashy Mouth," he was a keenly intelligent man and an astute politician.

In 1928 Long became governor, and even after his election to the Senate two years later he continued to rule Louisiana very much as he pleased. He dominated the legislature, curbed the press, and built a disciplined political machine. When people protested that he was violating the state constitution, Long replied, "I'm the Constitution around here now." Yet for every person who resented Long's dictatorial manner, there were many others who benefited from his reign. He improved the public schools, provided free textbooks, and initiated evening classes for adults; he built new roads, bridges, and highways; he eliminated the poll tax and property taxes on the poor. These reforms broke down the isolation of the rural poor, provided voters with tangible evidence of his accomplishments, and created jobs for political supporters. Unlike most other southern politicians, Long did not appeal to white supremacist sentiment. Once he harshly denounced the leader of the Ku Klux Klan: "When I call him a son of a bitch I am not using profanity, but am referring to the circumstances of his birth."

His advocacy of the "Share Our Wealth" program made Long a figure of national prominence in the 1930s. The government, he insisted, must "limit the size of the big men's fortune and guarantee some minimum to the fortune and comfort of the little man's family." To accomplish this, he proposed limiting individual wealth to $3 to $4 million, providing all citizens with a $5,000 homestead and a guaranteed annual income of $2,500, offering free education through the college level to all whose "mental ability and energy" qualified them, establishing a thirty-hour workweek, and financing generous old-age pensions through taxes on the rich. While this plan would not mean absolute equality, it would remove the most glaring inequalities. "So America would start again with millionaires, but with no multimillionaires or billionaires; we would start with some poor, but they wouldn't be so poor that they wouldn't have the comforts of life." In February 1934, Share Our Wealth clubs began forming; soon there were 27,000 claiming 4.7 million members. The movement's strength centered in Louisiana, Arkansas, and Mississippi.

The Share Our Wealth program went considerably beyond the Townsend plan. Long proposed a more sweeping change in economic relationships and assigned a more prominent role to the federal government than did Townsend. The Louisianan frankly advocated confiscating wealth in order to redistribute income. But in some respects the two resembled each other. Both Long and Townsend were charismatic leaders, both organized clubs that offered members a gratifying sense of personal involvement, and both promised a quick, certain path to good times. In addition, both appealed to those whom the New Deal had helped rather little. Long, who at first supported Roosevelt, broke with him decisively in 1935 on the grounds that the administration was proceeding too cautiously.

Roosevelt considered Long a veritable Pied Piper, leading people astray with spurious and impractical proposals. Nevertheless, in June 1935, the president moved somewhat closer to Long's position by asking Congress to impose high taxes on inherited wealth, corporate profits, and "very great individual incomes." When the president's message was read, Long declared, "I just wish to say 'Amen.'" Roosevelt's recommendations brought anguished cries from the business community, and by the time Congress finished watering it down, the Wealth Tax Act (1935) barely resembled Roosevelt's original proposal, much less Long's. Even as he borrowed a plank from the Share Our Wealth platform, the president attacked Long by denying him federal patronage, by encouraging the Treasury Department to investigate alleged financial wrongdoing in Louisiana, and by permitting his aides to speak their minds. "The

Senator from Louisiana has halitosis of the intellect," said Secretary of the Interior Harold Ickes; "that's presuming Emperor Long has an intellect."

None of this proved very effective. Then, in September 1935, a young doctor, Carl Austin Weiss, assassinated Long and was himself immediately killed by the senator's bodyguards. With its leader gone, the Share Our Wealth movement came under the control of Gerald L.K. Smith, a minister originally hired to organize the clubs. Smith, who had idolized Long (even wearing suits of clothes his mentor had discarded), appealed to similar hopes and exploited similar grievances. Smith cried, "Let's pull down these huge piles of gold until there shall be a real job, not a little old sow-belly, black-eyed pea job, but a real spending-money, beefsteak and gravy, Chevrolet, Ford in the garage, new suit, Thomas Jefferson, Jesus Christ, red, white, and blue job for every man!" By 1936 Smith, like Townsend, was prepared for a head-on clash with the administration. It came with the blessing of the "radio priest," Father Charles E. Coughlin.

## THE RADIO PRIEST AND HIS FLOCK

Father Coughlin had been assigned to the parish of Royal Oak, Michigan, in 1926. There he conducted a Sunday-morning radio program, *The Golden Hour of the Little Flower*, which at first consisted of inspirational readings and devotional messages. But in the early 1930s, with the depression worsening, Coughlin turned to economic and social issues. As he did, his audience grew rapidly. Each week more than 10 million listeners tuned in Coughlin's sermons. After every broadcast he received hundreds of thousands of letters and thousands of dollars in contributions. Coughlin enjoyed unusual latitude in his remarks because he had organized his own radio network after a Columbia Broadcasting System attempt to censor him in 1931 and because he had the solid support of his superior, Bishop Michael James Gallagher of Detroit.

Coughlin's position in the Catholic Church went far toward explaining his popularity, but he also set forth economic proposals that, if sometimes vague, proved highly attractive. He wanted to reform the monetary system by increasing the amount of currency in circulation, remonetizing silver, eliminating the Federal Reserve Banks, and replacing interest-bearing government notes with non–interest-bearing ones. He also favored nationalizing "those public necessities which by their very nature are too important to be held in the control of private individuals," providing a "just and living annual wage" for all workers, and imposing heavy taxes on the wealthy. "Modern capitalism as we know it is not worth saving," Coughlin said, but capitalism with its abuses eliminated would be very much worth saving.

In 1933 Coughlin, then a staunch Roosevelt supporter, asserted that "the New Deal is Christ's deal." Yet during the next two years he became disillusioned with the president. Coughlin particularly resented Roosevelt's failure to accept monetary management as the key to recovery, his advocacy of U.S. membership in the World Court, and his opposition to refinancing farm mortgages by issuing millions of dollars in greenbacks. Late in 1934, following the example set by Long and Townsend, Coughlin created the National Union for Social Justice to lobby for his economic program. By mid-1936, having concluded somewhat inconsistently that the New Deal both "protects plutocrats and comforts Communists," Coughlin announced the formation of the Union Party. It quickly gained the support of Townsend and Smith. Coughlin expected the party's nominee—William Lemke of North Dakota—to receive 9 million votes, enough to throw the presidential election into the House of Representatives.

Father Charles Coughlin, advocate of social justice, making an impassioned speech, 1938.
*(Time & Life Pictures/Getty Images)*

During the campaign Coughlin accused "Franklin double-crossing Roosevelt" of "flirting with Communistic tendencies" and predicted that Roosevelt's reelection would mean "more bullet holes in the White House than you could count with an adding machine." This rhetoric, however, failed to save the Union Party from a humiliating defeat. It received 892,000 votes, fewer than 2 percent of the total. In part this showing resulted from the party's inability to get on the ballot in several important states or to run a full slate of candidates for local office. In addition, Lemke proved a singularly uninspiring figure. Nor could Coughlin, Smith, and Townsend agree on policy and procedure. Expediency had made them allies, but a good deal of rivalry and suspicion remained. Millions of people who were attracted to economic panaceas would not back a hopeless third-party venture. The kind of support Coughlin and the others enjoyed could not be translated into votes on Election Day.

Dismayed by the outcome, Coughlin canceled future radio broadcasts, but his retirement proved brief. By 1938 he was back on the air with sermons that had taken on a distinctly new tone. Coughlin had employed nativist themes in the past, but never so prominently. He insisted that a conspiracy of international Jewish bankers threatened America. His magazine, *Social Justice*, carried the *Protocols of Zion* (a forgery depicting an alleged Jewish conspiracy to take over the world), termed Hitler's Germany "an innocent victim of a sacred war declared against her nine years ago by the Jews," and honored Benito Mussolini as "Man of the Week." In July 1938 Coughlin founded the Christian Front to combat communists and Jews. It prepared a Christian Index listing merchants who had pledged to patronize and employ other Christians as a means of curbing Jewish economic power. Coughlin, who had formerly denounced the anti-Catholic nativism of the Ku Klux Klan, ended by stirring up a vicious anti-Semitism.

## THE POPULAR FRONT

During the 1930s the American Communist Party gained a fairly wide influence, certainly wider than its membership (which hovered around 50,000) or its voting strength (which fell from 103,000 in the 1932 presidential election to 80,000 in 1936) would indicate. Party members controlled several large Congress of Industrial Organizations unions, including the United Electrical Workers and the Mine, Mill, and Smelter Workers; held responsible positions in the National Labor Relations Board and other government agencies; and gained a firm footing in the American Labor Party in New York State, as well as in other political organizations. Communist doctrines won a large audience among intellectuals. In 1932, for example, fifty-three prominent writers and artists—including Sherwood Anderson, Erskine Caldwell, John Dos Passos, Sidney Hook, Lincoln Steffens, and Edmund Wilson—endorsed the party's candidates, William Z. Foster and James Ford, explaining, "As responsible intellectual workers we have aligned ourselves with the frankly revolutionary Communist Party, the party of the workers."

Nevertheless, the 1930s hardly deserve to be called "the Red decade." The great majority of Americans remained hostile to communism, and most who joined the movement did so only briefly. The party consisted of a small cadre that remained steadfastly loyal and others who entered and left as through a revolving door. Surely one reason for this was the party's subservience to the Soviet Union. American Communist Party leaders consistently followed policies that conformed to Russian interests, not because they were hired Russian agents but because they believed that the needs of workers in America were identical with those of workers in the Soviet Union. They equated virtue with the Russian system and either rejected or discounted evidence of Stalinist terrorism. With every shift in party doctrine, those who could not adjust departed.

In the early 1930s, seeing themselves as revolutionaries, communists in the United States repudiated halfway measures and called for a dictatorship of the proletariat. They branded Franklin Roosevelt "an abject tool of Wall Street" and condemned the New Deal for striving "to hold the workers in industrial slavery." But in the summer of 1935, the party dramatically modified its approach. By then Stalin had identified Nazi Germany as the greatest potential danger. Accordingly, he urged communists to join liberals and socialists in an antifascist popular front. Communists in the United States worked diligently to soften their image. Their leader, Earl Browder, announced, "Communism is 20th-century Americanism." The party's view of the New Deal underwent a similar transformation. Communists praised Roosevelt as a Progressive and backed almost every one of his proposals.

These popular front tactics exacerbated divisions within the Socialist Party. In 1935 Browder invited socialist leader Norman Thomas to a debate in Madison Square Garden, with the proceeds going to the socialists. When Thomas accepted, old-guard socialists unjustifiably feared that he was ready to collaborate with the communists. By 1936 thousands had deserted the Socialist Party, whose membership dropped below 20,000. Thomas rejected other such overtures and, unlike Browder, kept up a steady attack on the New Deal. Roosevelt, he said, was trying to "cure tuberculosis with cough drops."

To those who urged him to support Roosevelt in the 1936 presidential election, Thomas replied, "The way to get Socialism is to proclaim the Socialist message, not to declare a moratorium on it during an election campaign." But his vote—which fell from 903,000 in 1932 to 187,000 in 1936—indicated that the New Deal had neutralized the Socialist Party's appeal. Thomas confessed as much. "Roosevelt did not carry out the Socialist platform," he declared, "unless he carried it out on a stretcher."

Before the signing of the Nazi-Soviet pact, Roosevelt did not consider domestic communism a major threat. Germany reached that agreement with Russia on August 23, 1939, and went to war with Great Britain and France in September. While the pact remained in force—until June 1941, when Hitler invaded the Soviet Union—communists in the United States completely reversed themselves, scrapping the idea of an antifascist popular front. They opposed American aid to the Allies, claiming that Great Britain and France were imperialist nations. They similarly opposed the buildup of defense industries, on occasion calling strikes to disrupt work in aircraft plants. Communists reverted to denouncing Roosevelt as "the leader and organizer of all reactionary forces in the country." The Communist Party paid a heavy price for this turnabout. Thousands of members, attracted by the popular front ideology, deserted the party in disillusionment. Many liberals who had cooperated with communists considered the party's justification of the Nazi-Soviet pact a symptom of its moral bankruptcy. Finally, the party's stance contributed to a Red Scare that swept the country after 1939.

## BLACK AMERICANS AND THE NEW DEAL

"People is hollerin' 'bout hard times, tell me what it all about," wailed a 1937 blues recording; "hard times don't worry me, I was broke when it first started out." In singing the blues, surely, people were laughing to keep from crying. The depression had a devastating impact on African-Americans, even on those who had never shared in the prosperity of the 1920s. Southern black farmers in the early 1930s scraped by on $300 a year. Of those employed in agriculture, four of every five did not own their land but worked as sharecroppers, tenant farmers, or wage hands. Lacking any security, they often lost their homes as hard times settled over the countryside. In the cities conditions were worse. The unemployment rate for blacks was from 30 percent to 60 percent higher than for whites, in part because of bias in hiring, but also because the jobs blacks had held in service occupations were often eliminated. Industries employing large numbers of blacks—such as building construction and bituminous coal—came to a virtual standstill. Desperate whites sometimes resorted to violence to displace blacks. On the Illinois Central Railroad, white firemen terrorized blacks, killing ten of them, to get their jobs. Whites also began taking jobs that blacks had formerly held as elevator operators, hospital attendants, cooks, waiters, bellhops, maids, and chauffeurs.

To people surviving at a subsistence level, the Roosevelt administration offered a ray of hope, primarily in the form of federal relief. Before 1933, localities administering relief often rejected black applicants; but the New Deal reversed this pattern. In 1935 nearly 30 percent of all black families were receiving some form of aid, and in certain cities the figure approached 50 percent. Proportionately, three times as many blacks as whites were on relief. New Deal programs sought to ensure fair treatment. The Works Progress Administration (WPA) enabled hundreds of thousands of African-Americans to weather the depression. Blacks accounted for more than two-thirds of the workers on its rolls in Norfolk, Virginia, where blacks made up less than one-third of the population. The Public Works Administration took a pioneering step by introducing nondiscrimination clauses, under which a contractor had to pay black workers a fixed proportion of the company payroll, based on the number of blacks in the labor force. Although other New Deal agencies often discriminated, on balance blacks received a share of federal assistance in proportion to their numbers, if not their need.

If the Roosevelt administration came to the rescue of jobless blacks, it proved less responsive to demands for legal equality and social justice. Little in Roosevelt's background suggested any such concern. He had served under the segregationist Wilson administration in the archsegregationist Navy Department; he made his second home in Warm Springs, Georgia, and apparently never questioned local mores; he accepted John Nance "Cactus Jack" Garner, a conservative Texan, as his running mate in 1932 and 1936. As president, Roosevelt maintained that economic recovery, not civil rights, would most effectively aid the largest number of blacks. He believed that New Deal legislation would be lost without the support of southern Democrats, who headed important congressional committees, and he recognized that the issue of civil rights for African-Americans was potentially a source of great friction within his party. Committed to a gradualist approach, Roosevelt reasoned that only education would finally eradicate racial prejudice. "We must do this thing stride by stride," he said.

Roosevelt took few such strides, however, during his first and second terms of office. Despite the angry protests of civil rights groups, New Deal programs in the South followed Jim Crow lines. The Tennessee Valley Authority segregated its work crews, hired only unskilled black laborers, and set up a model village that barred blacks. The Civilian Conservation Corps maintained segregated work camps. The National Recovery Administration, which in theory prohibited wage differentials based on race, in practice left loopholes whereby blacks could be paid less. The Agricultural Adjustment Administration's acreage reduction program led to the eviction of thousands of black tenant farmers. The Justice Department refused to prosecute lynchers under a federal kidnapping statute on the grounds that the victims were not taken across state lines for financial gain. Roosevelt branded lynching a "vile form of collective murder," but refused to support an antilynching bill that provided for a federal trial if states failed to prosecute, specified prison terms for members of lynch mobs, and made counties responsible for damages. In 1937, after a mob in Mississippi had set two blacks afire with a blowtorch, the House passed the measure. It was filibustered to death in the Senate in 1938 without protest from the administration.

Given this record, the president won a truly astonishing amount of support from African-Americans. In 1932 nearly three-fourths of them voted Republican; in 1936, more than three-fourths voted Democratic, and the percentage increased in the years that followed. New Deal

Mary McLeod Bethune. *(Library of Congress)*

relief programs—which primarily aided northern and urban blacks, who could vote, rather than southern and rural blacks, who could not—partially, but not fully, explain this shift. Certainly the president benefited when compared with his predecessor, Herbert Hoover, who, unlike Roosevelt, never even verbally condemned lynching. In addition, Roosevelt offered important government positions to such prominent blacks as Mary McLeod Bethune and Robert C. Weaver. Eleanor Roosevelt and other New Dealers spoke up forcibly on the subject of racial injustice. Partly because of his wife's prestige in the black community, Franklin Roosevelt received credit for the New Deal's achievements while escaping blame for its shortcomings.

Developments during the 1930s subjected the National Association for the Advancement of Colored People (NAACP), and the civil rights strategy it advocated, to a severe challenge. The NAACP had assumed that civil rights could be secured by lobbying in Congress and by arguing before the courts. Two events during the 1930s, however, weakened confidence in the possibility of ending Jim Crow through political and constitutional means. The first was the

# HALLIE FLANAGAN
## AND THE FEDERAL THEATER PROJECT

Hallie Flanagan, director of the WPA Federal Theater Project. *(Library of Congress)*

In 1935, as part of its expanded relief program, the Roosevelt administration initiated various projects to aid unemployed writers, artists, and actors. To head the Federal Theater Project, Harry Hopkins selected Hallie Flanagan, whom he had first met while both were undergraduates at Grinnell College in Iowa. She eventually became director of experimental theater at Vassar College, where she supervised some of the more imaginative productions of the early 1930s.

Under her guidance, the Federal Theater Project employed an average of 10,000 people a year for four years. Many of its plays had a frank social message. The "living newspaper" format, which vividly documented current issues, was well suited for this purpose. *Triple A Plowed Under* (1936) called for a New Deal for farmers, *Power* (1937) advocated a greater measure of consumer control over public utilities, and *One Third of a Nation* (1938) exposed the poverty and filth of big-city slums. Some productions met with huge popular and critical acclaim. A dramatization of Sinclair Lewis's *It Can't Happen Here* played to 275,000 people in four months; it grossed $80,000, even though the average ticket was priced at thirty cents. The Federal Theater provided new opportunities for black performers, who staged a jazz version of *The Mikado* and, under Orson Welles's direction, a version of *Macbeth* set in Haiti during the Napoleonic era.

Throughout its career the Federal Theater faced difficult problems. One concerned the competing demands of relief and art. Some unemployed people who clearly deserved assistance claimed to be "actors" even though they had little talent, and Flanagan sometimes felt obliged to give them jobs. In addition, disputes arose over the nature of the productions. There was built-in tension between the desire to appeal to a mass audience (particularly since public response was a means of justifying further appropriations) and the desire to stage avant-garde works that appealed to the actors' and directors' own aesthetic sensibilities.

There was yet another hard question: as a government agency, funded by the taxpayers,

The WPA Federal Theater Project production of *It Can't Happen Here*, New York, 1935. *(Franklin D. Roosevelt Presidential Library and Museum, Hyde Park, New York)*

how far could the Federal Theater legitimately go in advocating controversial views? Some critics denounced it for becoming a "veritable hotbed of un-American activities," and others alleged that its performances were obscene. Hostile congressmen snickered at such titles as *The Bishop Misbehaves* and *Old Captain Romeo's Four Wives*. Of *A New Kind of Love,* one Republican remarked, "I wonder what that can be. It smacks of the Soviets." In 1939, Congress killed the Federal Theater Project. Hallie Flanagan left to become a dean at Smith College.

The federal government did not again undertake a large-scale program of support for the performing arts until 1965, when Congress created the National Endowment for the Arts (NEA). Although it funded many popular programs, the NEA eventually ran into problems not unlike those encountered by the Federal Theater. By the 1990s, conservative congressmen assailed the NEA for funding exhibits by such artists as Andres Serrano and Robert Mapplethorpe, whose work, critics claimed, was "sickeningly violent, sexually explicit, homoerotic, antireligious and nihilistic." The beleaguered agency sought to appease outraged conservatives without alienating the artists, writers, and photographers it was supposed to encourage. In 1996 Congress cut its funding nearly in half, forcing the agency to scale down its activities.

## Web Links

**http://memory.loc.gov/ammem/fedtp/ftbrwn00.html**
An essay by Lorraine Brown, with links to articles and scripts.

**http://memory.loc.gov/ammem/fedtp/fthome.html**
Nearly 1,000 slides of posters, sets, and costume designs.

failure of the antilynching bill, which the NAACP had helped draft and to which it devoted a considerable portion of its time, money, and energy from 1935 to 1940. A second event that eroded the gradualist approach was the Supreme Court's decision in *Grovey v. Townsend* (1935). The Court held that the Democratic Party in Texas—and by extension elsewhere in the South—could exclude blacks from membership and thereby bar them from participating in primaries. The white primary did not violate the Fourteenth Amendment, the Court ruled, since the Democratic Party was a voluntary political association whose actions did not involve discrimination by a state. The decision effectively disfranchised blacks since in one-party areas the only meaningful contests occurred in primaries. The closed primary was an even more effective deterrent to voting than the poll tax or the literacy test.

The NAACP above all prized the goal of integration, yet during the 1930s this too came under fire. Led by W.E.B. DuBois, a number of black intellectuals advocated what one termed "the conscious development of nationalistic sentiment." DuBois, whose stand led to his resignation from the NAACP, continued to oppose forced segregation but saw distinct advantages in voluntary segregation. He asserted, "It is the race-conscious black man cooperating together in his own institutions and movements who will eventually emancipate the colored race." In his autobiography, *Dusk of Dawn* (1940), DuBois described his disenchantment with the view that education would wipe out prejudice. Convinced that racism was rooted in the subconscious and reinforced by economic self-interest, DuBois thought it pointless for a black minority to plead for justice from a white majority. Instead, blacks should set up their own institutions—schools, churches, hospitals, theaters—and a largely autonomous economy founded on socialist principles. DuBois's doctrine, although in some respects reminiscent of Marcus Garvey's, appealed to intellectuals rather than the masses, did not contemplate a return to Africa, and combined economic radicalism with racial nationalism.

DuBois's vision of a cooperative commonwealth never approached realization, as indeed it could not, given the lack of economic resources in the black community. The nearest any sizable group of blacks came to attaining perfect security was in the religious "heavens" of George Baker, who went by the name of Father Divine. In 1933 Divine, a preacher in Brooklyn and Long Island for more than a decade, moved to Harlem, where he attracted a huge following. Divine opened heavens—dormitory-like arrangements where his disciples lived and received adequate food and clothing as long as they worshiped their benefactor (and promised to abstain from sexual relations). His followers believed that Divine was God and that he and they were immortal. Those who died or became seriously ill were said to have stopped believing. Divine, the vast majority of whose followers were black but who also appealed to some whites, created a world in which racial conflict, indeed racial differentiation, no longer existed. He referred only to "people of the darker complexion" and "people of the lighter complexion." The names his disciples adopted similarly revealed their search for order and harmony: "Quiet Dove," "Perfect Love," "Sweet Music," and "Keep on Smiling." For thousands of blacks beset by racial, economic, or family troubles, Divine provided a way out, and many remained steadfast in their faith until his death in 1965. During the depression years, when millions followed political messiahs, it was hardly surprising that some turned to a man who claimed he was the True Messiah.

## WOMEN AND FAMILIES FACE THE DEPRESSION

"Where the folkways and old patterns of conduct are continued—that it is a man's job to support his family—husbands have been nagged and harassed to desperation," a welfare agency officer reported in 1931. "The degradation, the sheer fear and panic . . . have eaten into men's souls." "I did what I had to do," a housewife recalled of the depression years. "I think hard times is harder on a man." "I was going with someone when the depression hit," an unmarried woman remembered. "Suddenly he was laid off. It hit him like a ton of bricks and he just disappeared." "I feel like I was falling down a long dark shaft that has no end," a teenager told his caseworker. "It is both economically unfair and socially unjust to expect me to continue to support my family."

The depression's impact on family life became a subject of widespread concern. Familiar patterns of courtship and marriage seemed to fall apart. The marriage rate fell in 1929 and did not start to rise until 1934. Often marriages were postponed until hard times had passed or simply never occurred. The divorce rate declined as income fell, but desertion increased. "Mr. Raparka asked [his wife] for money to go to New York in search of a job," sociologist Wight Bakke reported in *Citizens Without Work.* "He has not been heard of since." The birthrate, which had been dropping throughout the 1920s, plunged even further. It fell from 21.3 births per thousand persons in 1930 to 18.4 in 1933. Contraception became more popular, birth control clinics multiplied, and in 1936 a federal court decision made it legal for doctors to distribute contraceptive information and devices, except where prohibited by state law. The demands of the Great Depression appeared to have succeeded where birth control reformers had not.

Case studies revealed that new patterns of domestic life developed within families that had suddenly slipped downward in economic status. In some cases, where relationships had always been stable, families drew into themselves, curtailing outside activities. "Family members have to do things with and for each other," Eleanor Roosevelt wrote in 1933, "and the result is that the clan spirit grows." In other cases, clan spirit disintegrated. When unemployment struck, disconcerting authority shifts often occurred at home. Depression affected male heads of household who lost their jobs. "Working around the house was not all profit to the unemployed man," sociologist Eli Ginzburg reported. "By taking on feminine duties he widened the breach between the old life and the new. His failure was underlined by the transgression of sex boundaries." In study after study, case analysts described the transformation of former "breadwinners" from family head into "just another member of the family." Women seemed less affected when family income dropped, since they retained much the same roles they had held before the Great Depression struck.

In *Middletown* (Muncie, Indiana), sociologists Helen and Robert Lynd reported, unemployed men hung about the street, lost their sense of time, and dawdled helplessly. At home, however, "the women's world remained largely intact and the round of cooking, housecleaning, and mending became if anything more absorbing." Domestic routines took on new significance, especially when family survival depended on housewives' frugality. "Making Do" became an important 1930s adage. Women traded depression recipes, restyled old clothes, took in boarders, ran kitchen beauty parlors, and started other household businesses. Older children sometimes contributed to family income if they could find jobs. But wives were most likely to become the family's major new wage earners.

Women's entry into the depression labor force was hardly popular. Once jobs became scarce, Americans voiced opposition to wives who worked outside the home—and implicitly deprived a male family head of income. Congress prohibited more than one family member from taking a federal service job. State and local governments rejected married women who applied for government posts. In 1931, three out of four school boards refused to hire wives as teachers and many dismissed women teachers who married. The American Federation of Labor urged employers not to hire women who had working husbands. Public opinion surveys, such as the new Gallup poll, echoed such injunctions; respondents declared that wives of employed men should remain at home.

But despite continued pressure against married wage earners, women were less likely to be unemployed than men and were more likely to take jobs for the first time. In the 1930s, the number of workingwomen rose 25 percent, and the majority of new workers were married women, precisely those who were urged to remain at home. One reason for this unexpected development was that opportunities for female employment did not contract as much as those for men. The depression's worst impact was on heavy industry—autos, steel, and mining— where few women were employed. The sectors that employed many women, however, such as sales, service, and clerical work, were less affected and tended to recover more quickly. Most important, men did not seek jobs in what were considered women's fields. The sexual division of labor that usually handicapped women on the labor market suddenly offered a new measure of protection.

Such protection did not extend to black women workers, whose unemployment rates were higher than those of any other group; it did not affect applicants for federal work relief, where male heads of household were favored; and it rarely helped professional women, whose aspirations were now limited. Career ambitions faded, and so did feminist demands for equal rights and equal opportunity. Still, women's employment record reversed the expectations of depression-era Americans. Denunciations of the working wife were counteracted by both family need and, in some cases, new advantages on the employment market. As a result, in the 1930s, women entered the labor force at twice the rate of men.

Women also played new roles in social welfare and political life. During the depression, new welfare agencies opened up at all levels of government and social workers were suddenly in demand. Several women with expertise in social welfare assumed high-level federal government posts. The leading example was Labor Secretary Frances Perkins, the first woman cabinet member, who had a long career in social welfare. Since the Progressive Era, Perkins had worked in settlement houses and for the New York Consumer's League. In 1928, she had been appointed state industrial commissioner by Franklin Roosevelt. As a cabinet member, she did not expect "to gain anything materially," Eleanor Roosevelt explained in 1933, but "to render a public service to . . . the workingmen and women in their families."

Similar experience in social welfare was evident in the careers of almost all the New Deal's high-level women appointees, such as Florence Allen, the first woman appointed to the federal court of appeals; Ellen Woodward, who headed women's work relief projects under the Civil Works Administration; Mary Anderson, head of the federal Women's Bureau; and Mary W. Dewson, head of the Women's Division of the Democratic National Committee and later a member of the Social Security Board. Like Frances Perkins, these new officeholders considered themselves social reformers more than feminists. Eleanor Roosevelt, who campaigned for women's appointments, promoted their careers. "The steady increase of women's influence," she wrote to a friend, "tends to ameliorate bad social conditions." Such influence waned after 1936, when New Deal receptivity to reform dwindled. But the Roosevelt administration had given women more high-level government jobs than had any previous administration. It also propelled into view the most politically sophisticated woman reformer ever to reside in the White House.

During the 1930s, Eleanor Roosevelt capitalized on a decade of experience in Democratic Party campaigns, the League of Women Voters, and other women's organizations, such as the Women's Trade Union League. Increasingly influential in New Deal politics, she became a model of activism. In 1933, she began holding her innovative weekly White House press conferences, limited to women reporters. She also defended the interests of unemployed women, supported the establishment of summer work-relief camps for women, campaigned for the end of Washington's alley slums, worked on the federal homestead program, and aided thousands of correspondents who wrote to her in an unprecedented volume of mail. This pace of activity only increased. As political strategist and presidential adviser, Eleanor Roosevelt helped organize the 1936 campaign, served as a spokeswoman for the disadvantaged, and emerged as a forthright liberal, often taking stands to the left of her husband. By defending black pressure groups, pacifists, and the National Youth Congress, she created her own constituency and simultaneously relieved President Roosevelt of some pressure from the left. Finally, whether visiting coalmines, testifying to Congress about migrant labor, or campaigning against racial discrimination, she was constantly in public view. By the end of the 1930s, through her press conferences, radio talks, and popular syndicated newspaper column, "My Day," Eleanor Roosevelt had become one of the most prominent figures in public life. Although her role was controversial, her causes were ceaselessly publicized by women reporters, who commended her "instinct for civic and social reform" and credited her with "humanizing the New Deal."

## THE CONSERVATIVE RESPONSE

There were, of course, many Americans who did not sympathize with the New Deal and who were distinctly unimpressed by either Franklin or Eleanor Roosevelt. The business community constituted one important source of opposition, although sentiment in the business community was never monolithic. Several industrialists endorsed Roosevelt's policies, but organizations such as the National Association of Manufacturers and the Chamber of Commerce consistently fought the New Deal, particularly after 1935. By then, speakers at the association's meetings were talking about the need to rid Washington of "economic crackpots, social reformers, labor demagogues and political racketeers." These critics charged that deficit spending undermined the nation's credit, that the tax on undistributed corporate profits curbed initiative, that the growth of executive power endangered individual liberties, and that the Wagner Act weighted the scales too heavily on labor's side. Roosevelt stirred up class antagonism, business executives complained, by his unfair references to "economic royalists" who sought control of the government for selfish purposes.

The president believed that business critics failed to perceive the true intent, and effect, of his policies. He compared himself to one who jumped off a pier to save a rich gentleman from drowning; at first the gentleman was grateful, but he later complained bitterly that his silk hat was lost. Whether or not the New Deal rescued the capitalist system, it certainly enabled business to make higher profits than it had under Hoover. Despite all the fuss about fiscal irresponsibility, Roosevelt reluctantly turned to deficit spending as a last resort when nothing else seemed to work. Nor did the New Deal redistribute wealth. The share of disposable income held by the rich did not change significantly from 1933 to 1939. Taxes, while higher than in the past, were hardly crushing. Late in the decade they ranged from 4 percent on incomes of $10,000 to 32 percent on incomes of $100,000. "It is the same old story of the failure of those who have property to realize that I am the best friend the profit system ever had, even though I add my denunciation of unconscionable profits," Roosevelt wrote.

In 1934 conservatives created the American Liberty League to mobilize public sentiment against the New Deal. Over the next two years the league enrolled 125,000 members, spent $1 million, and distributed 5 million pieces of literature. In order to appear nonpartisan, it recruited several prominent Democrats. The American Liberty League formulated an essentially conservative indictment of the New Deal. It denounced Roosevelt as a dictator, although it had difficulty deciding whether he more nearly resembled a communist or a fascist. The league held that the welfare state aided the improvident and unfit at the expense of the hardworking and virtuous and was therefore immoral. It exploited popular reverence for the Constitution and the Supreme Court. Roosevelt's sweeping triumph in the 1936 election, however, discredited the league, which had found itself in the position of insisting that the people break sharply with the practices of the past four years and dismantle the welfare state. Roosevelt, by contrast, could promise continuity and stability. Only the initiatives he took in 1937, especially his plan to enlarge the Supreme Court, gave conservatives another chance.

## "COURT PACKING"

At the time of his second inauguration, Franklin Roosevelt seemed to stand at the pinnacle of his political career. Yet his second term witnessed a sharp decline in New Deal fortunes. In some ways, the very size of his congressional majorities—the House contained 331 Democrats and 90 Republicans, the Senate 76 Democrats and 16 Republicans—encouraged factionalism and discord. Also, relatively large numbers of Democrats were elected in 1936 from safe districts (that is, by a margin of more than 5 percent) and were therefore less responsive to the wishes of party leaders. But Roosevelt's problem stemmed less from the composition of Congress than from what he wanted it to do. This became apparent in February 1937, when he unveiled his plan to reform the Supreme Court. Asserting that the Court carried too heavy a workload, the president proposed to add an additional justice for each one who did not retire at the age of seventy. A maximum of six new positions could be created, and the Court would revert to a smaller size upon the death or retirement of an elderly member.

The president took this stand chiefly because the Court had struck down crucial reform legislation. It had ruled against the National Recovery Administration and the Agricultural Adjustment Administration, and in June 1936, by a narrow 5-to-4 margin, it agreed that a New York minimum-wage law violated the due process clause of the Fourteenth Amendment. Roosevelt believed that the same narrow reasoning would lead the Court to invalidate the Wagner Act and the Social Security Act, both of which were on the docket. It also appeared that federal regulation of wages and hours, another item on the New Deal agenda, would not pass the judges' scrutiny even if Congress approved it. Roosevelt believed that the four conservatives on the Court—Willis Van Devanter, George Sutherland, James McReynolds, and Pierce Butler—were busily reading their own political prejudices into the Constitution under a cloak of judicial impartiality.

The president's decision to make an issue of the justices' ages, when he really objected to their ideology, offended many, including eighty-year-old Justice Louis D. Brandeis. Yet in seeking to enlarge the Court, Roosevelt chose the only course that seemed feasible. He rejected the alternatives—constitutional amendments requiring a two-thirds vote of the Court in order to declare an act unconstitutional, permitting Congress to override Court decisions, or broadening the legislative authority to regulate the economy. Roosevelt knew that three-fourths of the state legislatures would never approve any of these proposals, and certainly not soon enough to help. Besides, in Roosevelt's view the Court, not the Constitution, needed changing.

The proposal triggered the most bitterly fought dispute of Roosevelt's presidency. Advocates said that the Supreme Court was already "packed" with reactionaries who were frustrating the popular desire for social reform as expressed in the election of 1936. There was nothing sacred about the number nine, they continued, for the Court's size had varied in the past. Legislation that affected millions of people should not stand or fall on the whim of a single judge. Opponents responded that the Court, far from obstructing the New Deal, had invalidated only a few measures, and badly drawn ones at that. Roosevelt had never received a mandate to pack the Court, since he had studiously avoided the subject during the campaign. Finally, they pointed out that Roosevelt's plan would set a dangerous precedent. If a liberal president could restructure the Court to suit his fancy today, what would stop a conservative president from doing the same thing tomorrow?

In the spring of 1937 the plan lost whatever momentum it had when the Court—largely because Justice Owen Roberts switched to the liberal side—upheld the Social Security Act and other vital reform measures. In *NLRB v. Jones and Laughlin*, the Court sustained the Wagner Act by a 5-to-4 vote. The majority implicitly overturned earlier decisions by holding that the commerce clause was indeed broad enough to cover federal regulation of manufacturing. In *West Coast Hotel Co. v. Parrish*, again by a one-vote margin, the Court approved state minimum-wage laws. Chief Justice Charles Evans Hughes asserted that "reasonable" regulation, adopted in the interests of the community, by definition fulfilled the Fourteenth Amendment's due process requirements. In May 1937 Justice Van Devanter's resignation gave Roosevelt his first Court appointment. The administration continued to back a compromise permitting the appointment of one additional justice each year for every member who reached the age of seventy-five. This seemed likely to pass because most senators assumed that Roosevelt would nominate their colleague, Majority Leader Joseph Robinson of Arkansas, to fill the first vacancy. In July Robinson died of a heart attack and the Senate quickly defeated the bill.

The Court debacle injured Roosevelt's standing with Congress and the public, although many who would have broken with him for other reasons merely used the episode as a convenient pretext. The struggle over the Court divided the Democratic Party by alienating a number of liberals, aroused widespread distrust of Roosevelt's leadership, and convinced Republicans that their best strategy was to maintain a discreet silence while Democrats battled among themselves. But Roosevelt did not come away empty-handed, for the Supreme Court in 1937 finally put its seal of approval on the New Deal. Roosevelt would appoint five justices during his second term—including Hugo Black, William O. Douglas, and Felix Frankfurter—and after they took their seats, judicial barriers to the welfare state came tumbling down.

## THE WANING OF THE NEW DEAL

From Roosevelt's vantage point, administrative reform was hardly less important than judicial reform. In 1936 he had appointed a committee to study administrative management. It reported in January 1937, urging Congress to furnish the president with six assistants, expand the civil service system, improve fiscal management, and establish the National Resources Planning Board as a central agency to coordinate government programs. The committee also suggested creating two new cabinet positions (welfare and public works), changing the name of the Department of the Interior to the Department of Conservation, and giving the president broad authority to transfer agencies, including certain functions of the independent regulatory commissions. In this fashion the committee hoped to find a permanent home for New Deal agencies and provide a suitable administrative apparatus for the welfare state.

But reorganization provoked a storm of opposition when it came before Congress in the spring of 1938. Roosevelt's critics charged that the measure would clamp "one-man rule" on the nation and succeeded in frightening large numbers of people. After squeaking by the Senate, the bill went down to defeat in the House of Representatives when more than a hundred Democrats deserted the president. Congressmen had various reasons for opposing the measure, including a desire to reassert legislative prerogatives, placate pressure groups, and protect their existing channels of access to administrative agencies. The conflict over reorganization resembled the earlier one over the Supreme Court in that both measures failed to elicit support from a sizable constituency, opened Roosevelt to the charge of seeking dictatorial power, divided liberals, and led to stinging presidential defeats. In 1939 Congress passed a mild measure that enabled Roosevelt to establish the Executive Office of the President and to streamline the bureaucracy. But the sweeping changes he favored were not made.

Democratic opposition to Court reform and reorganization crossed sectional lines. But three other measures—relating to housing, wages and hours, and civil rights—divided the Democratic Party into rural and urban, northern and southern factions. The Wagner Housing Act (1937), which authorized expenditures of $500 million to aid the construction of low-cost units, passed only after southerners had extracted concessions limiting the appropriation, the number of dwellings to be built, and the cost per family. The Fair Labor Standards Act (1938) similarly catered to the South, which wished to protect its competitive position as a cheap labor market. The measure regulated child labor and established a minimum wage of forty cents per hour and a forty-hour workweek, but it exempted domestic workers and farm laborers and allowed regional wage differentials. The antilynching bill never had a chance against a Senate filibuster engineered by southern Democrats. Measures that appealed to the New Deal's northern, urban constituency won little support from rural and southern representatives.

The administration's response to the recession of 1937–1938 added to the disenchantment with reform. In the fall of 1937 the economy went into a tailspin. Over the next ten months, millions of people lost their jobs. The slump occurred primarily because the administration, in attempting to balance the budget, had cut expenditures sharply. Yet Roosevelt resisted new deficit spending. Unlike the Keynesians, who favored unbalanced budgets in slack periods, Roosevelt believed pump priming to be appropriate in 1933, "when the water had receded to the bottom of the well," but doubted its worth in 1938, "with the water within 25 or 30 percent of the top." Not until April, when it appeared that economic conditions would ruin the Democrats in the fall elections, did the president listen to advisers who favored additional spending.

He then asked Congress to authorize a $3.75 billion relief appropriation. But the damage had already been done. Those who had lost their jobs or whose businesses had failed blamed the Democrats, not the Republicans, and concluded that the time for further innovation was past.

The president suffered yet another reversal in his attempt to purge the Democratic Party in the 1938 primaries. Roosevelt fought unsuccessfully to unseat Senators Walter George of Georgia, Millard Tydings of Maryland, and Ellison D. "Cotton Ed" Smith of South Carolina. Many southerners appeared to resent the president's intrusion into local affairs, while those benefiting most from New Deal relief programs and presumably most sympathetic to the president—blacks and poor whites—hardly participated in Democratic primaries. Opinion polls indicated that even among the unemployed and those on relief a bare majority disliked the White House's intervention. The purge claimed only one victim. John O'Connor of New York City, chair of the House Rules Committee, was defeated by a local politician friendly to the New Deal. In the November elections Republicans went on to win a smashing victory: they gained eighty-one seats in the House and eight in the Senate. Since all Democratic losses took place in the North and West, southerners emerged in a much stronger position. For the first time, Roosevelt could not form a majority without the help of some Republicans or southern Democrats.

Congress assembled in January 1939 and wasted little time in disposing of the president's program. To demonstrate its resentment at what it judged the attempted politicization of relief, Congress passed the Hatch Act (1939), prohibiting all government employees except a few high-ranking executive branch officials from engaging in political campaigns. The House abruptly cut off funds for the Federal Theater Project, which, because most of its activities centered in a few large cities, was highly vulnerable. The tax on undistributed profits, which the business community bitterly resented, was repealed outright. Congress also refused to increase expenditures for public housing. When the administration requested $3.86 billion for self-liquidating public works projects, the Senate trimmed the amount substantially, and the House voted not even to consider it. Recognizing how far the pendulum had swung, Roosevelt became more cautious. He opposed efforts to expand federal contributions to the Social Security program in order to equalize benefits, disapproved proposals for additional deficit spending, and withheld support from a national health bill that would have provided aid for maternity and child care, hospital construction, and "general programs of medical care."

## NATIVISM AND THE APPROACH OF WAR

In the period from 1937 to 1941—years marked first by economic dislocation at home and then by international tension abroad—the United States experienced a sharp upsurge in nativist sentiment. This affected the New Deal because in the minds of some people the Roosevelt administration was playing into the hands of the very groups that seemed to pose the gravest danger—communists, Jews, and labor agitators. Charges that the president had surrounded himself with dangerous advisers and had embraced an alien ideology were by no means new, but after 1937 they were voiced more frequently and accepted more widely. By 1940 the administration itself had grown concerned enough to crack down sharply on suspected subversives. But it did not succeed in quelling popular fears.

In 1937 workers in the Congress of Industrial Organizations adopted radical tactics to gain traditional goals of union recognition and improved conditions. Labor's new weapon,

Members of the nascent United Auto Workers (UAW) union during a sit-down strike in the General Motors Fisher Body Plant in Flint, Michigan. *(Sheldon Dick/Getty Images)*

the sit-down strike, terrified property-conscious Americans. No fewer than 477 such strikes, involving 400,000 workers, took place in 1937, the most important of which was the General Motors sit-down in Flint, Michigan, in January. Most Americans assumed correctly that the union's occupation of a factory violated the law, but concluded erroneously that the automobile workers were inspired by revolutionary intent. Two out of every three people favored outlawing sit-down strikes and employing force against the union. "Armed insurrection—defiance of law, order and duly elected authority is spreading like wildfire," protested one group of citizens. Because Roosevelt refused to call out federal troops to evict the strikers, he was accused of cringing before the forces of anarchy and disorder.

With the outbreak of World War II in September 1939, Roosevelt became worried about the possibility of subversion by fascist agents or by communists (who were then defending the Nazi-Soviet pact). Congress and the administration outdid each other in tracking down potentially disloyal groups. In March 1940, Roosevelt approved the fingerprinting of all aliens applying for visas as temporary visitors, and two months later he authorized the use of wiretaps against anyone "suspected of subversive activities." In June Congress passed the Smith Act, which required aliens to register and made it a crime to conspire to teach or advocate the violent overthrow of the government. Congress also required all political organizations subject to foreign control to register with the attorney general. The government prosecuted

Communist Party leader Earl Browder on the technicality of using a fraudulent passport; he received an unprecedented four-year jail sentence.

At the same time, Roosevelt increasingly shifted his emphasis from domestic reform to foreign policy and national defense. By 1940 his chief legislative goal was to obtain approval for assisting Great Britain and France. This, given isolationist strength in Congress, required the backing of southern Democrats. As one conservative southerner put it, the president had begun "cultivating us in a very nice way." Similarly, Roosevelt's interest in readying plans for economic mobilization in the event of war moved him to mend fences with the business community. In August 1939 he appointed a War Resources Board composed mainly of representatives of big business and headed by Edward Stettinius of United States Steel. Roosevelt, however, came to fear that the board's proposals might dilute his own authority in wartime and did not make them public. In May 1940, when he set up a National Defense Advisory Commission to expedite production, he again turned to Stettinius and to William S. Knudsen of General Motors. By 1940 the process of repairing relations with the business community and southern Democrats alike was well under way.

By 1940 the agenda of American politics had been transformed, with foreign policy replacing reform as the central issue. The presidential campaign that year reflected this change. The international crisis persuaded Roosevelt to seek a third term and gave the Democrats an excuse to nominate him. The Republicans chose Wendell Willkie, who, while a critic of many New Deal policies, accepted much of the welfare state. Moreover, as a spokesman for the internationalist wing of the Republican Party, Willkie endorsed the main outlines of Roosevelt's foreign policy, refusing, for example, to make issues of aid to Great Britain or the peacetime draft. The tense international situation undoubtedly worked to the president's advantage, although Willkie did surprisingly well with 22.3 million votes to Roosevelt's 27.2 million. But during the campaign, Roosevelt made his most famous and, given the events of the following year, his most unfortunate promise: "I shall say it again and again and again: Your boys are not going to be sent into any foreign wars."

CHAPTER EIGHT

# 1929–1941

## The Big Breakdown—
## The United States and the World

A small boat rescues a seaman from the USS *West Virginia* at Pearl Harbor, Hawaii, December 7, 1941. *(Library of Congress)*

The Great Depression ripped apart the treaty agreements so carefully built during the 1920s to preserve world peace, for the pacts had utterly depended on a smoothly working economic system. The collapse of 1929 not only destroyed the political arrangements, but it created such chaos and disillusionment that fascists and radical leftists replaced moderate governments in Germany, Spain, and Japan. Extremists did not grasp control in the United States, however. In a remarkable performance, Americans continued their allegiance to the traditional economic-political system, even though it was producing the most miserable and inhumane conditions in the nation's history. Franklin D. Roosevelt's foreign policy mirrored that moderation. But the United States started down the road to Pearl Harbor between 1929 and 1932. FDR was unable to find an exit from that road.

## "MAD DOGS" AND ENGLISHMEN:
## THE MANCHURIAN CRISIS OF 1931–1932

In June 1931 President Hoover tried to stabilize Western money markets by suggesting a one-year moratorium (postponement) on the collection of reparations from Germany and war debts from France and Great Britain. "Perhaps the most daring statement I ever thought of issuing," as Hoover recalled, was too daring for the French. They insisted on keeping the hatchet of reparations above German heads. When Paris stalled, the president's policy collapsed. In July the German banking system came apart, then Great Britain's economic system went into a tailspin, the French government fell, and panic struck Europe and the United States. In Asia, Japan took its first step toward World War II by invading Manchuria.

The Japanese had been especially hard-hit by the depression. Their economy depended on overseas markets, which by 1931 had largely disappeared. Exports to the vital U.S. market, for example, dropped 30 percent in 1930. Japan's liberal government, like liberal regimes elsewhere, was undercut and then destroyed by the collapse. By early 1931 dynamic political factions led by ambitious militarists demanded that Japan find its salvation not in the sick Western trading community, but in its own empire. Since 1905 Tokyo had controlled and developed South Manchuria. North Manchuria, however, was coming under the domination of Chiang Kai-shek's new regime in China. Chiang and a rapidly multiplying Chinese population even endangered Japanese control of South Manchuria. In September 1931 the Japanese militarists took affairs into their own hands. After a brief skirmish between Chinese and Japanese troops along the South Manchurian railway, Japan's army launched a full-scale invasion of North Manchuria. Tokyo had bloodily repudiated its pledge at the Washington Naval Conference to maintain the open door.

Hoover and Secretary of State Henry Stimson were trapped. Throughout the 1920s America's Far Eastern policy had depended on a cooperative Japan, particularly when the only alternatives as partners were a "revolutionary" China and the Soviet Union. Hoover privately remarked that he had some sympathy for the Japanese, for they faced a "Bolshevist Russia to the north, and a possible Bolshevist China" to the west. Some officials wanted Japan handled gently because it was holding back the Chinese tide. "The Chinese are altogether too cocky," the American ambassador in London told the Japanese ambassador. "What you people need to do is to give them a thoroughly good licking to teach them their place and then they will be willing to talk sense." In December 1931 Japan's militarists overthrew the civilian regime and accelerated the Manchurian offensive; yet nearly a year later Stimson, who knew that "the situation [in Japan] is in the hands of virtually mad dogs," urged a moderate response so that "the little group of militarists" could not "make us a bogey in the whole matter."

During the next ten years the United States single-handedly tried to protect its interests in the Far East. China was undependable, Russia too revolutionary, and Great Britain hesitant and no longer a major Pacific power. The only alternatives were stark: warring against Japan, working out something somehow with Tokyo, or else admitting that the United States had no vital interests in the area. No American president has ever opted for this third alternative. As the Japanese drove deeper into Manchuria in late 1931, Stimson discussed possible economic sanctions (for example, cutting off the considerable American oil and metal exports to Japan), but Hoover refused. The president feared that sanctions would inevitably lead to war. The League of Nations investigated the outbreak, indirectly called Japan the aggressor, refused to recognize Japan's establishment of a Manchukuo puppet state in Manchuria, and then watched hopelessly as Tokyo responded by quitting the League. Stimson refused to work formally with the League. His main effort was to coordinate an Anglo-American reaffirmation of the Nine-Power Treaty backed by an increase of military strength in the Pacific. That policy collapsed when the British decided to work through the League of Nations while privately trying to appease Japan. From 1931 until Pearl Harbor in 1941, Great Britain, whose primary concerns lay in Europe, would support American actions against Japan only if it was certain the United States would accept the possible consequence of war and be willing to fight Japan virtually alone. Otherwise the British were prepared to make deals with the Japanese, and consequently the United States refused in turn to trust the British.

## NEW ORDER TO NEW DEAL

Hoover made one final attempt to put the pieces back together. Between 1930 and 1932 nearly every nation withdrew inside itself, erected tariff walls, and attempted to follow autarchic economic policies. In 1930 the United States passed the Hawley-Smoot bill, the highest pro-tective tariff in its history. A more extreme example of autarchy was Britain's construction of the Imperial Preference system in 1932. Through a series of bilateral pacts, the British government and members of the Commonwealth promised to give one another favored trad-ing privileges, thus largely excluding such third parties as the United States from traditional markets in Canada, Australia, and South Africa. The United States bitterly fought such poli-cies, not only because they gravely hurt trade, but also because they injected the government into the realm of private enterprise. In 1932 Hoover counterattacked by proposing an inter-national conference in London that would negotiate war debts, reparations, and disarmament. The president hoped that settlement of the debts could be used to pressure Great Britain and France into accepting liberal trade policies.

Before the conference could convene, however, Franklin D. Roosevelt moved into the White House. When Hoover and Stimson asked Roosevelt to accept their policies in the Far East and the proposed London conference, the new president agreed not to recognize Manchukuo, but absolutely refused to commit himself on economic issues. During his first eight months in office he rejected Hoover's international approach, most dramatically when he destroyed the London conference by refusing to tie American tariff and monetary policy to any inter-national agreement. Believing that the American economy might be able to resurrect itself if it were not tied to a disintegrating world economy, Roosevelt allowed the war-debt issue to die, took the country off the international gold standard, and began tinkering with the dollar to raise its purchasing power. None of these devices sufficiently spurred the economy. "Yes, it is the zero hour in Washington," critic Edmund Wilson observed in early 1934. "The first splendor of the New Deal has faded. . . . The emergency measures which revived our morale have not achieved all that they have promised."

By the spring of 1934 Roosevelt gave up his experiments and returned to Hoover's assumption that recovery required a booming American export trade. Quite clearly the domestic economy would not further improve without measures—some of which smacked too much of socialism for Roosevelt's taste—that would radically change the nature of the system. The president's only alternative therefore was to find help outside the system itself, that is, in the world marketplace.

Two major differences, however, separated Roosevelt's foreign policy from Hoover's. Roosevelt was dealing with a world rapidly compartmentalizing into closed, government-controlled blocs. Japan's Manchukuo and the British Imperial Preference system, for example, were not open to American competition. More ominously, in January 1933 Adolf Hitler assumed power in Germany. Within three years he worked out exclusive, government-controlled trade arrangements in Europe and Latin America that made it difficult for private American traders to compete.

These developments led to the second distinguishing—if not revolutionary —characteristic of New Deal policy: the government had to involve itself directly, for example by giving subsidies to private business that needed help in the marketplace. Hoover had avoided such direct involvement at all costs, fearing that it would change the nature of the system itself. Roosevelt believed that such danger could be averted. Moreover, he had little choice; if Americans were to find economic salvation overseas, they could compete against Germans, Japanese, and British governmental policies only if the U.S. government provided similar aid. That, of course, raised the grave danger that if conflict arose in the marketplace, the governments themselves would become fully involved in the struggle.

The guiding genius behind this policy was Secretary of State Cordell Hull. An ardent Wilsonian and former congressman from Tennessee who prided himself on complete command of the Tennessee mountaineer's earthy vocabulary, Hull was named secretary of state because of his influence on Capitol Hill. He was driven by an obsession to reopen the clogged channels of trade. Only when high tariffs, currency manipulation, and the power of state trading enterprises were obliterated, he believed, could individual freedoms be restored and wars averted. Hull was certain that friction between economic blocs inevitably led to political conflict. He therefore set out to replace such closed blocs with an open, multilateral trading system that had freely convertible currencies (instead of monies manipulated by the state) and that allowed private business concerns to buy and sell anywhere they chose. Hull used this standard of freer trade to judge nearly every diplomatic move he made between 1933 and his retirement in 1944, a standard that led him to condemn Germany in the 1930s, Japan in 1941, and the Soviet Union in 1944. This policy is central to an understanding of why he and Roosevelt came to define these three nations as enemies politically as well as economically.

Between 1934 and 1939 more legislation was enacted in Washington to find markets abroad for American surpluses than in any similar period in the nation's history. Two measures stand out. The Reciprocity Act of 1934 was Hull's pet project. It sharply reversed post-1920 policy

## EDWARD R. MURROW
## AND THE RADIO

"Radio is a recent innovation that has introduced profound alterations in the outlook and social behavior of men," two noted psychologists concluded in 1935. This dramatic view was accurate, even though commercial radio was just fifteen years old. The first national networks were formed in the mid-1920s by the National Broadcasting Company (NBC) and Columbia Broadcasting System (CBS), breakthroughs that led Secretary of Commerce Herbert Hoover to establish a governmental licensing and regulatory agency in 1927. He was concerned that radio be responsible: "It is inconceivable that we should allow so great a possibility for service, for news, for entertainment . . . to be drowned in advertising chatter." That was a forlorn hope. Radio advertising grew in popularity even during the depression. Albert Lasker, king of the advertising agents, tripled sales of Pepsodent by having the toothpaste sponsor the most popular 1930s program, *Amos 'n' Andy*, in which two white actors impersonated black minstrel-show types. Radio standardized habits of living, speech, and taste in a nation once famous for its distinct regions and diversity.

Edward R. Murrow outside the BBC's Broadcast House, from which Murrow beamed his broadcasts, London, May 1940. *(CBS Photo Archive/Getty Images)*

Until the 1930s radio broadcast little news. NBC did not have a single daily news series. It believed its job was to entertain the entire family while leaving current affairs to newspapers. Franklin D. Roosevelt changed this situation with his "Fireside Chats" in 1933. With a voice perfectly suited for the new medium, his broadcasts were so successful that, in the words of a columnist, "The President has only to look toward a radio to bring Congress to terms."

As Europe moved toward war, news services increased until in 1937 CBS sent twenty-eight-year-old Edward R. Murrow to Europe to establish continent-wide broadcasts. Born in Polecat Creek, North Carolina, he had moved west to study at Washington State College, where the nation's first courses on radio were offered. As Murrow left for Europe, a CBS executive protested, "Broadcasting has no role in international politics," but should limit itself to radioing "the song of a nightingale from Kent, England," a program that had been voted the "most interesting broadcast" of 1932. Murrow destroyed such illusions. CBS's coverage of the 1938 Munich crisis was followed hourly by millions.

Its effect was noticeable a month later when the network produced Orson Welles's ver-

Franklin D. Roosevelt during a fireside chat in Washington, DC, 1935. *(Franklin D. Roosevelt Presidential Library and Museum, Hyde Park, New York)*

sion of *War of the Worlds*, a story of invaders from Mars landing in New Jersey. Welles utilized the news bulletin-spot interview techniques used during the Munich crisis. Within a half-hour after the program began, New Jersey residents filled the highways heading out of the state, two Princeton professors had rushed out to study the invaders, and a Pittsburgh woman, crying "I'd rather die this way than that," was stopped before she could take poison. News broadcasting had come of age.

Murrow built a staff in Europe headed by Eric Sevareid and Howard K. Smith. His most famous programs occurred during Hitler's air blitz of London in 1940 and 1941. His rich, quiet, understated voice began each broadcast with "This—is London." He followed with graphic accounts that tried to "report suffering to people [Americans] who have not suffered" by providing eyewitness testimony of bombing ("that moan of stark terror and suspense cannot be encompassed by words"). Pioneering new uses of the microphone, he once simply put it on a London sidewalk while sirens shrieked, antiaircraft guns fired, and people hurried to shelters. As the foreign policy debate in Washington intensified, Murrow shrewdly helped the pro-interventionist forces by emphasizing Churchill's greatness and England's bravery while reporting British belief that Americans were the last hope for democracy. As American poet Archibald MacLeish wrote of Murrow, "You burned the city of London in our houses and we felt the flames that burned it. You laid the dead of London at our doors and we knew the dead were our dead."

Murrow brought a new dimension to radio, for he used it to educate and mobilize society. Even after his death in 1965, his style and ideals shaped news broadcasting in television as well as radio.

**Web Links**

CBS News websites devoted to Murrow and his most famous programs—

*Person to Person*: **www.cbsnews.com/person-to-person/** and
*See it Now*: **www.cbsnews.com/video/watch/?id=1065699n**.

by giving the president power to reduce or raise tariffs by as much as 50 percent in bargaining with other nations for reciprocal reduction of tariff barriers. The policy also included the unconditional-most-favored-nation principle: trade favors given to one nation would automatically be given to all others that did not discriminate against American trade. That principle made it impossible for two nations to gang up economically against a third. If used successfully, the reciprocity act would be like a giant economic wrecking ball, swinging in all directions to batter down tariff and other state-created barriers that Hull and Roosevelt so hated. Reciprocity pacts with fourteen nations helped accelerate exports between 1934 and 1938 by over $500 million. Imports, however, lagged; this meant that other nations were not selling enough to Americans to obtain the dollars needed to buy increased U.S. exports.

As during 1928 and 1929, therefore, a dollar shortage threatened to stunt the growth of the world, and consequently the American, economy. In 1934 Roosevelt established a government-operated Export-Import Bank through which government credits would be made available to foreign customers so they could purchase U.S. exports. Funds to finance foreign trade would now be provided by the government, not just by the private bankers, who had proven unequal to the job in the 1920s. American tax dollars were lent overseas for the purchase of American goods. These acts creating the reciprocity policy and the Export-Import Bank proved so beneficial that both were renewed and expanded into the twenty-first century.

## AREAS OF SPECIAL INTEREST: LATIN AMERICA AND THE SOVIET UNION

These economic initiatives were aimed at every corner of the world, but the New Deal selected several areas for special attention. Between 1933 and 1938, Roosevelt and Hull devoted great energy to making North and South America "good neighbors," in FDR's words. During those years U.S. imports from Latin America leaped 114 percent to $705 million, while exports to South America rocketed 166 percent to over $640 million. In 1932 the United States accounted for 32 percent of Latin American trade, but after the reciprocity legislation took effect, Americans enjoyed 45 percent in 1938. Politically, Roosevelt continued Hoover's policy of noninterference militarily. A major step occurred at the Montevideo Conference in 1933 when Hull, somewhat against his will, pledged the United States not to carry out further military interventions.

The increased economic leverage was providing Americans with an alternative diplomatic weapon. Cuba provided a classic example. Since 1901 the Platt Amendment had given officials in Washington the right to send troops to Cuba. Control became firmer between 1919 and 1921, when depressed sugar prices ruined plantations and Americans invested heavily in Cuban sugar. Throughout the 1920s a dictator protected these interests, but by 1933 the economy had collapsed and left-wing movements challenged the government. After thirty-five years as an American protectorate, Cuba's trade with the United States had dropped 50 percent since 1929, the island's sugar sold for one-tenth of a cent per pound, and 500,000 of Cuba's 4 million people searched for work. In September 1933 junior army officers under Fulgencio Batista overthrew the government and put a liberal politician into the presidency.

The regime was indeed too liberal for the State Department, which thought it saw communists creeping into power. Hull and Undersecretary of State Sumner Welles, a close friend of Roosevelt, asked him to make a show of force in Havana harbor. The president refused. He had a better alternative. Between 1933 and 1934 FDR and Batista—who desperately needed economic help—agreed to pump life into the Cuban economy by opening the American sugar market to Cuban cane at prices above those in the world market. Other foreign-produced sugar was effectively excluded from the United States. American consumers thus paid extra for their sugar, but Batista lived up to his part of the deal by placing a more conservative president in power in Havana. The policy worked so well that in 1934 Roosevelt felt he could safely repeal all of the Platt Amendment but the part giving the United States the Guantanamo Naval Base. At the same time, Washington also promised to give the Philippines independence in ten years, but again carefully made economic arrangements to protect American interests on the islands.

Roosevelt pursued the same economic approach toward Russia, but with much less success. After frequent consultation with William Bullitt, who had returned from the French Riviera and private life in Philadelphia to advise him, the president recognized the Soviets in November 1933. He had to overcome strong opposition from the American Legion, the Daughters of the American Revolution, Roman Catholic Church leaders, the American Federation of Labor, and, most important, his own State Department. Hull swore that no deals could be made with a state-controlled economy. He also argued that the Bolsheviks would try to interfere in American domestic affairs, as he believed they had in Cuba during the 1933 revolution. Roosevelt did, however, receive strong support from businessmen, who argued that the potentially vast Russian market could help rescue Americans from the depression. Bullitt became the first U.S. ambassador to the Soviet Union.

The Soviets welcomed FDR's initiative, but for very different reasons. They were less interested in trade than in working out a common policy to contain Japan. Since 1931 the Soviets, fearful that Tokyo's militarists would move from Manchuria into Siberia, had desperately searched for friends. One Moscow official remarked that Russia and the United States must join in "breaking [Japan] as between the two arms of a nutcracker."

Within two years after diplomatic relations were resumed, Moscow–Washington relations turned sour. Trade did not prosper because no agreement could be reached on proper credit arrangements. The Soviets became disillusioned when the State Department went out of its way to assure anxious Tokyo officials that recognition was not in any way directed against Japan. Roosevelt and Bullitt plainly informed Russian leader Joseph Stalin they would make no anti-Japanese alliance. Washington preferred to consider a deal with its old friend Japan rather than work with the mysterious, revolutionary Soviets. In 1934 Stalin gave up on the United States. He began negotiating with Japan, joined the League of Nations, and—too late—reversed his attitude toward Hitler (whom Stalin had dismissed as a fool in 1932) in a last-ditch try at working out antifascist alliances with Eastern and Western governments. Russia and the United States continued to go in opposite directions until Hitler startlingly threw them together in 1941.

## THE FAILURE OF POLITICAL NEUTRALITY

Between 1933 and 1937 the Japanese carefully refrained from further aggression, but tightened their grip on Manchuria. When Roosevelt attempted to help China in late 1933 with wheat, cotton, and airplanes, Tokyo slammed back with the so-called Amau Statement of 1934, which warned that since foreign aid to China could "acquire political significance," Japan had the right to act unilaterally to maintain "peace and order in Eastern Asia." The State Department again reiterated the Nine-Power Treaty principles for an open door in China, but Japan threw that treaty on the scrap heap by excluding American oil and other interests from Manchuria. By late 1934 Tokyo demanded that the Five-Power Treaty principles be changed to allow Japan parity with the American and British fleets. When this was refused, the Japanese withdrew from the agreement and accelerated the building of their navy and fortifications in the Pacific.

In 1936 Tokyo found new friends. During the previous year Benito Mussolini's Italy had suddenly ravaged the small African nation of Ethiopia. When the League of Nations and the major powers offered little response, Hitler embarked on his own campaign of aggression. The self-proclaimed führer, determined to rectify the 1919 peace conference's dissection of Germany, marched unopposed to reclaim the Rhineland in 1936. During that summer civil war erupted in Spain between the five-year-old republic and the conservative army-church forces led by Francisco Franco. Within a year Hitler and Mussolini funneled vast aid to Franco while the republic obtained major help only from the Soviets. Great Britain and France remained on the sidelines of what they preferred to believe was only a civil war, and the United States followed their example. Franco then overthrew the Spanish Republic and established his own dictatorship. Germany was clearly on the move. In November 1936 the Japanese signed with Hitler the Anti-Comintern Pact, which secretly called for joint consultation if either party were attacked by the Soviets; both parties promised not to make treaties with Russia. Italy joined the pact in 1937. Japan now had friends and security on its Russian flank if it wanted to move into China or areas to the south.

The United States responded to these developments with a series of neutrality laws. A Senate investigation headed by Gerald Nye (Republican of North Dakota) revealed during 1934–1935 that private American bankers had become closely involved with the French and British war efforts during 1915–1917. No evidence demonstrated that President Wilson's policies had been directly shaped by the bankers, but the conclusion was too easily drawn that the United States had been shoved into world war by the profit lust of a few. Congress responded with the 1935 Neutrality Act: when the president declared that war existed, no arms, ammunition, or items of war were to be shipped to any belligerent, and American ships could not transport such supplies to a belligerent. In 1936 Congress passed a second Neutrality Act that prohibited loans to nations involved in war. A year later, in response to the Spanish conflict, other Neutrality Acts forbade Americans from traveling on the vessels of belligerents and applied these various provisions to civil wars.

But one major change appeared in the 1937 legislation. In response to Roosevelt's complaint that the acts tied his hands, and because the damming up of these items threatened vital parts of the country's economy, a "cash-and-carry" provision was added allowing nations to obtain nonmilitary supplies if they paid cash and transported them home in their own ships. Americans, in other words, hoped to avoid wars while making money from them. Obviously the cash-and-carry clause also helped Great Britain and France since in any European war their navies would control the Atlantic. As Japan soon demonstrated, however, the Neutrality Acts were written to prevent the previous war, not the next one.

In July 1937 the Japanese army attacked northern China in an effort to build a buffer area around Japan's puppet state of Manchukuo. The Neutrality Acts were useless, for whereas Americans wanted to help China, the Japanese fleet controlled the western Pacific and hence could take advantage of the cash-and-carry provision. Roosevelt tried to escape from the dilemma by refusing to declare that a war existed in Asia. The neutrality provisions consequently did not take effect. He meanwhile desperately searched for ways to aid China.

On October 5, FDR delivered a "quarantine speech" in Chicago, the center of political isolationism. The president talked vaguely about quarantining aggressor nations, but offered no specific policies. A majority of Americans probably supported Roosevelt's call, but the howls of opposition that arose drove Roosevelt and Hull to disclaim any intention of immediate action.

In December 1937 Japanese planes attacked an American gunboat, the *Panay*, as it stood guard over Standard Oil tankers in China's Yangtze River. Two Americans were killed. Roosevelt strongly protested, and Japan apologized, but the president then tried to take the offensive. In the House he waged a bitter and successful struggle against a constitutional amendment proposed by Louis Ludlow (Democrat of Indiana), which if passed would have required a national referendum before a declaration of war unless the United States itself were attacked. The following month Roosevelt proposed a 20 percent increase in the U.S. naval fleet and began rebuilding Guam and other Pacific bases.

## THE FAILURE OF THE NEW DEAL

After these small successes the president had to turn from foreign policy to a crisis at home. In early 1937 he believed that the American economy had recovered sufficiently so that some New Deal measures could be cut back. He especially hoped to balance the budget, a move that would dry up vast federal monies that had been priming the economy. As Secretary of the Treasury Henry Morgenthau phrased it, "This was the moment, it seemed to me, to strip off the bandages, throw away the crutches, and see if American private enterprise could stand on its own feet." Roosevelt pulled government money out too rapidly, however, and like a patient drained of blood, the economy staggered, then collapsed into the most precipitous decline in American history. In nine months industrial production dropped 33 percent, payrolls 35 percent, industrial stock averages 50 percent, profits 78 percent. Only unemployment rose, spiraling upward 23 percent. The domestic New Deal had no other medicines to offer. Roosevelt, one of his cabinet members noted, "did not know which way to turn." But something had to be done rapidly, for the crisis went beyond economics. Harry Hopkins, one of FDR's closest advisers, declared, "This country cannot continue as a democracy with 10 or 12 million people unemployed. It just can't be done."

Roosevelt's massive spending program on the navy and later on a 5,500-plane air force provided one response to the crisis. By 1939 defense spending was putting Americans back to work again, although 10 million remained unemployed as late as January 1940. The full-scale war economy after 1941 would finally solve the terrible economic problems that the New Deal could never sufficiently remedy.

Another response to the crisis was the traditional hope of finding expanded foreign markets for the vast surplus of American goods. China provided the greatest potential market. "Probably never in its history has China offered greater promise for [U.S.] future trade, industry, and general economic progress," a Commerce Department official told a gathering of American businessmen in mid-1937. The Japanese invasion threatened that dream and more: if the Japanese developed a large cotton industry in northern China, then, Secretary of Commerce Daniel C. Roper warned Roosevelt in late 1937, American exports would drop so low as to require "a recharting of the economy of the South and definite Federal production control procedures." Several years later a correspondent of the *New York Times* substituted rubber for cotton, but came up with the same conclusion: "The future of China and the future of the United States in Asia may very well be determined by whether or not those rubber tires that roll on the Chinese roads are made in Akron or in Osaka [Japan]."

Secretary of State Hull was caught in the middle of this maelstrom. In 1936 he had been impressed with the advice from John A. Hobson, the great historian of imperialism, that the "last large possibility of maintaining capitalism lies in the Orient." It was doubtful, Hobson continued, that in exploiting this lush market "the Americans will care to play second fiddle to the Japanese, whose character and behavior are so baffling to the Occidental mind." That advice fitted perfectly with Hull's view that an open-door approach, rather than Japanese exclusiveness, was the only method to develop a healthy global trade, world peace, and the American economy. In November 1938, however, Hull suffered a severe setback when Japan proclaimed a Greater Asia Co-prosperity Sphere, based on anti-bolshevism, which aimed to close off the Far East. It was, Tokyo claimed, an Asian equivalent to the American Monroe Doctrine in the Western Hemisphere. Hull feared that all of Asia would go the way of Manchuria. "In our opinion," he sweepingly declared in late 1938, "an endeavor by any country in any part of the world to establish itself in favor of a preferred [economic] position in another country is incompatible with the maintenance of our own and the establishment of world prosperity." That statement was the cornerstone of American foreign policy.

How to drive Japan from its "preferred position" was the central problem, compounded in early 1939 by statistics showing Japan to be America's third-largest customer. During a severe depression, such trade was not to be lightly discarded for the mere potential of the China market. Japan, moreover, had long been Washington's and London's most dependable ally in the Far East, a bastion against revolution. A war to protect the open door in China, on the other hand, could spawn new revolutions and be bloody as well as long-lasting, particularly if the Japanese and Germans coordinated their efforts. "We would like to help China if we knew how, of course," Secretary of the Interior Harold Ickes summed up the cruel dilemma in late 1938, "without running the risk of our own involvement in war."

Two alternatives emerged. The first, championed by Hull and his State Department advisers, urged continued effort toward a cooperative policy with Japan. Only then, Hull believed, could traditional multilateral cooperation be maintained for propping open the door to Far Eastern markets. He believed that an international trade agreement based on his beloved reciprocity principle would restore economic cooperation and—as Hull's reasoning ran—therefore result in a political agreement. Once brought within such a trade-political network, Japan could find necessary markets peacefully, continue to receive strategic goods from a friendly United States, and quit its evil partnership with Hitler.

A second and quite different answer came from Henry Morgenthau and the Treasury Department. Morgenthau reasoned that Japan's militarists were uncontrollable and too ambitious to settle for a friendly division of the Asian market. He urged direct bilateral aid to help China drive back the invader and bitterly criticized Hull's complicated multilateral, cooperative approach ("while he was discussing it, one country after another goes under").

Roosevelt at first equivocated between the two alternatives but told Morgenthau in late 1938, "Henry, these trade treaties [of Hull's] are just too goddamned slow. The world is marching too fast." The secretary of state's approach was also undercut when Japan insisted that only it and China could settle Chinese affairs; third parties were not wanted. Morgenthau

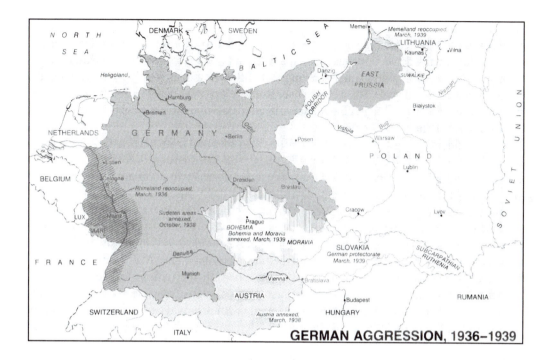

**GERMAN AGGRESSION, 1936–1939**

won a victory in 1938 when FDR agreed to send a $25 million credit for China's war effort. Then in July 1939 Morgenthau won a major triumph when Hull finally agreed to terminate the 1911 commercial treaty that governed trade with Japan. Roosevelt was so happy with Hull's acquiescence that he blurted out, "Cordell, I feel like kissing you on both cheeks." Morgenthau next pushed for an embargo on oil, but Hull resisted. No more would be done until Hitler had begun World War II.

## THE GHOST OF 1919

As European peace disintegrated after 1935, Roosevelt offered only suggestions for disarmament or economic conferences. Not even the British would accept such proposals. The Conservative government of Prime Minister Neville Chamberlain embraced instead the policy of appeasement, a dirty word during the post-1945 era but not in the 1930s, for it meant adjusting the wrongs inflicted on Germany by the 1919 peace conference. In this sense Roosevelt and most Americans were also appeasers. Like Europeans, they were belatedly conscience-stricken by the harsh penalties pressed on Germany and so stood paralyzed as Hitler's armies moved into adjoining territories during the mid-1930s. Also like Chamberlain, Roosevelt believed that compromises could be made with Germany and Italy, especially through the personal, private, and manipulative diplomacy that each leader preferred to more traditional methods.

When the Munich crisis flared in September 1938, Roosevelt encouraged Chamberlain to talk with Hitler. The president refused to take the side of either the German dictator, who demanded annexation of the Czechoslovak Sudetenland area containing several million Germans, or the Czechs (supposedly supported by Britain and France), who did not want to surrender their only defensible frontier area. On September 9, Roosevelt angrily made clear to reporters that Americans had no moral commitment to defend European democracies. Chamberlain finally decided to make a dramatic flight to Munich for talks with Hitler, a decision that resulted in Chamberlain's agreeing that Hitler should have his way. FDR wired the prime minister, "Good man." But a month later Roosevelt confessed to the cabinet his "shame" for supporting the Munich agreement and ordered the acceleration of plans for sending war goods to Great Britain and France.

The president's disillusionment with Hitler also resulted from Nazi activities in Latin America. German businesses, including the powerful Lufthansa airline, scored repeated successes in Latin American markets. An assistant secretary of commerce observed during 1938, "It used to be said that trade follows the flag. Observing world affairs today we might more appropriately say that political ideologies follow trade." As the Germans entered Latin American markets, traditional U.S. markets disappeared, a loss especially felt during the economic crisis of 1938. Roosevelt responded with increased government assistance to American businesses and pushed for a common anti-Axis front. His success was marked in the 1938 Declaration of Lima, when all the nations in the hemisphere agreed to cooperate fully against outside threats. A year later, after war began in Europe, the Americas agreed on the Declaration of Panama, which created a "safety belt" of nearly a thousand miles around the hemisphere in which there were to be no hostile acts by non-American belligerents.

By 1940 the only outstanding hemispheric problem was again the Mexican revolution. In March 1938, Mexico finally nationalized all foreign oil companies. Hull angrily urged quick action against "those Communists down there." The previous U.S. pledges of nonintervention, however, and Roosevelt's fear that a tough policy would turn Mexico toward Japan and Germany, moderated Washington's response. A settlement was finally reached in November 1941, when Mexico agreed to pay $40 million in back claims and establish a committee of experts to settle compensation for the oil companies. In return, the United States helped finance Mexican currency and extended a $30 million Export-Import Bank loan to build a large section of the Pan-American Highway from Mexico into Guatemala. Mexico was restored to the anti-Axis front that the United States was so anxious to forge.

Otherwise appeasement was a disaster. History catches and controls every decade and never more tragically than when the 1919 treaty paralyzed the anti-Hitlerian nations during the 1930s. One nation finally broke away. On August 23, 1939, Stalin signed a nonaggression treaty with Hitler in which they agreed on the division of Poland and the Balkans. Since 1937, Stalin had tried to negotiate a security agreement with France and Great Britain. This had foundered on French and British anticommunist hatred and the refusal of the Poles and Romanians to entrust their existence to Russian hands. Stalin had also carried out a gigantic blood purge of his supposed political enemies. He probably exterminated several million Russians. This brutality turned many Westerners, even Communist Party members, against the Soviets; a typical American magazine account was titled "Stalin, Portrait of a Degenerate," in which he was compared—unfavorably—with the famous Chicago killer Al "Scarface" Capone. Among the victims of the purge were leading Red Army officers. Western officials concluded that in any conflict the weakened Russian forces would be virtually useless. Hitler perceived Russia differently, for a treaty with Stalin would free Germany from the danger of a two-front war. Americans viewed these events incredulously, at first dismissing the Nazi-Soviet pact as a

Secretary of State Cordell Hull, Undersecretary Sumner Welles, and Adolf A. Berle Jr. *(left to right)* going to the White House with the unsigned Neutrality Proclamation in 1939. *(Thomas D. McAvoy/Time & Life Pictures/Getty Images)*

mere "grandstand play" designed by Stalin to frighten the West, then agreeing that there must be no difference after all between communism and fascism.

On September 1, 1939, nine days after the Nazi-Soviet pact was signed, Hitler invaded Poland. Great Britain and France, which had guaranteed Poland's boundaries, declared war on Germany. World War II had begun. After an impassioned congressional debate, Roosevelt won a modification of the Neutrality Acts. The arms embargo was changed to cash-and-carry in order to help the Allies, but loans remained illegal. Unlike Wilson, FDR never asked Americans to be neutral in thought and deed. He did, unfortunately, insist that his policies would keep the United States out of war, even as he was tying the country closer to the Allies.

In November 1939, Russia invaded Finland to obtain strategic areas along the Finnish-Soviet boundary. Despite State Department urgings, Roosevelt refused to break diplomatic relations with Russia, although he placed a voluntary, or "moral," embargo on airplanes and gas ticketed for the Soviets. An important side effect soon appeared. Spurred by war orders, American employment jumped 10 percent in late 1939 as production rose sharply. World War II rescued the economy.

## THE TRIALS OF UNNEUTRAL NEUTRALITY

The German blitzkrieg through Poland was followed by a lull, or "sitzkrieg," during winter and early spring of 1939–1940. In May, Hitler suddenly occupied France and the Low Countries. By June, his forces stood triumphant on the English Channel. Only the British remained to face the Nazis. Winston Churchill, who throughout the 1930s had repeatedly condemned appeasement, replaced Chamberlain as prime minister and mobilized Great Britain for a last-ditch fight. In the Pacific, Japan took advantage of the French and Dutch disasters to make demands on French Indochina and the Dutch East Indies. By September the struggle truly became global, for Japan, Germany, and Italy signed a tripartite mutual assistance pact clearly aimed at the United States. Americans now faced the prospect of a two-front war if they went to the rescue of Great Britain.

Roosevelt and his advisers concluded that Germany, not Japan, posed the gravest threat and that Great Britain must have top priority for war supplies. That policy continued to govern American actions until 1945. Protecting Great Britain, however, also meant safeguarding the European colonial empires in South and Southeast Asia, which produced the vital rubber, oil, and metals for the Anglo-American war effort. Japan, therefore, could not be allowed to strike to the south. Roosevelt initially responded by proposing an unbelievable building program to construct 50,000 planes and build over a million tons of ships. In September 1940 he made an executive agreement with Churchill by which fifty U.S. destroyers were sent to Great Britain in return for ninety-nine-year leases on British naval bases in the Western Hemisphere. This act required considerable political courage, for Roosevelt had decided to run for an unprecedented third term and was confronting strong criticism for his earlier aid to Great Britain.

The opposition to FDR's policies was led by the America First group made up of anti–New Deal industrialists (such as Henry Ford and Sterling Morton of Morton Salt), old Progressives (such as Senator Burton K. Wheeler of Nebraska and journalist Oswald Garrison Villard), and public figures who warned of dire military and political consequences should the nation be sucked into the war (such as flying aces Eddie Rickenbacker and Charles A. Lindbergh and historian Charles Beard). On the other side, the Committee to Defend America mobilized pro-Allied sentiment to aid the Allies. The committee vowed that it wanted to stay out of war, but argued that keeping Americans away from the battlefields required sending vast aid to nations resisting fascism. Roosevelt was fortunate in that the 1940 Republican presidential nominee, Wendell Willkie, sympathized with the Committee to Defend America by Aiding the Allies and so refused to condemn the president for helping Great Britain.

During the 1940 campaign FDR stressed that he did not intend to involve the country in war. After the election, however, he stepped up American assistance, often with the public assurance that it would somehow lessen the need for Americans to fight. Roosevelt was trapped. He knew the American system could not long survive in a fascist-dominated world, but he feared making strong public statements because of his estimate of antiwar sentiment, especially on Capitol Hill. When one ardent interventionist urged more action, the president replied, "Whether we like it or not, God and Congress still live." He consequently committed the United States to the Allies while issuing public explanations that fell short of the truth.

Roosevelt moved rapidly in 1941 against the Axis. In March he pushed the Lend-Lease Act through Congress so that the country could be "the arsenal of democracy" and send vast amounts of goods to Great Britain regardless of its inability to pay for the supplies. The act was aimed, he said, at keeping "war away from our country and our people." Senator Wheeler called lend-lease "the New Deal's triple-A foreign policy: it will plow under every fourth American boy." Roosevelt promptly shot back that this was "the rottenest thing that has been said in public life in my generation." But moving supplies to Great Britain through Nazi submarine–infested seas of the North Atlantic soon required the president to send American convoys to protect the supply ships. He ordered such convoying as far as Iceland, despite telling a press conference in late May that he had no plans to permit the U.S. Navy to accompany British vessels. By late summer he secretly ordered American ships to track German submarines and report to British destroyers. When one submarine turned and fired a torpedo at the *Greer*, which had been following the German vessel for three hours, Roosevelt said that the attack was unprovoked and implied that henceforth U.S. ships should feel free to shoot on sight. In November U.S. ships were armed and carrying goods to Great Britain. The nation was all but formally at war.

## THE LAST STEP

The formal, constitutional declaration of war ironically resulted from an Asian, not a European, crisis. After Japan threatened Indochina in July 1940, Roosevelt restricted the export of oil, aviation fuel, and scrap metals to Japan. This was a major step, for cutting off Tokyo's main source of these goods could force the Japanese to seize the oil and mineral wealth of South Asia. Yet Tokyo proceeded cautiously. In March 1941 Japan freed itself from the threat of a two-front war by signing a five-year nonaggression treaty with Russia. Hitler was stunned. Great Britain had been tougher than he expected, and he had failed to reach agreement with Stalin on dividing booty in the Balkans, so Hitler had decided to invade Russia. Despite the Tokyo-Moscow pact, the German dictator struck the Soviet Union on June 23 and by early winter had driven to within thirty miles of Moscow. Only the United States remained to keep Japan from taking what it wanted in the Far East.

In July 1941 the Japanese invaded Indochina and Thailand. Roosevelt froze Japanese assets in the United States, thus stopping nearly all trade. Hull had negotiated with Japan throughout mid-1941, but no agreement could be reached on three points: Tokyo's obligations under the Tripartite Pact (Hull demanded that Japan disavow its alliance with Germany); Japanese economic rights in Southeast Asia; and a settlement in China. The secretary of state mumbled to friends that "everything is going hellward," but he refused to give up hope that Japan would be reasonable. Roosevelt supported Hull while restraining cabinet members, such as Morgenthau, who wanted to have a showdown with the Japanese. The president desperately needed time to build American strength in both the Atlantic and the Pacific.

Averting an immediate clash, Hull nevertheless stuck to his demands that Japan get out of China, Indochina, and the Tripartite Pact. The Tokyo government of Fuminaro Konoye, under tremendous pressure from the Japanese military, was reaching the point of no return. American economic pressure was building. Konoye either had to meet Hull's demands and

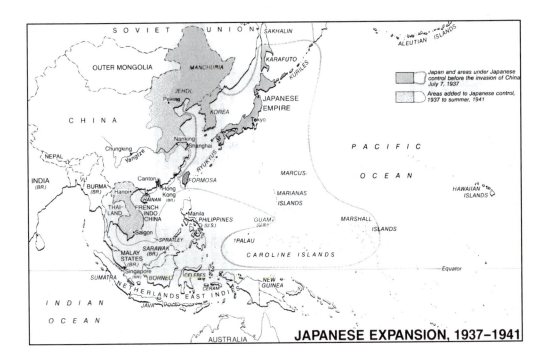

JAPANESE EXPANSION, 1937–1941

restore normal trade with the United States or remove all restraints and conquer the rich resources to the south. In August, Konoye made a final attempt at conciliation by asking Roosevelt to meet him personally to thrash out the problem. FDR was initially attracted, but Hull convinced him the conference would be worthless unless Japan agreed before the meeting to acquiesce to Hull's earlier demands. Konoye naturally refused such preconditions. In early October, Konoye's civilian government was swept aside and replaced by the military regime of General Hideki Tojo.

There was one last effort to avert war. In November the Japanese offered to leave Indochina and implied that they did not feel bound by the Tripartite Pact. In return they demanded vast American economic aid. The United States had cracked the Japanese diplomatic code, so Hull knew that this was the final offer. He rejected it, declaring on November 26 that Japan must in addition evacuate all troops from China and agree to an open-door policy in the Far East. This Japan would not do. The next day Tojo's regime decided to attack the United States on December 7 in a surprise raid on the Pearl Harbor naval base. At no time did the Japanese government harbor any hope of actually conquering the United States. Japan hoped instead that after a large portion of the American fleet was destroyed, Roosevelt would want to avert further conflict and be willing to talk more agreeably about China and trade.

Washington officials knew that Japan was preparing to attack, but they believed that the strike would be against Southeast Asia only. Some, such as Secretary of War Henry Stimson (whom Roosevelt had appointed in 1940 in a bipartisan and pro-Allied gesture), even hoped that the Japanese would attack in the southern Pacific, for the United States would then be justified in declaring war to protect the Philippines. On December 7, 1941, Japan instead struck in the mid-Pacific, crippling American naval forces in a matter of minutes with the worst losses they had ever suffered in a single engagement. More than 3,500 men lost their lives in the attack on Pearl Harbor as six large battleships and numerous auxiliary vessels settled to the bottom of Hawaiian waters.

Pearl Harbor was caught unprepared because of a massive breakdown in military intelligence and communication, not because Roosevelt or Stimson conspired to use the navy as bait so that Japan would attack and thereby enable the administration to take a united country into war. No administration plans to begin a war by losing nearly half its navy. When FDR asked Congress on December 8 to declare war against Japan, he did not think it possible to declare war on Germany, even though Hitler remained the primary objective of American policy. Many Americans, especially in the Midwest, wanted vengeance on Japan but were not yet ready to become embroiled in Europe. Hitler solved Roosevelt's dilemma on December 11 by declaring war on the United States. He did so in part because he had long promised the Japanese to honor their 1940 treaty, but more important because he felt that the United States was already fighting against him without a declaration of war. Hitler's unbounded ego apparently demanded that he, not Roosevelt, take the initiative in the life-and-death struggle.

The breakdown of intelligence at Pearl Harbor was remarkable. Washington's last telegram to the base on December 7 said nothing about a possible attack on Hawaii, went by slow commercial cable after a delay in transmission through military communications, and was finally delivered to authorities by a Japanese-American on a motorbike nearly seven hours after the strike. It was a symbolic end to the decade. The economic system had broken down by 1931, spawning fascism in Japan and Germany. The 1922 Washington Naval Conference Treaty system had consequently broken down, allowing Japan to destroy the open door in Asia. The 1919 peace arrangements had broken down, turning Hitler loose in Europe while Chamberlain and Roosevelt wrung their hands. The American economic system had broken down, leaving the New Deal a failure until it was rescued by war spending. American foreign policy had broken down, leaving Hull uttering platitudes about restoring peace by restoring an international marketplace that had not worked properly since before World War I. The Constitution's checks and balances had broken down, allowing FDR to send Americans to kill and be killed on the high seas eight months before the formal declaration of war while he explained publicly that each step toward war was really a step away from war. After a decade like that, the intelligence breakdown at Pearl Harbor is easier to understand if, like the others, difficult to justify.

# Guide to Further Reading

Beisner, Robert L., ed. *American Foreign Relations Since 1600: A Guide to the Literature.* 2nd ed. 2 vols. Santa Barbara, CA: ABC-CLIO, 2003. This guide is available and updated online.

Norton, Mary Beth, and Pamela Gerarde, eds. *The American Historical Association's Guide to Historical Literature.* 3rd ed. New York: Oxford University Press, 1995.

**http://historymatters.gmu.edu**
Created by the American Social History Project/Center for Media and Learning/Graduate Center of the City University of New York. This site provides a gateway to Web resources, listing more than 1,000 annotated Web sites on American history, and includes 1,000 primary documents and images.

**www.blackpast.org/?q=african-american-history-bibliography/**
A bibliography of African-American history.

**www.cnr.berkeley.edu/departments/espm/env-hist/us-hist.html**
A bibliography of environmental history.

**www.digitalhistory.uh.edu**
Developed by the University of Houston, the Chicago Historical Society, the Museum of Fine Arts in Houston, the National Park Service, and the Gilder Lehrman Institute of American History, this Web site provides a wealth of information about writings on all aspects of American history.

**www.digitalhistory.uh.edu/modules/mex_am/bibliography1.html**
A bibliography of Mexican-American history.

**www.library.yale.edu/rsc/american**
A selected bibliography of new works in American history arranged by topic as well as by historical period.

# Index

# About the Authors

**Walter LaFeber** is the Andrew Tisch and James Tisch University Professor Emeritus at Cornell University. His publications include *The New Empire: An Interpretation of American Expansion, 1865–1898* (1963, 1998); *America, Russia, and the Cold War, 1945–2006* (10th ed., 2007); *The Deadly Bet: LBJ, Vietnam, and the 1968 Election* (2005); *The American Age: U.S. Foreign Policy Since 1750* (2nd ed., 1994); and *Inevitable Revolutions: The United States and Central America* (2nd ed., 1991). He is a Stephen H. Weiss Presidential Teaching Fellow at Cornell.

**Richard Polenberg** is the Marie Underhill Noll Professor Emeritus of American History at Cornell University. He is the author of *Reorganizing Roosevelt's Government, 1936–1939* (1966); *War and Society: The United States, 1941–1945* (1972); *One Nation Divisible: Class, Race, and Ethnicity in the United States Since 1938* (1980); *Fighting Faiths: The Abrams Case, the Supreme Court, and Free Speech* (1987); and *The World of Benjamin Cardozo* (1997). He is the editor of *America at War: The Home Front, 1941–1945* (1968); *Radicalism and Reform in the New Deal* (1972); and *The Era of Franklin D. Roosevelt, 1933–1945* (2000). He is a recipient of the Clark Award for Distinguished Teaching and is a Stephen H. Weiss Presidential Teaching Fellow at Cornell.

**Nancy Woloch** is the author of *Women and the American Experience* (4th ed., 2006) and *Muller v. Oregon: A Brief History with Documents* (1996); coauthor of *The Enduring Vision: A History of the American People* (6th ed., 2008); and editor of *Early American Women: A Documentary History, 1600–1900* (2nd ed., 2002). She teaches history at Barnard College, Columbia University.